BYRON'S DAUGHTER

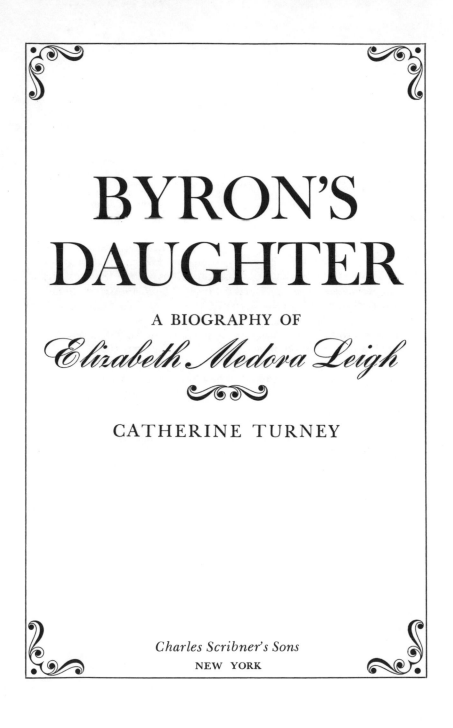

BYRON'S DAUGHTER

A BIOGRAPHY OF

Elizabeth Medora Leigh

CATHERINE TURNEY

Charles Scribner's Sons

NEW YORK

To my sister
who also is named Elizabeth

Contents

List of
Illustrations

William, Fourth Lord Byron, 1669–1736,
m. 1720, Frances, daughter of Lord Berkeley of Stratton *

William, Fifth Lord Byron, 1722–98
m. 1747 Elizabeth Shaw

William 1749–76
m. his cousin, Juliana Elizabeth Byron

William, d.
1794

John 1756–91
m. 1. 1779 Amelia, Baroness Conyҽ
2. 1785 Catherine Gordon of
Gight (d. 1811)

1. Augusta Mary Byron
1784–1851
m. 1807 her cousin,
Col. George Leigh

Georgiana Augusta b. 4 Nov. 1808	Augusta Charlotte b. 9 Feb. 1811	George Henry John b. 3 June 1812	Elizabeth Medora b. 15 April 1814	Frederick George b. 9 May 1816	Amelia Marianne b. 27 Nov. 1817	Henry Francis b. 28 Jan. 1820

* Lord Berkeley of Stratton had two daughters; the elder married John
Trevanion, of Caerhays, Cornwall, the younger, Lord Byron.

Medora Leigh's Family

John, Admiral R.N. 1723–86 ("Foulweather Jack")
m. his cousin, Sophia Trevanion *

George Anson 1758–93
m. 1779 Henrietta Dallas

Frances
m. Gen. Charles Leigh

Col. George Leigh
m. 1807 his cousin,
Augusta Mary Byron

2. George Gordon
Sixth Lord Byron
1788–1824 *m.* 1815
Anne Isabella Milbanke
(1792–1860)

George Anson
Seventh Lord Byron
1789–1868 *m.* 1816
Elizabeth Chandos-Pole

Augusta Ada Byron
1815–52
m. 1835 William Lord King (1805–93),
created Earl of Lovelace, 1838

Byron Noel
Viscount Ockham
1836–62

Ralph Gordon Noel
1839–1906
Baron Wentworth
and Earl of Lovelace

Anne Isabella Noel
Fifteenth Baroness Wentworth
1837–1917

Introduction

THE LIVES OF LORD BYRON, LADY BYRON, AND THE HONOR-able Augusta Leigh—the three people who had the greatest influence on Elizabeth Medora Leigh's complex background and history—have been dealt with by an ever-increasing number of biographers. Most of them refer in some way to "Medora Leigh." Yet her story has never been told for its own sake but only as it pertains to the lives of others, such as her aunt, Lady Byron, and her mother, Augusta Leigh. When Elizabeth Medora Leigh was two, Byron left England, never to return, so she cannot be said to have known him, despite the profound effect he would have upon her life. Due to the "shameful" circumstances of her birth—she was the illegitimate child of an incestuous relationship—she had great obstacles to overcome, which were made doubly difficult by the times in which she lived and the importance of her family connections. The truth of her background was kept a secret from the world until twenty years after her death, although it became known in her lifetime to a considerable number of people close to the Leigh family and to Lady Noel Byron's circle.

My interest in George Noel Gordon, Lord Byron, began many years ago when I read *The Glorious Apollo,* a fictionalized biography by E. Barrington. From then on I read every biography about Byron as it appeared in bookstores or on library shelves. *The Life of Anne Isabella, Lady Noel Byron* by E. C. Mayne was my first real introduction to Medora Leigh, but it is so biased in favor of Lady Byron that it shows Medora in a very bad light. The story of this fascinating but ungrateful and often disagreeable girl piqued my curiosity. It struck me that E. C. Mayne's portrayal of Medora Leigh was based too much on Lady Byron's reactions and on the conclusions expressed by her in letters and journals, as well as on the reactions of her friends and cohorts. Before reaching my own conclusions I decided to try to find other sources of information.

Twelve years of digging and delving have only increased my sympathy and affection, even admiration, for Elizabeth Medora, or Libby, as I have come to think of her. It was the name used by her family, the name she also seemed to prefer. I feel it suits her mercurial personality better than the more exotic Medora, which nobody called her after she was three. Medora was the name of one of Byron's ill-starred, passive Oriental heroines, the childhood sweetheart of Conrad "The Corsair." Certainly, Libby's life was ill-starred, but passive she could never have been with her heritage. Undoubtedly she made many grave mistakes and deserved some of the tribulations that beset her; in some respects she could be called a nineteenth-century delinquent. Yet after a thorough examination of available facts about her life, one is amazed to see that she came through as well as she did and eventually was able to redeem herself. Seldom has there been a more unfortunate example of the exploitation of a child to serve the selfish interests of those who professed to love and protect her.

As with any list of source material, this note cannot fully acknowledge the contributions of many busy people who took the time to answer my requests for information and were willing, whenever possible, to share their knowledge. I refer especially to letters from the following esteemed biographers of Byron: Professor Leslie Marchand, Professor Ernest J. Lovell, Jr., Doris Langley Moore, and Peter Quennell. Mr. Quennell also sent me an old photograph of Elizabeth Medora's birthplace, Six Mile Bottom, which he gave me permission to use.

Dr. A. L. Rowse, the distinguished biographer of Shakespeare and Marlowe, whom I met at the Huntington Memorial Library in San Marino, California, gave me interesting information about the Trevanion family in Cornwall. He also put me in touch with Mrs. Rosamund Clerk, granddaughter of Henry Trevanion's legitimate daughter Ada, who sent me some fascinating personal details of Henry's family.

I am indebted to Miss Christine Hawkridge, Senior Assistant Archivist, County Record Office, Truro, Cornwall, for sending me important facts dealing with the Trevanion family and Caerhays Castle, and a copy of the Trevanion family tree. In this connection, I want to thank my friends the Honorable Cecil Howard and Mrs. Howard for putting me in touch with Miss Hawkridge.

Mr. Derek Brown, District Librarian of Esher, Surrey, provided me with a wealth of nineteenth-century data which he culled from local documents and historical accounts. This material dealt with the then village of Esher, where Lady Byron made her home for several years at Moore Place. The material also dealt with Ockham Park, the country estate of the Earl and Countess of Lovelace. The Countess, Ada, was Byron's only legitimate child.

My thanks go also to Sir Berkeley Ormerod of the British Information Service, New York, for suggesting sources that provided me with facts about Captain Joseph Barrallier, i.e. the Public Record Office, London, and the War Office Record Centre, Hayes, Middlesex. And I am grateful to my friend Don Moore for guiding me to Sir Berkeley Ormerod.

Mother Mary Clarissa, D.C., of St. Vincent's Academy, Shreveport, Louisiana, was kind enough to send me valuable background data about the Cistercian Order, Daughters of the Cross, and its activities in nineteenth-century Brittany.

My friend Beulah Roth was most generous of her time in helping me in the translation of *Le Secret de Byron* by Roger de Vivie de Regie which deals with Elizabeth Medora's life and last years in France; without it this biography would have been incomplete. Through Mrs. Roth I was also given the name of Mrs. Francis Wormald, Newmarket, England, who sent me interesting local lore about Elizabeth Medora's birthplace.

I want to express my gratitude to my friends John D. and Harriet Weaver who were the first to suggest that I undertake the research necessary for the writing of this biography. And all my thanks to my friend John Collier for his endless patience in reading the various drafts of the manuscript and giving me invaluable advice and suggestions.

I take this opportunity to acknowledge the debt I owe to some of my friends who, in their own way, gave me their encouragement and support which made it possible for me to complete this book: Pauline and Herschel Daugherty, John Dyett, Doris Gilbert, Marian Hanisch, Maxae and Cecil Kersten, Lenard Kester, Raymond Friday Locke, Katherine and Michael Meehl, Dr. and Mrs. Norman Nixon, Everett Riskin, Walter Schmidt, Jan and Marian Stachowski, Alice Young, and Jeane Wood.

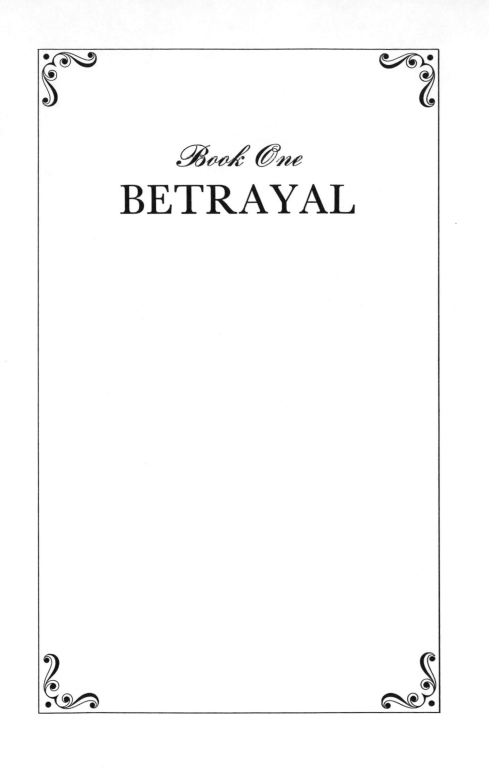

Book One

BETRAYAL

I

My hope on high—my all below.
Earth holds no other like to thee,
Or, if it doth, in vain for me:
For worlds I dare not view the dame
Resembling thee, yet not the same.
The very crimes that mar my youth,
This bed of death—attest my truth!
'Tis all too late—thou wert, thou art
The cherish'd madness of my heart!

—THE GIAOUR

Elizabeth Medora Leigh born at
Six Mile Bottom April 15th 1814.
Christened there, May 20th 1814 by
the Revd. C. Wedge. Sponsors—
The Dss. of Rutland   Mrs Wilmot
and Lord Byron.

ENTERED IN HER BIBLE BY THE
HONORABLE AUGUSTA LEIGH

APRIL 15, 1814, WAS NOT AN UNUSUAL DAY IN ENGLAND as days went. The news was full of Napoleon's abdication and the glory of the Duke of Wellington, while off in America the Royal Navy was giving a good account of itself against the stubborn Yankees who refused to admit that Britannia ruled the waves. There was trouble on the home front, but it would soon straighten out. Men who prided themselves on work done with their own hands resented the new machines which did the same work in half the time. These malcontents vented their

3

wrath by wanton destruction of the machine, and they had the audacity to lay most of the blame on the long and costly war in Europe. This, despite the fact that the war had brought about the downfall of the Emperor of France, and France had been for centuries their enemy. Napoleon would make one more desperate try, but in June of the following year Waterloo would be his finish. As far as England went, however, God was in his heaven and all was right with the world.

On the road between the Newmarket racecourse and Cambridge, at Six Mile Bottom, stood the country house of Lieutenant Colonel George Leigh of the Tenth Dragoons. Colonel Leigh had seen military service in Spain during the Peninsular War but at the moment he was back in England. His wife, Augusta, had some reason to consider this particular day fairly important because she was in the throes of giving birth to her fourth child. The baby proved to be a girl who would be christened Elizabeth Medora Leigh.

The Colonel was off in Yorkshire; he was seldom home during the racing season except when the meets were held at Newmarket. The birth of a child was hardly a reason for remaining at Six Mile Bottom. The house was comfortable enough but already too small for a growing family, and inasmuch as the Leighs were always afflicted with money troubles the place was not kept up too well. The Colonel, alas, had a passion for betting and traveled in a circle of men who were far richer than he, men who were also cronies of the Prince Regent. The result was that the Colonel was always up to his ears in debt and quite unable to provide properly for his wife and children. He simply took it for granted that Augusta would manage on her own—and she did—up to a point.

In London it was the height of the season; the stately London houses of the aristocracy—Holland House, Melbourne House, St. James's Palace—all were open and providing brilliant entertainment for those who belonged. There was a young man in London who belonged, but his thoughts were not on waltzing parties; he was anxiously awaiting news from Six Mile

Bottom. The young man had good reason to be anxious because, he, George Gordon, Lord Byron, was the father of the child. If the Honorable Augusta Leigh had been merely the country wife of a wandering husband, seduced by the attentions of the most sought-after young bachelor of the year, the birth of Eliza-beth Medora Leigh would not have caused undue comment in the circles comprising Society, even with those in the know. It was an oft-told joke that Lady Oxford's children bore a re-markable resemblance to some of her husband's friends! Hand-some young gentlemen were allowed to sow as many wild oats as they pleased as long as they behaved with reasonable propri-ety, or with such impudence that they provided a subject for conversation. But this was no ordinary love affair, and though it was not generally known, there were just enough people who did know to insure its being the worst kept secret of the year. The Honorable Augusta Leigh was Lord Byron's half-sister. Both had the same father, and in his day he too had provided his own share of juicy scandal.

Handsome Captain John Byron, a direct descendant of the noble Byrons of Newstead, had been known as "Mad Jack." He was not mad in the true sense of the word (though insanity ran in the family), but he was wildly reckless and spendthrift, having gone through the sizable fortunes of two wives with such speed that one avalanche of debts was barely paid before an-other set came due. This rash extravagance coupled with a tem-pestuous love life did not augur well for the emotional stability of his children, and their chances for a normal existence were lessened even more by the instability of the two mothers. Augusta's mother was the Baroness Conyers, a beautiful girl who married the Marquis of Carmarthen (later fifth Duke of Leeds), bore him three children, then eloped with Mad Jack. After being divorced she married Captain Byron, and then a short time after giving birth to Augusta, she died. During this all too brief period, the dashing Captain went through every penny of his wife's fortune. There was nothing else to do but find another heiress, and he found her very soon. She was

Catherine Gordon who was by no means as worthy a conquest as the Baroness Conyers, but she was indirectly descended from the Stuarts and possessed a considerable fortune which made up for her lack of great beauty. In three years of marriage, Mad Jack spent all her money, and during this disillusioning period she presented him with a son christened George Gordon. Catherine Byron did possess some strength of character, and was by nature a thrifty Scotswoman, but she was hot-tempered and inordinately proud.

Such was the heritage of Medora. From her mother she inherited a violent emotional nature and a complete lack of money sense; from her father she inherited the same emotional nature plus fierce pride, temper, and a liking for money. From both her parents she received the Byron charm and good looks; from neither did she receive the inner security which might have helped her over the rough spots, for the simple reason that emotional security had never been the lot of either of her parents.

Not that there was much foreboding in the mind of the newborn infant's mother, once she saw that the little creature was not born deformed, a monster, or any of the age-old horrors which were supposed to be the fruit of incest. Augusta was never a deep woman and contemplation was not one of her attributes. As far as she was concerned, she'd had her adventure, but now it was over and no harm done. She was really quite fond of "that impossible gentleman," [1] her husband, and would be until many years later when circumstances ruled otherwise. She had been determined to marry the gallant Colonel Leigh, who was also her cousin, and had waited three years for him until he was in a position to take a wife. He had turned out to be almost as spendthrift as Mad Jack Byron, which would seem to prove the old adage that girls marry men who are like their fathers. She muddled along, making allowances, bringing up her children as best she could, and refusing to face facts because reality was too unpleasant. It was thus with her in the spring of 1813—a woman of twenty-nine whose life was more or less in a stalemate, doomed to unimportance—until she came face to face with the man who was to change her life beyond any possibility of return or hope of salvation.

She had seen little of her half-brother George since they were children. He had lived with his mother in Aberdeen and Augusta had ended up under the protective wing of her maternal grandmother, Lady Holdernesse. She was five years older than her brother and remembered him with the tolerant affection of an older sister who was too busy with her own pursuits to give much thought to that rather pudgy, lame boy with his Scotch burr and his crabby mother. He was a sensitive, proud boy who attached much more importance to the occasional letters and rare meetings than Augusta was capable of doing. He had barely known his father before the gallant Captain left his disillusioned wife and lost himself on the Continent, but he knew his mother only too well, and suffered greatly at her hands. She had suffered too, at the hands of her husband, and her disposition was irascible; the worst type of woman to bring up a sensitive child, hugging him one moment, raging at him the next, calling him a lame brat. His right leg was wasted and a bit shorter than the other (some say because of infantile paralysis, others blame Mrs. Byron's excessive modesty at the time of the accouchement), but whatever the cause, it kept him from the regulation boyhood games, and he became dreamy, a voluminous reader, prone to moods of alternate gaiety and depression. The title came to him when he was nine, and part of his inheritance was Newstead Abbey, but his mother was too poor to live in it or up to it, so the boy had the humiliation of being not only title-poor but land-poor. The letters from Augusta were precious to him, and they corresponded from time to time all during his adolescence, his years of travel after coming into a small sum of money, his return to London. And then —overnight he became famous, and he was the social idol of the year.

At long last Augusta grew curious about this brother of hers. In some of her letters she had hinted that her marriage was not all it should be, for the Colonel loved not only the races but the dubious charms of chambermaids, and on more than one occasion Byron had replied that she could always pay him a visit if she needed a change of scene. In July, 1813, she took him up on it. He was glad to make her welcome, for his latest affair with the amusing Lady Oxford had just ended, and he was happy to break the ennui of a London summer out of season. Neither of them expected anything too exciting out of the visit, but they were delighted with each other from the moment they met.

Augusta found a divinely handsome young man whose halting gait only added to his romantic appearance. Yet he was not a pale, poetic creature capable only of scribbling verses and lounging about in drawing rooms. He was robust, of middle height, with powerful shoulders and arms as a result of his prowess as a swimmer. He was also an excellent boxer, very much a man's man in all ways.

Byron found a woman not conventionally beautiful but exactly his type, with a soft, voluptuous body, a mouth with the full, pouting Byron underlip, large dark eyes, and long silky black hair. She was shy like him, loved to poke fun at pomposity, enjoyed parlor games, had a merry way about her, laughed at anything and everything. Even her conversation pleased him, full of half-finished sentences and exclamations, most of it childish and artless; her mind flitted from one thing to another like a hummingbird.

In truth, she was like a bird which had been caged and now was free. It was wonderful to be taken everywhere by the most popular man in London who was obviously proud to be seen with her. She did not stay with him in his Bennett Street rooms, but she visited him every day—and all day. He had a housekeeper named Mrs. Mule, an elderly woman who looked like the witch of Endor, and there was the faithful Fletcher, his manservant, so everything was proper. She met his friends, went everywhere with him, had a grand time. She enjoyed herself so much that she remained three weeks rather than a fortnight, as was the original plan. He followed her to Six Mile Bottom within a few days, visited her twice, in fact, and persuaded her to come back to London for another visit. On the surface they seemed to be a delightful couple, more devoted perhaps than most brothers and sisters, but it was a romantic, paradoxical age in which sentimentality and cynicism walked side by side, and it was often difficult to separate one from the other.

Together these two basically frustrated people had found surcease from that awful inner loneliness which besets the insecure; they had become passionate lovers. When the seduction was accomplished is not known, but from all that was said and written by Byron, it was fairly soon after they met, and once a *fait accompli* it was all-consuming. It could not have been difficult for Byron to overwhelm Augusta; he had learned a great deal about the art of conquest and love from various ladies he met in his Grecian travels as well as from such charmers as Lady Caroline Lamb and Lady Oxford. The more deadly art of mental seduction he had learned at the feet of Lady Melbourne. Now, having become Byron's hummingbird, the artless, amiable Augusta (or Guss as he nicknamed her) fluttered helplessly, caught up in a tempest of passion which she had not really expected or desired and which, in a way, she feared even as she abandoned herself. She had only wanted to make her "baby Byron" happy, but now she found she was loved as few women would ever be loved and it was all too much for her. Byron loved her with an intensity which consumed him; Augusta loved him as much as she could. If he could have somehow contrived to keep his passion a secret, things might have leveled off in the course of time, but he was so possessed by this new and powerful experience that he could not resist taking Lady Melbourne into his confidence.

Lady Melbourne was one of the social arbiters of London, a perfect product of her time, now too old for romance though she had many vivid memories. She was only too willing to sponsor and become the confidante of the young man whose audacity and beauty were enough to intrigue any woman, regardless of age. Nothing delighted Society more than a good scandal. She could sit on the sidelines and watch with cynical detachment the agonized progress of Byron's love affair with her son's wife, Lady Caroline Lamb. Later she could encourage Byron's cursory interest in her young niece Annabella Milbanke though she was well aware that the serious, innocent young girl was not right for him.

Byron could not help being flattered by the marked attention of a woman of Lady Melbourne's assured social position; a woman, moreover, who was still a charmer. She was on the tall side, "full of grace and dignity, an animated countenance, intelligent features, captivating manners and conversation." [2] Small wonder that Byron was delighted to become one of her circle of intimates and to exchange innumerable letters with her. The trouble was that he abandoned discretion and wrote in detail about his liaison with Augusta—which he should not have done and Lady Melbourne should not have encouraged, and which he would later regret.

Unfortunately the redoubtable Lady Melbourne's vicarious enjoyment of the pleasure and pain of love came to a full stop at the thought of incest. She wrote to Byron severely that it was "a crime for which there is no salvation in this world, whatever there may be in the next." She also blamed Augusta for allowing it to happen, as women are likely to do in such cases, but Byron took all the blame:

> She was not aware of her own peril until it was too late, and I can only account for her subsequent abandon by an observation which I think is not unjust, that women are much more attached than men if they are treated with anything like fairness or tenderness.

Fairness and tenderness had not been Augusta's lot with her husband, but when she found herself pregnant and knew that only one person could have been responsible, she was dismayed; back at Six Mile Bottom by the latter part of August, she tried to settle down into some semblance of decorum. Her brother, however, could not behave decorously at any time; he gloried in the fact that she was going to have his child, telling it not only to Lady Melbourne but in a more guarded manner to other people. With those others he merely said that he was passionately in love with a woman who was with child by him and if it were a girl she would be named Medora. Medora was one of the characters in *The Corsair,* a tale of incestuous love on which he was at work. His friends knew this. They could put the puzzle together if they wished, but they tried not to, and there were those who would never admit that they believed it despite all the evidence.

Augusta's attempt to stem the tide of this headlong passion was none too successful. At one period Byron planned to take her abroad but gave it up through the efforts of Lady Melbourne. In December Augusta came up to London for a few days and Byron accompanied her back to Six Mile Bottom. Colonel Leigh was the only one involved who was not an indefatigible letter writer, so little is known about what he was doing and thinking during this hectic period.

All we know about him is through other people's letters, in which he is usually dismissed with a tolerant shrug. That he could have strong opinions and act with dispatch will be seen later, but at this time he seems to have worn his horns with bland indifference. His only sign of vexation was due to his wife's spending too much time away from home instead of being at his disposal if and when he dropped in. Probably it never occurred to him that his wife was still desirable; he had been taking her for granted as many other husbands have done—to their sorrow. There was nothing unusual about Augusta's being in the family way. He was glad to escape and allow his brother-in-law to keep her company, play with the children, and scribble poetry when the mood seized him. He did not like Byron and the feeling was mutual, but where the chance of making a touch was concerned, the Colonel was willing to rise above his prejudices, and Byron *had* been generous on more than one occasion.

Byron got along well with the children. While he was working on *The Corsair* they were in and out of the room at all hours, not in the least awed by their "Uncle By," and he endured these distractions with great good nature for a man so easily irritated by trifles. On sunny days he sometimes wrote outside, and generally sat beneath a huge tree which in due time became known as "Byron's tree." [3] Friends and acquaintances of the Leighs were amazed to see him there, deep in thought, unmindful of the screams and laughter of the Leigh children and their playmates. People would twit him about it. Never loath to put himself in the worst possible light for the sake of the sensation it caused, he retorted that he abominated children and entertained the greatest respect for the character of Herod. There would be a great shaking of heads and shrugging of shoulders. What next would the rascal say?

In February, 1814, Augusta was seven months along, and Byron took her with him to Newstead as any doting husband might do: give his wife a holiday away from complaining servants and noisy children. Newstead Abbey was a few miles from Nottingham, in Sherwood Forest of Robin Hood fame, a magnificent example of pure Gothic beauty though the building was falling into decay. Byron had done what he could with his limited means to restore the Abbey, but he could not do it completely. He had been able to furnish a bedroom for himself which looked out on the lake which was half covered by reeds and surrounded by woods. A few other rooms were furnished for guests, and one room served as his study and drawing room, but otherwise the vaulted corridors were empty—haunted, too!

A ruined abbey with the added fillip of a ghost; nothing could have pleased him more. He loved the place with a passion, and to be there alone, except for the servants, with an agreeable companion whom he also loved, provided one of the happiest times of his discontented life. That year, 1814, became known as the "year of the Great Frost." It started in February with a heavy snow which continued to fall for six weeks. All over England there was great suffering from the bitter cold, but at Newstead, before a blazing fire, it was heaven for Byron and Augusta. For ten days they were snowbound, which was a perfect excuse to make the ten days stretch into a fortnight.

True, there were moments when the sense of mortal sin plagued him, for he had been brought up in the harsh Calvinistic dogma of the Church of Scotland from which he never entirely freed himself. He was impelled to talk about it with Augusta, his partner in this same dark sin, but he was wasting his time. She veered away as she always did from unpleasant subjects. Oh, my stars! was there not enough trouble without deliberately searching out more? Soon she would succeed in making him laugh. He called her "Goose" because of her aimless gabbling, and her lack of depth never seemed to pall on him because, with all her foolish chatter, he knew that she idolized him with the mindless devotion of a dog. He was a great lover of dogs. He also enjoyed the companionship of intelligent women such as Lady Melbourne, Lady Oxford, later Mary Shelley, Madame de Staël, and Lady Blessington. He was a fascinating conversationalist judging from the number of accounts testifying to his pungent wit and shrewd observations about life and people as well as his mordant humor. The thing which saved Augusta from becoming a bit wearing was that she was never with him long enough. Ten days here, a fortnight there, then back to the family life he could never share completely.

Their idyll at Newstead came to an end, she returned to Six Mile Bottom, he to London, but in March she begged him to come to her as her confinement drew near. Colonel Leigh was away; she was plagued with vague fears, needing the fairness and tenderness which only Byron could provide. He remained a few days, had to return to London, but his thoughts were with her. Then came the news—a girl!

With tumultuous relief he imparted the glad tidings to

Lady Melbourne, and when she must have asked if all the danger in this ill-starred romance had been worthwhile, he answered:

> Oh, but it is worthwhile, I can't tell you why, and it is *not* an Ape, and if it is, that must be my fault; however, I will positively reform. You must however allow that it is utterly impossible I can ever be half so well liked elsewhere, and I have been all my life trying to make someone love me, and never got the sort I preferred before. But positively, she and I will grow good and all that, and so we are *now*, and shall be these three weeks and more too.[4]

He could not betray his true ecstasy to his worldly but disapproving friend—he had to inject a sly note—but he poured out his exultation in one of the most passionate declarations of love ever written, part of which is quoted here:

> I speak not, I trace not, I breathe not thy name,
> There is grief in the sound, there is guilt in the fame;
> But the tear which now burns on my cheek may impart
> The deep thoughts that swell in that silence of heart.
>
> Too brief for our passion, too long for our peace
> Were those hours—can their joy or their bitterness cease?
> We repent, we abjure, we will break from our chain,—
> We will part, we will fly, to unite it again!
>
> Oh! thine be the gladness, and mine be the guilt!
> Forgive me, adored one!—forsake if thou wilt;—
> But the heart which is thine shall expire undebased,
> And *man* shall not break it—whatever *thou* mayst.

There it was for all the world to see, and if Augusta could have responded with the same fierce scorn of public opinion—but alas! she was no Isolde. She was only an average woman who had the misfortune to be loved by a far from average man. Poseur that he was about many things, there can be no doubt that he loved her with great truth and sincerity and would go on doing so as long as he lived. But the very qualities which endeared her to him were not sustaining qualities; she had neither courage nor conviction and in the end life destroyed her.

As for their child who was christened Elizabeth Medora Leigh (and considered a Leigh by those not privy to the truth), she was doubly a Byron, and the Byrons were "mad, bad, and dangerous to know." Yet she might have weathered the exigencies of life with happier results had her father been less rash and her mother more responsible. Even before she was conceived, however, a chain of events had started which were to involve her parents with another person outside the Byronic orbit who was likewise destined to play an all-important part in Medora's life.

2

There was Miss Millpond, smooth as summer's sea,
That usual paragon, an only daughter,
Who seem'd the cream of equanimity,
Till skimm'd—and then there was some milk and water,
With a slight shade of blue too, it might be,
Beneath the surface; but what did it matter?
Love's riotous, but marriage should have quiet,
And being consumptive, live on a milk diet.

                —DON JUAN

DURING HIS HECTIC ROMANCE WITH AUGUSTA, BYRON HAD kept up a desultory correspondence with Lady Melbourne's country niece, Anne Isabella Milbanke (Annabella for short), who resided at the family home in Seaham, then a little seaport village in the county of Durham. As was the custom for the daughters of country squires with noble connections, Annabella came down to London for the season and attended a waltzing party given by her cousin, Lady Caroline Lamb, in March, 1812. This was her first glimpse of Byron though she did not actually talk to him until the following month. In her diary she wrote that she was "much pleased by the humanity of his feelings." She told her mother that he was without exception more agreeable in conversation than any person she ever knew. She considered him a "very bad, very good man, with impulses of sublime goodness which broke through his malevolent habits." Later in her diary she told herself that she was not bound to him by any strong feelings of sympathy until she heard him say,

"I have not a friend in the world." That it was said for effect never occurred to her. She had just turned twenty, a self-contained girl, pretty in a healthy, rosy-cheeked way, with a dainty graceful figure, utterly without artifice and full of high-minded disapproval of the antics of Society. Her avowed reason for going to London was to attend lectures on the density of the earth. Her Aunt, Lady Melbourne, and Byron promptly dubbed her the Princess of Parallelograms. In spite of this inclination toward pedantry, she was an intelligent talker though somewhat given to lofty thoughts. Unfortunately for Annabella, she was also intensely romantic.

Byron, jaded by female adulation and still enmeshed reluctantly with Lady Caroline Lamb, found this naive girl with her surprisingly masculine mind an interesting challenge. She had a number of things to recommend her. Edward Noel, Lord Wentworth, was her maternal uncle and on his death her mother, Lady Milbanke, would inherit his wealth and the arms of Noel. On Lady Milbanke's death all would pass to Annabella who was the only child. At this time the Milbankes were merely comfortably fixed but with great expectations, so Annabella would be a good catch. Byron had comparatively little money in this period, and though his worst detractors never suggested that he planned to marry for money, he had the realistic attitude about marriage which was typical of that time. If one must marry, it was sensible to marry an heiress, especially an heiress with titled connections.

He was not in love with Annabella, but he did admire her and perhaps made the mistake of many rakehells in believing that marriage to a good woman one respected but did not love would work out to everyone's advantage. He proposed in October of that year. She turned him down in a tactful way which did not close the door on the future. It was the age-old maneuver of a proud girl who knew herself to be deeply in love but did not want to appear too eager.

Contrary to the generally accepted idea that she was a prim little bluestocking lacking feminine allure, she had a number of suitors far more eligible socially and financially than Byron, and in at least two cases the suitors were genuinely involved emotionally. In 1811, a year before she met her Nemesis, the Honorable George Eden, son and heir of Lord Auckland, proposed and was rejected. The Eden family were close friends of the Milbankes and remained so despite the awkwardness of the situation. George remained loyal too and stayed a bachelor until death, many believing he never got over Annabella.

Another young man was William John Bankes, heir to a large estate and with an income of eight thousand pounds a year. He had been at Cambridge with Byron and kept up the friendship. One day he came to Byron in a state of great distress, bursting into such a flood of tears that it took time for him to control himself enough to explain the reason for his sorrow. He had been refused by Miss Milbanke! "Is *that* all?" answered the surprised Byron. "Perhaps then it will be of some consolation for you to know that I have also been refused by Miss Milbanke." [1] Inwardly he resented her refusal, but he was still intrigued by her.

In his Journal for November 29, 1813, Byron mentioned that he "had a very pretty letter from Annabella which I answered." He went on to say that she was "a very superior woman, and very little spoiled . . . very kind, generous and gentle, with very little pretension." That did not mean, however, that he was thinking of asking her a second time to marry him—he was then involved in his consuming love for Augusta. Had it not been for Annabella's persistence, the friendship might have withered from neglect.

After the birth of Medora, Lady Melbourne and Augusta both urged Byron to make a choice and settle down, in the preposterous belief that marriage would straighten things out. He promised to give it some thought, but that was all. He scraped together three thousand pounds which he gave to Augusta, ostensibly to pay off the Colonel's gambling debts but actually as a present in return for Medora. In July, 1814, he trundled Augusta and all the children off to Hastings for some sea bathing and in August he took them to Newstead. While there, Augusta kept after him to make up his mind about a bride. Several eligible heiresses were considered and a few formal offers were made, but fortunately for the heiresses, the offers were turned down. Meanwhile there were those letters from Annabella, long and full of worthy sentiments but on the dull side. Byron responded gallantly, though it is doubtful that he read them from start to finish.

Annabella was now the aggressor in her own oblique way, puzzled and not a little hurt by his change in attitude, though she made no reference to it. How humiliated she would have been, had she known of his offers to other girls. All she did know was that he did not seem to be involved in some new love affair; he was spending the summer with his sister and family, and what could be wrong with that? If anything, it augured well for his future as good husband material. Many a young fellow had settled down into wedded happiness, once he'd sown his wild oats. At Newstead Augusta continued to prod her reluctant brother until he wrote the fatal letter to Annabella which was more a guarded inquiry into the state of her feelings than an outright proposal. Annabella, alas, grabbed the bait: "I am and have long been pledged to myself to make your happiness my first object in life. If I can make you happy, I have no other consideration—."

Beautiful, moving words they were but written to a man who already possessed a woman who was making him happy.

The letter arrived at Newstead while Byron and Augusta were at the dinner table. He glanced through it, turned pale, then handed it to Augusta, saying wryly, "It never rains but it pours." She read the letter, handed it back and said brightly, "It is the best and prettiest I ever read." [2] This astonishing exchange sealed Annabella's fate as well that of Augusta, Byron, and their child. To do Byron justice, he knew almost immediately that he had made a grave mistake, but it was too late to back out. The terms of the marriage contract were already being drawn up, and the lawyers on both sides were shrewd bargainers. One day Annabella would have an income of close to eight thousand pounds a year, in those days a fortune, although it would belong to her husband to spend as he saw fit. Byron was more than generous in his settlement though it meant having to sell his beloved Newstead. To the world all appeared to be going according to custom but seldom has an engaged man dawdled so long before paying his betrothed the obligatory visit.

He tarried until late August at Newstead, wandering hand in hand through the park with Augusta, feeding the swans on the reedy lake, carving his initials along with hers on an old elm tree, or playing with his little daughter, now five months old. The fond parents had pet names for her—Mignonne—or "Do" which was short for Medora.³ At that time her first name, Elizabeth, was not used. They fancied they could see a strong family resemblance. The baby did have the luminous eyes of the Byrons; her hair was dark like her mother's rather than chestnut like her father's, but she had the pouting lower lip and the rounded chin of all Byrons. It was an enchanted time; the empty corridors of the old abbey rang with the screams of laughter of Georgiana and George, the young Leigh children. Yet it was a sad time too, for Byron and Augusta, because it would be the last time in their lives when they could be together without the presence of an outsider.

In late October Byron left London for Seaham to pay his betrothal visit, stopping en route at Six Mile Bottom. Colonel Leigh was at home for it was during the Newmarket racing season, and he twitted his brother-in-law by saying that they were laying bets at the track that the marriage would never come off. This remark plus the Colonel's unaccustomed presence was enough to drive the prospective bridegroom out of the house, and on November 2 he arrived at Seaham.

He had never cared much for Annabella's mother and now he found her a managing woman known in the vicinity as a "water finder." ⁴ Nothing could have aroused his sense of ridicule more than the sight of this officious woman trudging about with her divining rod. Actually, Judith Milbanke (née Noel) had been a charming, attractive young girl with many admirers. Women considered her a steadfast friend and trusted her because of her intense devotion to her husband. They were a great success socially, which went to Judith's head as time passed. She began to show signs of dogmatic assertiveness; her opinions were *right*. It was a trait which, alas, she encouraged in her daughter.

It was Annabella's misfortune to be the only child of a couple who had been childless for fifteen years—and to compound her bad luck, her mother was forty when she arrived in the world. Thus she was her parents' adored little girl, and the very familial loyalty which made Judith a good wife worked against her when it came to bringing up a child. Annabella became Perfection Incarnate. No man could possibly be good enough for her, especially not Byron, the intimate friend of Judith's sister-in-law, Lady Melbourne. Judith disapproved highly of Lady Melbourne's past indiscretions. It was a well-founded rumor, for example, that William Lamb, her favorite son (who one day became the illustrious Lord Melbourne, Queen Victoria's first prime minister and adviser), was really the son of Lord Egremont, one of Lady Melbourne's former lovers. Judith Noel was very strait-laced about such matters, and eventually Annabella would also be. But on the subject of Byron Judith had no influence over her daughter.

Annabella was in the grip of her first powerful sexual attraction; she *had* to marry Byron so that she could call him hers exclusively. And like any young girl in this state she was tremulous, easily hurt, frightened by the unladylike longings which burgeoned within her, wanting desperately to please and be pleased. Byron could have handled this aspect of the relationship, but Annabella was also a bluestocking who loved to talk abstractions with her poet, a pastime least likely to succeed with a man whose chief requirements in a woman were sexual abandon and an ability to laugh. He did, however, experiment with the former as much as he dared, and then he wrote to Lady Melbourne that his betrothed's passions were stronger than they had supposed. He did not fare nearly so well with laughter.

So he grew bored, a dangerous state of mind for him. It made him moody, sometimes intractable. He talked a lot about his sister, saying that Guss treated him like a child and spoiled him. "You remind me of her when you are playful," he told his fiancée. It was a hint which Annabella would have been wise to follow up, but she could not change her nature. The constant companionship of this deadly serious girl with her calm gray-blue eyes and didactic tongue drove him crazy with exasperation. She was so damnably sure of herself, so much the apple of her parents' eyes; it became a pleasure to take her down a peg or two. "If you had married me two years ago, you would have spared me what I can never get over," he told her darkly, then added in a low, malevolent tone, "I will be even with you yet." *That* startled her out of her composure which was what he wanted, and so he laughed it off. She could not laugh it off so easily.

There came a moment when she was prescient enough to realize that they were ill-suited and she gave him the opportunity to get out of the engagement as gracefully as possible. He did not grasp the chance which might have spared both of them endless torment and regret. According to Annabella's later statements, he was so shocked that he fainted dead away. Perhaps he did, but it could well have been one of his grand gestures. One can almost see him clasping his hand to his marble brow and collapsing at her feet, fully aware of the sensation it would cause. Whether it was pride, fear of reprisals from Augusta and Lady Melbourne, or some more sinister reason which held him back is not known.

And so, on January 2, 1815, these two woefully opposite people were married in the drawing room of the Milbanke house. "If I am unhappy, it will be my own fault," said Annabella to her mother as she went toward the carriage which was to take them on their honeymoon. John Cam Hobhouse, Byron's closest friend and best man, handed the bride into the carriage, then held out his hand in parting to the groom. Byron clung to it as a drowning man clings to a rock, was still clinging to it as the carriage moved away. Hobhouse wrote years later that he felt he had "buried a friend." [5]

While Byron was less than a week married and staying at Halnaby Hall (the honeymoon abode), Augusta wrote to him that she was in a state of great agitation at the hour of his wedding. Later when it was time to ask the newlyweds for the usual visit she made up all manner of excuses; the house was not large enough, someone else was coming, the children had colds, the servants were grumpy, anything to postpone the meeting. She had seen Annabella once when they attended the same social gathering but they had never met. She had read her letters full of sentiments and sermons which were very pretty and all that, but what was she really like? Suppose she was shrewd as well as moral! Augusta would have to be careful and set a good example so that her "baby Byron" would be careful, too. Not that she dreamed of renewing the old relationship. *That* was finished, but the residue of love remained: the memories which can trip one up. Augusta had never worried about her husband who had his own share of pitfalls to avoid, but Annabella had nothing to hide. Her mind would probably be full of her husband and all things relating to him; she might be jealous as all brides are, and jealousy is hydra-headed with a thousand eyes and ears.

Since she was Byron's only close relative she had to extend the expected invitation after considerable pressure from her brother. Some strong premonition of disaster must have plagued her when the sound of carriage wheels came to a stop in front of the house that fatal Sunday, March 12. She did not run down the stairs and meet Lord and Lady Byron in the hall. It would have been wiser had she done so for he came in first, "to prepare Guss" as he told Annabella who remained outside in the carriage. A more worldly girl might have wondered why it was necessary to "prepare" his sister for the arrival of his bride. He was upset by not finding Augusta in the hall and "returned in great perturbation" to hand out his wife.

When Augusta did come down the stairs she was ill at ease, greeting Annabella nicely but not kissing her. Byron's expression became black with one of his sudden tempers which he later excused by saying he'd just received a letter about some problem connected with the sale of Newstead. Despite the foreboding nature of this meeting, Augusta was pleased by her first impression of Lady Byron who seemed eager to be her friend and not in the least prim or standoffish. Augusta could not know then what she would know later, that Annabella's cordial manner hid wretched unhappiness. She had gone through experiences which would have unnerved a woman with less strength of will and she was to endure worse.

What is known of the saga of the honeymoon are the bitter memories of Lady Byron, described vividly in journal, diary, letters, confidences to friends. Byron wrote his own version in his Memoirs of which more will be told later, but since they were never published and only read by a handful of people sworn to secrecy, little is known of his side of the disaster. In public he contrived to give the impression that all had gone much better than expected and he was a happy man, chafing a little at being tied down, but still content with his lot. Lady Byron had no such sanguine impression.

"I will be even with you yet," he had warned her, and he made good his threat. After the carriage left Seaham he burst into "a wild sort of singing" and never spoke a word until the carriage rolled into the town of Durham, many miles distant. She could not know that wild singing was his way of covering up despair. A few years later, after he placed the drowned body of his friend Percy Shelley on a funeral pyre and watched it consumed to ashes, he rode through the night wildly singing.

Despair he must have felt on that grim drive, seated beside a girl he did not love and to whom he was tied for life. He felt remorse, too, for sacrificing her on the altar of expediency, but a guilty conscience is no insurance against resentment. Her abject silence and obvious bewilderment aroused the devil which always lurked within him, and the less she fought back the more bored and devilish he became. After their wedding supper he asked his bride "with every appearance of aversion" whether she planned to share the same bed with him. "I hate sleeping with any woman, but you may if you choose." A statement not calculated to arouse bride-like anticipation, but she chose.

At some time during the night he started out of his sleep. The bed was canopied in red and through the crimson curtains he saw a taper still burning at the end of the room. "Good God," he cried out, "I am surely in Hell." [6]

He probably *was* in Hell, though not necessarily because of his frustrated passion for Augusta. Byron had homosexual tendencies. Throughout his life he waged a battle against them which was never entirely won. At Cambridge he formed a passionate attachment for a choir boy named Edleston which was reciprocated. Edleston died of consumption while Byron was off on his Childe Harold wanderings in Greece. On his return he learned of the tragedy and was deeply griefstricken. Such youthful passions for one of the same sex are common occurrences, but in most cases they run their course, and the two involved settle down in the regulation way. But Byron's instinct for self-dramatization, his strong sexual appetite and curiosity, plus his belief in the Byron destiny of doom all militated against his doing anything in a regulation way. As he was wont to say, the lure of the forbidden was always a force in his life. Still, he had to be careful. Despite his reckless innuendoes about his passion for Augusta and his delight in causing sensation, there were limits beyond which he dared not go. There was a conventional streak in his nature and a certain snobbery which made him anxious to keep the good opinion of people who would have shuddered away from him had they known his secret. A few of his close friends knew about it—Tom Moore, for one— and Augusta. There seems to be no doubt that she protected him on occasion and worried about him; it may indeed have had something to do with her anxiety for him to marry.

In this connection, it is necessary to understand the attitude toward homosexuality which prevailed at the time. According to law, sodomy was a hanging matter. The Prince Regent, the absolute ruler of Society, abhorred homosexuality although he was an enthusiastic devotee of so-called natural vices. There were, of course, those in the upper echelons who practiced "unnatural vices," but they lived under the constant threat of blackmail and exposure. Such a misfortune could mean social ostracism if it became generally known, though not necessarily the death penalty. Then as now, wealth and the right connections came in handy; the aristocracy and gentry took care of their own by a conspiracy of silence—until scandal became too noisome to hide. In that case, the best plan was to take an extended sea voyage to faraway places until things simmered down.

Augusta's knowledge and acceptance of Byron's "tendencies" bound him to her all the more closely. With her he could be natural. His ego demanded the adulation of women and the excitement of conquest, but he was always more at ease around men. It is significant that the women he preferred were generally older than he, most of them willing to keep things on a platonic basis. Caroline Lamb, who abandoned herself to him with reckless passion, felt the sting of his cruelty. Toward the end of his life he was able to adjust himself to a close relationship with a loving woman, the young Contessa Guiccioli, but the half-friendly, half-passionate understanding given him by Augusta was "the sort he preferred."

Now he was married. The full import of the disaster became all too clear during the dreadful honeymoon at Halnaby Hall. There she was, the omnipresent bride, expecting to be cuddled and fawned upon by a doting bridegroom, at his side day and night. Except for the retinue of doting Milbanke servants, he was alone with Annabella. If he had been able to talk things out, she *might* have understood, but it is probable that he did not understand himself. All he could do was to blame her for his misery, and she reacted with the inevitable hurt feelings, soon coming to the conclusion that he had hated her all along. It was not true. He hated himself, and as always happens in such cases, he projected this self-hatred on his defenseless wife.

One day he said, "I will live with you—if I can—until I have got an heir—then I shall leave you. I only want a woman to laugh and don't care what she is besides. I can make Augusta laugh at anything. NO ONE makes me happy but Augusta." There were times when he roamed about the place like a caged tiger, raging at Annabella for having turned him down that first time, hinting at monstrous crimes committed in the past, threatening to be unfaithful as often as he pleased, and she could have all the lovers *she* pleased for it made no difference to *him*. He knew he was behaving like a fiend, and there were times when he would be overcome by remorse. Then he would hold her in his arms or make her sit upon his knee while he told her she was a "good Pip—a kind Pip—the best wife in the world." With the Byron penchant for nicknames he called her Pippin (Pip for short) because of her rosy apple cheeks, which were paler and thinner now. Augusta would have taken it all in stride, returned his kisses, held him close as a mother would a child, said some nonsensical thing which would make him laugh. Annabella could not match mood for mood; she had suffered too many shocks, too many blows to her pride. If, just once, she had ignored these dagger thrusts or shrugged them off with a laugh or quip—but she took them literally. "If you wouldn't mind my words, we shall get along very well together," he cried out with exasperation, forgetting that most of his words were said for one purpose only: to be minded. If by chance she did manage a smile, it was generally at one of his foibles and was resented accordingly. We know little about *her* foibles because she was too busy speaking or writing in her own defense in the days ahead, but many of her words betray a complacency and smugness which would have irritated almost any bridegroom. Even her eating habits were calculated to drive him crazy with impatience. She ate slowly, methodically; he finished a meal in two minutes and had to watch her intermin-

able mastication. Small wonder that one of his pet aversions was
to watch women eat. She was interested in philosophical subjects; he was bored by the abstract. She theorized; he was a doer.
She scorned superstition; he believed in omens and portents,
beliefs instilled in him during childhood by a Scottish nurse
who regaled him with nightmarish tales of goblins and ghosts.
He would not begin a journey on a Friday for it would mean
certain disaster. One cold night they were standing outside in
the garden of Halnaby Hall, watching a wisp of cloud drifting
toward the moon. "If it crosses the moon, I shall be ruined," he
said. "If it doesn't, all will be well." It crossed the moon.

By the time they were on their way to Six Mile Bottom,
Annabella had resigned herself to being an unloved wife. She
was the stuff that martyrs are made of and had reached a state
of almost mystical sublimation in which she would use all her
strength to "save" her husband from the abyss. And she would
make it her business to be a friend of his sister (the only one
who made him happy), despite those stirrings of jealousy which
she refused to recognize. As they approached Six Mile Bottom,
Byron was kinder than he had ever been; he seemed to pity her
as if he, like Augusta, had some premonition of disaster. "You
married me to make me happy, didn't you?" he asked. "Well,
you *do* make me happy." It made her happy too; perhaps the
last real happiness she was to know with him.

The previous weeks had been Purgatory—now she was to
know Hell. At least she was prepared; Augusta was not. After
dinner that first evening, Byron began to drink brandy; the
steady deliberate drinking of a man who is trying to escape his
own thoughts, or to gain courage enough to live with them. All
the frustrations and resentments of the past weeks, even months,
came into the open, not so much in rage as in a wild, savage
glee at the consternation he was inflicting, not on Annabella
but *Augusta*. She'd wanted him to marry, hadn't given him a
minute's peace until he wrote that damned letter which brought
them all to this miserable pass. She was responsible and now she
was going to share his suffering. There were oblique references

to the past, mysterious looks and ogles from eyes bleary with drink, coarse innuendoes which mystified Annabella and terrified Augusta, climaxed by his ordering his wife to go to her room. "We don't want *you*, my charmer." Later when he staggered into the bedroom, he said, "Now I have *her,* you will find I can do without *you,* in all ways."

Annabella was too naive at this time to understand fully what he meant; Augusta had tried to keep the situation under control by attempting to laugh off his remarks, though Annabella noted that sometimes she seemed literally to "sink from desperation." At a much later time Augusta told Annabella that he had tried to renew the old relationship, but she refused. Judging from his behavior during this visit and references made in one of his letters, Augusta continued to stand firm. The only explanation for his incredible behavior during those two weeks is that he may have suffered a form of nervous collapse induced by too much brandy and constant association with the woman who had been half-mother, half-lover to him, and who now withheld herself.

Annabella was surprised to see how well her short-tempered, difficult husband got along with the children and noted the tenderness in his expression whenever he looked at the baby of the family. "Do" would be a year old in a month, a pretty little thing with her big eyes and pouty mouth. One evening Annabella, Augusta, and Byron were all together and "Do" was for some reason still with them and not relegated to the nursery. Byron turned suddenly to his wife, pointed at the baby, and said, "Do you know that is my child?" [7] She was so taken aback that she could not speak but she saw Augusta's dismay. So did Byron. Delighted at the shock he caused, he warmed to the subject and began counting impishly on his fingers, calculating beyond a doubt that the Colonel could not possibly be the father.

Apparently it was smoothed over and Annabella elected to ignore the remark. Later Augusta warned Byron that he was doing and saying things which would have made any other woman suspect, surely the understatement of all time. For Annabella did suspect a great deal more than she admitted, but she took care to seem unobservant, perhaps through fear of more reprisals from her husband.

Hindsight can be a trap for the unwary. Annabella was not a fool; she had pride, she had right on her side. Why did she stay in that house and endure one humiliation after another? The answer lies partly in her upbringing and the times in which she lived, but mostly in herself. A girl who said, "If I am unhappy it will be my own fault," was not likely to run home to mother. That would prove she had made a mistake; her parents had never really approved of the match. She had a high regard for her own good sense and judgment and she was stubborn when people did not accept her evaluations as gospel truth. Everyone who ever came up against her had reason to regret it, if she decided they were wrong. She was as inflexible as iron. Snap her heart in two, yes; bend it—never.

Now married, and still desperately in love, she could not face facts. She was mesmerized by the Byron spell which would hang over her as long as she lived. Byron, Augusta, Elizabeth Medora—all of them bewitched her. Three times she dragged herself free, as an animal frees its maimed foot from a trap by gnawing it off. But incredibly, while Byron was stirring his brew of gall and wormwood, Annabella and Augusta closed ranks against their common enemy. This weird alliance cannot be explained away by saying that misery loves company. The truth is that Annabella, through some neurotic compulsion, was invariably drawn to the wrong people for her. Augusta responded by loving Annabella in her own meandering way as she loved everyone who was close to her.

They walked through the snow in the park surrounding the house, talking endlessly of one subject: how to deal with *that man*. At first Augusta made light of his aberrations; his bad temper was due to his silly diet, starving himself for days to keep down his weight, then wolfing a large meal and suffering the pangs of indigestion. As Annabella began to confide the story of her honeymoon in all its pitiful detail, Augusta was appalled but still veered away from the truth, begging the unhappy girl to try and understand him, make allowances as *she* did. She was kindness itself, but she was also thoughtless. One day a package arrived from London for Augusta which contained two gold brooches. They were adorned with mysterious crosses and each held a strand of Augusta's hair entwined with one of Byron's. Byron and Augusta wore these identical brooches, and he could not resist making sly comments for Annabella's benefit. "Does she know what these crosses mean?" He was referring to Augusta's habit of ending her sentences in letters with little crosses rather than periods; letters to *him,* that is. Annabella must have known what the crosses signified, but she refused to give him the satisfaction of admitting it, nor did she want to harbor disloyal thoughts about Guss, for Guss was her friend and ally. Yet she was deeply wounded and the wounds festered, spreading an insidious sickness of the soul. Byron's constant turning of the screws even wore down Augusta's patience and once she sighed bitterly and said, "You don't know *what* a fool I've been about him." When Annabella answered that no matter what Augusta did it could not be so *very* bad, Augusta shook her head. "You love me because you do not know me."

And so the days wore on. Byron knew the two women were talking about him and analyzing every word and action. The thought of Guss, "The Princess of Aimless Chatter," attempting to carry on a conversation with his dogmatic "Princess of Parallelograms" must have afforded him some sardonic amusement, but he still counted on good old Guss to take his side. If, in his saner moments, he regretted his betrayal of the woman he purported to love above all others, he had an odd way of showing it.

Two weeks were enough for Augusta and she made it clear that the visit must come to an end, though she made it equally clear that it was not Annabella's fault. The two women parted on affectionate terms. Within four days Guss was starting to make allowances for her brother. "His nerves and spirits are very far from what I wish them," she wrote a friend. "I think the uncomfortable state of his affairs is the cause." She referred to his financial affairs, trouble with selling Newstead and other such matters. Fortunately for her own peace of mind she possessed an elastic conscience.

Back in London and settled in their apartment at 13 Piccadilly Terrace, a smart address, Annabella hoped that things would take a turn for the better. Byron could see his men friends, serve on the Greenroom Committee of Drury Lane, and enjoy other such diversions. For a man who possessed Byron's sexual tendencies, the free and easy company of the theater must have been a welcome relief. Annabella was now pregnant which was a hopeful sign, for she might present him with the heir he wanted, and then he might be kinder to her. But things did not improve. In company they appeared to be a happy couple; his friends all commented on his attentiveness to his wife as he hung over her chair at social gatherings or handed her tenderly into the carriage. To all who would listen he extolled this "best of wives." Byron was no hypocrite, and he did have a conscience which he often resented but could not always ignore. Perhaps he was trying to save his wife's pride, or he may have found her less exasperating when he was not alone with her. Whatever he did in public was not enough to offset his behavior in private as far as Annabella was concerned. Most of the time he was "perfectly ferocious," drinking far too much and staying out too late with his rakehell friends. Then would follow days, sometimes a week, of kindness. When she had to visit her family for a brief time, his letters were unfailingly kind and tender. Away, he could appreciate her good qualities; at home, she drove him mad.

In April Annabella invited Guss to pay them a visit, hoping that her presence would make life easier, but it was Six Mile Bottom all over again. To make matters more unbearable, Byron seemed to enjoy his sister's company heartily. A perpetual state of nonsense existed between them (according to Annabella), and since she could not join in because nonsense was not her forte, she sat in judgment. Some of the nonsense shocked her; Byron was a habitué of the Greenroom these days, and the humor of the theater has never been known for its decorum. Guss affected a certain prudery in Society, but she was not prudish by nature and enjoyed a good laugh. She would sit up half the night with Byron after Annabella had been ordered to her room where she lay in bed, listening to the gales of merriment below, sobbing herself to sleep in a torment of jealousy and suspicion. It was insensitive of Augusta but she might have been trying to keep the peace. Annabella might also have learned a few lessons from this, but one cannot learn to be funny and gay.

During this period Augusta was appointed lady-in-waiting to Queen Charlotte, aged seventy, who had borne the King nine sons and six daughters in over half a century of marriage. Formerly Princess Charlotte of Mecklenburg, she and George III were well suited; both were of Germanic background and shared a love for cozy domesticity. It made for a dull Court, however, particularly for the friends of the Prince of Wales, and Queen Charlotte was a stodgy female who bored her ladies-in-waiting to the point of stupefaction. Since 1811 she had been parted from her husband, now blind and hopelessly insane, and under constant guard. The Prince of Wales was now Regent but he treated his old, lonely mother with the deference due a Queen. In spite of the ghastly dullness, it was still an honor to be appointed a lady-in-waiting, particularly in Augusta's case because it entitled her to a spacious apartment in St. James's Palace and a modest emolument of twelve hundred pounds a year.

While preparing for her new position at Court, Augusta stayed with Annabella and Byron at Piccadilly Terrace, a visit which would last more than ten weeks, longer than expected or desired by Annabella who finally hinted that enough was enough. Nevertheless the two women continued to write affectionate, chatty letters to each other. In one, Annabella said that

Byron had made his will, providing handsomely for "his dear Guss" and of course Annabella's "dear Guss." Once she mentioned that "By" was going to visit La Tante (Lady Melbourne) of whom Annabella did *not* approve. She was shrewd enough to feel that the old lady's influence was not necessarily salubrious.

Early in November, worn down by despair and approaching confinement, she begged Augusta to return. Guss was also well along in her fifth pregnancy, but she heeded her sister-in-law's cry of distress. She found Annabella unable to cope with her husband who was consorting with the women at Drury Lane and threatening to make one of them his mistress and bring her into the house. In justice to him, he had some excuse for this behavior. In addition to Augusta, Annabella had asked her former governess, Mrs. Clermont, to stay in the apartment, and this woman was anathema to Byron. He felt, rightly, that she was spying on him and gossiping maliciously, which indeed she was. To make matters worse, Augusta decided to invite Captain George Anson Byron, R.N., the heir presumptive, to stay in the house, too. That eminently decorous gentleman was Byron's cousin who seemed to be on good terms with his famous relative, though no two people could have been more disparate in character and temperament.

Never could a man have felt more alone in a crowd than Byron. To compound trouble, his finances were in wretched condition, creditors after him night and day. Annabella's uncle, Lord Wentworth, had died in April, and his fortune and estate of Kirkby Mallory had gone to Lady Milbanke who now resumed her maiden name of Lady Noel. All that stood between Annabella's inheritance of eight thousand a year was her mother who persisted in remaining hale and hearty.

Between the creditors and the constant presence of an unhappy wife and her reproachful cohorts, Byron behaved as if he had lost his reason. Augusta was the only rock to which Annabella could cling, but one evening Byron treated Augusta "with a familiarity which shocked and astonished" his wife to such an extent that she was finally convinced that all her nagging, dreadful suspicions were true. What this "familiarity" was she never disclosed, but in view of everything she had seen and heard, it seems (to misquote) a bit like straining at a camel and swallowing a gnat.

She said nothing to Augusta, having convinced herself that Byron had been the seducer and poor Guss the submissive victim in the best tradition of sentimental novels, but she taxed Byron with it in no uncertain terms. He admitted it was true, that it would go on being true, and Annabella would have to submit to it. She warned him that it was mortal sin, a crime against God and man; his reply, calculated to shock her, was to say that mortal sin was its very attraction, that "he had worn out all the *ordinary* forms of sin and longed for the stimulation of a new vice." He warned her that she dared not leave him or accuse him because "the world has made up its mind that By is a glorious boy, and the world will go for By—right or wrong." [8]

On December 10, 1815, the baby was born, not the son he wanted but a daughter who was christened Augusta Ada, though always called Ada. During Annabella's long and agonizing labor, the man who had been so fair, so tender and so anxious about the birth of that other daughter remained downstairs, getting drunk, popping soda water corks at the ceiling and singing bawdy songs. At least that is what Mrs. Clermont and Annabella claimed he was doing, though his friends denied most of it. Bailiffs were camping at the door and gossip was rampant. The world was waiting to spring at the throat of "the glorious boy."

In January, 1816, Byron wrote a note to his wife, suggesting it would be better for her to go to her parents at Kirkby Mallory and to take the child with her, as soon as she could travel. Nine days later she and the baby were ready to leave. Byron and Augusta were in the drawing room when Annabella entered. "Well, Byron," she said, "I have come to say good-bye," and held out her hand. He refused to take it and fled to the mantelpiece where he leaned with studied indifference, an instinctive gesture whenever he was unsure of himself. He glanced at the two women with a faint smile. "When shall we three meet again?" "In Heaven, I trust," was Annabella's quiet answer. Then she was gone. This was Annabella's version of the parting.[9]

It was not the version which Byron gave to Hobhouse. He said that he and Belle had a spat after which he dashed off a note asking her to leave, not forever but only to be away while he was breaking up the household. They patched up their quarrel and lived on conjugal terms until she left.[10]

Regardless of which version is true, they had separated for the moment, but Augusta still remained in the apartment. She was not the same old Guss, always ready for a laugh. She was heavy with child and worried about the gossip which was increasing day by day. Byron thought it would blow over and set about trying to induce Annabella to return to him, via letters as kind as his words had been cruel. Her answers were the wifely little missives of a devoted spouse who has gone to visit her parents. She signed some of them "Pip," his pet name for her.

The unfortunate girl was dreadfully torn, pacing the floor in an agony of indecision, his letters clenched in her hand. Had she been left to her own decisions she might have gone back to him because she was still desperately in love while knowing in her heart that it would never work. She had to contend with her mother, however, who had been shocked by her first sight of her daughter's hollow eyes and wasted cheeks. Annabella was strong enough to nurse the baby, but she was broken in spirit. Finally she told her parents what she had endured, and she confided many intimate details to Mrs. Clermont. That lady was horrified to such an extent that from then on she pictured Byron as a monster of depravity. There was no longer any question of Annabella's returning to Byron; her parents would not have allowed it.

Lady Noel looked about for a suitable lawyer to handle legal separation proceedings. After interviewing the highly recommended Dr. Stephen Lushington, she engaged him on the spot. "I would not but have seen Lushington for the world," she enthused. "He seems the most *gentlemanlike,* clear headed and clever Man I ever met with—." [11]

After he took charge there was never a chance for a reconciliation. Lushington became a close friend and adviser of Annabella's and in the future would also figure importantly in Elizabeth Medora's life. Nevertheless, for a time, Annabella tried to avoid a legal separation, preferring to think her husband insane and not responsible for his behavior. After a medical doctor talked at length with Byron he gave his opinion that there was no evidence of insanity.

Byron's friends, meanwhile, had been hearing flamboyant rumors about the reason for the separation. Hobhouse states that "when they heard the most positive assertions that the cause . . . was an addiction on the part of Lord Byron to vices of the most disgraceful and abominable nature, (they) were obliged to communicate the intelligence . . . to Byron." [12] These rumors were circulated by Lady Byron's adherents— although she steadfastly maintained that she had adopted "a policy of silence" in public. Privately she was anything but silent. Having decided against reconciling with her husband, she had to convince herself and others that she was *right* in her decision. At the time she made no specific accusations against Augusta, but gossip was rampant about Mrs. Leigh's part in the marital breakup, with Caroline Lamb doing her share of adding fuel to the fire.

When Byron heard all the accusations against him, he did not knuckle under as expected. Hobhouse states that

> B resolved to make a public defense. . . . From that time on all threats of public exposure ceased. Instead Lady B's advisers begged for a private arrangement—she and her friends talked of the cruelty of dragging her into a public court—although her father had been the first to threaten it (in a letter to B).[13]

And so the reasons were never made public, which proved in the long run to be a great disservice to everyone involved.

Conjecture is more titillating than truth. So far, the gossip had been more or less confined to those in the upper echelons of Society who were acquainted with the people involved. But when it was learned that legal papers were being drawn, and the public at large could gloat over gossip items in the newspapers, Society bared its collective teeth.

Those who had smarted from Byron's ridicule; those who had read *The Bride of Abydos, Lara, The Corsair,* all with a recurrent theme of incest; those who heeded Caroline Lamb's chatter—all of them fell upon his reputation and tore it apart, along with that of his sister. He had some good friends who stood by him, but the world, *his* world, turned its back or cut him to his face. Colonel Leigh, to everyone's surprise, stood by his wife staunchly, discrediting all rumors which came his way. Hobhouse and Tom Moore tried to intercede for Byron with Annabella, but it was useless. She had made up her mind.

Byron did not want to sign the separation papers, though his lawyer Hanson had done very well for him financially. He would still inherit what was agreed upon in the marriage settlement, after Lady Noel's death. He could keep what he already possessed. It was not the money which interfered with signing the papers. Belatedly he realized what he had done to his beloved Guss; to sign would be tantamount to admitting that the welter of rumors was true. To protect Augusta's reputation he went about London to the few houses still open to him, claiming that he could not understand why his wife had left him, that there was no basis for her accusations, that she was being manipulated by his enemies. He wrote letters to her in which he humbled his pride and entreated her to come back. There was even a brief interlude when he told Hobhouse and Moore that he would be willing to go to Kirkby Mallory to plead with Annabella in person if it were not for the presence of Lady Noel. At last he accepted the fact that Annabella was adamant. He signed the papers.

Augusta stood by him though she moved to St. James's to avoid further gossip. Colonel Leigh was annoyed—he wanted her home where she belonged—but to do him justice he seemed to appreciate her position. He came to London and stayed with her. At Kirkby Mallory, Annabella felt "apalled at the desert which seemed to spread before me—the touch of every hand seemed cold." She wrote innumerable letters to Augusta, and in one of them she asked, "Are you still my sister?" Augusta, in return, wrote lengthy epistles to Kirkby Mallory in which she went into detail about Byron's health, state of mind, and social life—what there was of it. Annabella, in fact, had a considerable number of friends, including George Anson Byron, who acted as her informants during this period. If they thought they were keeping their activities from Byron, they were mistaken. He was only too aware although he pretended ignorance.

A week before he signed the papers, Augusta came to bid him farewell. It was Easter Sunday, the day before their daughter's second birthday, but their thoughts were not on her. Byron was leaving in less than two weeks for Dover, to sail from the country which had turned against him. Augusta was going back to Six Mile Bottom. Their parting was heartbreaking; he had a presentiment that he would never see her again. After she had gone, he wrote to Annabella:

> More last words—not many—and such as you will attend to —answer I do not expect—nor does it import—but you will hear me. I have just parted from Augusta—almost the last being you had left me to part with. Wherever I may go—and I am going far—you and I can never meet again in this world —nor in the next. If any accident occurs to me—be kind to Augusta—if she is then nothing—to her children—.[14]

On April 23, 1816, he left England. Back at Six Mile Bottom, Augusta took up her life again, the same old life of grumbling servants, debts, a wandering husband, five children. Annabella was alone with the child Ada, Byron's legacy to her. Her life had come to a full stop—at twenty-four.

All unknowing of the havoc she had helped to cause and would add to later, Elizabeth Medora played with her toys, toddled through the house after her brothers and sisters, safe in the untroubled world of childhood. Eight years were to pass before another important event cast its shadow on her life. They seem to have been happy years, for happiness is seldom recorded, and nothing is mentioned about her during that period. But all around her snares were being set, not for her, though she would be caught in them along with the intended victim. And so, once again, events not directly connected with her but important to her future must be included in the story of her life.

3

The thorns which I have reap'd are of the tree
I planted; they have torn me, and I bleed.
I should have known what fruit would spring
From such a seed.

—CHILDE HAROLD'S PILGRIMAGE

In THE MIDDLE OF MAY, 1824, SAD NEWS WAS RELAYED TO Six Mile Bottom. It came from Mrs. Leigh in London where she was busy with her duties as lady-in-waiting to Queen Charlotte. The news was relayed to the children.

Uncle By was dead. His friend John Cam Hobhouse had been awakened out of a sound sleep to receive a note to that effect from another of Byron's friends, Douglas Kinnaird. Hobhouse had dispatched someone to St. James's to tell Byron's sister. Later in the day he came in person to discuss certain matters and to give Augusta the letter containing the fatal news. It was from Byron's faithful valet Fletcher, sent from Missalonghi, Greece, and it related in painful detail his master's last illness. Hobhouse and Augusta decided it would be best to send Captain George (as he was called), now the seventh Lord Byron, to inform Byron's widow who was living in a country house outside Beckenham, Kent.[1]

Later, Annabella wrote that when she saw Captain George arriving in the chaise—alone—she had a premonition that he was there to tell her of Byron's death.[2] For some weeks prior to this she had been arranging her papers relative to the mar-

41

riage and separation. The new Lord Byron was perhaps not fully prepared for the depth of her feelings on hearing the news. He offered to procure the various letters and dispatches if she so wished. She admitted that she had "no right to be considered by Byron's friends," but she "did have her feelings" and wanted to see the account of her husband's last moments.[3]

At Six Mile Bottom Georgiana (called Georgey) and George, the two oldest Leigh children, remembered their Uncle By well though they had not seen him for eight years. Now he was gone forever. He had died April 19 and it had taken all this time for word to arrive. He had financed an expedition to free Greece from Turkish rule, had given his money, his health, and his life to the cause of Freedom. It was a stirring story which would excite any child's imagination.

Georgey in particular could recall many happy times with her uncle at Newstead, at the seashore, and on a few occasions when she accompanied her mother on visits to Piccadilly Terrace during his year of marriage. She told her young sister Elizabeth Medora—Libby—about him.* If Libby recalled her Uncle By at all it would have been a subconscious memory. Although she probably listened attentively to whatever Georgey had to say about him, she was more interested in the fact that he had died four days after her tenth birthday.

She was very close to her sister Georgiana despite the seven years' difference in their ages. In temperament they were not at all alike. Georgiana was a shy, retiring girl. Libby was full of vitality, loaded with that overworked word charisma, which was also a Byron attribute, but she also had her share of the Byron hot temper. She was the Colonel's "favorite child," [4] and indeed, Libby had no reason to suspect that the Colonel was not her father. She was fond of him in spite of his spells of harshness and "had greater influence over him than anyone else when he

---

* When Elizabeth Medora was around three, the name of Medora and the pet name "Do" were dropped by the family. From then on she was called Libby except when she was referred to as Elizabeth by people other than her immediate family.

was violent." [5] She adored her mother, "dearest Moe" as she was called by her family. It was impossible not to love Moe though Augusta was no longer as attractive as she was when Byron knew her. She was forty-one and had given birth to seven children. One of them, the second daughter, named Augusta Mary, had been a source of great anguish to her parents because she proved to be of "weak intellect" and had to be "put away" in a nursing home for such children. Apart from the natural un-happiness which such a tragedy would cause, Augusta had to pay two hundred pounds a year to the asylum. She had taken on weight and was inclined to be blowsy, but she still had her lovely big eyes (extremely myopic) and her lovable personality. Everyone was fond of her and most were willing to overlook her part in the Byron separation scandal. It was felt that she had troubles enough with her husband, "that very helpless gentle-man" as Byron termed him. Not only did the Colonel expect her meager income to include a valet to attend to his needs but Augusta was also supposed to make good his debts and use her influence in high places to mend his fences with the Prince Regent after a falling out.

Assuredly Colonel Leigh had not improved with age. He was a tyrannical father to his sons except when he dragged them off to Newmarket during the racing season so that he could initiate them into betting and other dubious diversions. Poor Guss could not control him and her little income of eight hundred pounds a year was stretched beyond the vanishing point. The children were accustomed to bill collectors and irri-tated servants, but now that Uncle By was dead and gone things might improve. They had been told that he had provided for them in his will, and children being acquisitive creatures, the conjectures about future benefits probably occupied their minds more than the death of their famous uncle.

With Augusta it was always first things first, and at the moment she was concerned with the problem of Byron's Memoirs. During her meeting with Hobhouse, he had said that the first duty of everyone was to protect her brother's fame, so—what to do about those Memoirs? Byron had given them to his friend Tom Moore, but Moore, chronically short of cash, had sold them to Byron's publisher, Murray, for two thousand guineas. Hobhouse was indignant about that, and Augusta, always a straw in the wind, was indignant, too. Hobhouse knew the contents of those pages and feared that their uncomprising honesty might cause trouble. Augusta had never seen them, but she was alarmed. She had suffered under the lash of her brother's honesty, which was a more agreeable word than "indiscretion," and she was not anxious for more trouble. She learned that Moore, Kinnaird, and Murray wanted them to be preserved, in a vault if necessary, but not destroyed. Some time before his death Byron had written to Lady Byron, asking her to read the Memoirs since she was mentioned in them, and to make whatever notes and deletions she thought proper. Lady Byron had refused to have anything to do with them. So the decision was handed over to Augusta. For reasons of his own, Hobhouse wanted them destroyed, and it was not difficult to convince Augusta that this was the only sane thing to do. She seems not to have read them either; she took the word of Hobhouse. In her defense she had already experienced more than her share of unearthing painful memories, as will be told later. Also it is possible that she feared there might have been some hints about that other side of her brother's life. According to reports he had been less discreet once he left England, especially during his period of debauchery in Venice, and also in Greece. Augusta thought the Memoirs should be burnt. After a great deal of argument, Augusta and Hobhouse had their way.[6]

Thus the Memoirs of a great man, certainly the outstanding personality of his time, were cast summarily into the flames. What they might have told us about his feelings during his ill-fated marriage, his thoughts about Augusta, Medora, friends and foes; all were lost to the world. The few who did read them always swore that he was eminently just in his evaluations of his marriage. Unwittingly Hobhouse did his friend a great injustice because for many years the world had only Lady Byron's version which grew more bitter and one-sided as she grew older. Ironically for her, she got the blame for the destruction of the Memoirs. People had indeed turned against the glorious boy for a while, but now he had become a minor deity. The world passed judgment on Annabella as an unyielding and unloving wife; just as her husband prophesied.

When Byron's body arrived from Greece at the end of June, 1824, there was a crowd at the dock. Many wished to view the remains, for then, as now, the world had its share of morbid sensation seekers. Among those close to him, only Augusta had the courage to look upon him in death, and she wept at the sight of those chestnut curls shot through with gray. Young men all over England and the Continent wore black arm bands.

The funeral cortege moved slowly through the country lanes toward the little churchyard at Hucknall Torkard near Newstead (his beloved Newstead now in other hands) where he was to be buried beside his ancestors. All along the way there were groups of mourners as well as the merely curious who watched the black-plumed horses drawing the hearse followed by empty carriages. The aristocracy was giving homage in spirit if not in the flesh.

Lady Byron did not attend the funeral though she had wept bitterly as poor, faithful Fletcher tried to tell her of Byron's last moments. Almost his last words had been "Go to Lady Byron—tell her—," but the rest was mumbled and unintelligible, and Fletcher was too honest to make up a message. In vain did she beg for him to try to remember. That lost message was to haunt Annabella to the end of her long and lonely life. On July 16 all that was mortal of George Noel Gordon, sixth Lord Byron, was laid to rest, dead at thirty-six. He was free. Not so Annabella, Augusta, Elizabeth Medora. They were left to "reap the bitter harvest."

Augusta's share of this harvest and indirectly Elizabeth Medora's had rooted and sprouted within two months after Byron's departure from England eight years before. There must have been many times during that period when Libby was mystified by the preoccupied, even erratic behavior of her "dearest Moe." How often Libby and the other children saw her at her desk, writing letter after letter with her long feverish scrawl, stopping to think, pushing back the heavy hair from her forehead with a hand which trembled, and then with a quick sigh, attacking the paper again. Or when the post arrived there were those letters she would open nervously, lips twitching. Sometimes she tossed the pages on the desk with a sudden gust of anger, sometimes with a sigh of despair. Even letters from Uncle By did not always make her happy; too often they made her weep. Libby would throw her arms around her Moe with the quick emotion of a child, but she would still be embarrassed —for Moe. Mothers are supposed at all times to behave like mothers, not like other people. Libby was too absorbed in her growing pains to comprehend that Moe was also enduring pain at the hands of two women who professed to be her best friends. One of them was Lady Byron, the other was the Honorable Therese Villiers, Augusta's lifetime confidante. If anyone had accused them of subjecting a fellow human being to needless torment they would have been genuinely appalled. They were only trying to "save" her. Since Mrs. Villiers would play an important part in Libby's future, one should know something about her.

In spite of her French name she was an Englishwoman, born Theresa Parker in 1775, and a sister of Lord Borington who was created Earl of Morley in 1815.[7] In 1798 she married George Villiers, third son of the Earl of Clarendon. They had four sons and a daughter. From childhood she had known Augusta as well as Augusta's half-sister Mary, Lady Chichester. She was nine years older than Augusta but was her closest friend. In 1813, when Augusta paid her first visit to Byron in London, she stayed with Therese. In the light of subsequent events she seemed not to have confided in Therese about her intimate relationship with her brother, but then it was scarcely a suitable topic for discussion, even with a friend like Therese.

Therese Villiers was a warm-hearted, worldly woman who moved in the Prince Regent's orbit. She had, in fact, pulled a few wires with the Prince on Colonel Leigh's behalf, after Waterloo when he had to find another position. Therese had met Annabella before she married Byron, but it was a casual meeting which might have ended there had not Augusta brought them together. There was an age difference of nineteen years between Mrs. Villiers and Lady Byron, and their temperaments were completely opposite, but Annabella was always impressed by Augusta's high ranking friends who seemed so assured and sophisticated to a little country lass from Seaham. The real friendship began when Therese wrote to Annabella on February 26, 1816, anent Augusta. To quote part of her letter:

> . . . from the conviction I feel that your affection for Augusta is unchanged and your good opinion of her undiminished, I am persuaded you will be anxious to do her justice in the eyes of an ill-natured world; justice which *no one but yourself* can render her. — amongst the many very malicious and caluminous reports which are now most industriously circulated in London respecting your separation from Lord Byron, there is *one* which is in the *highest degree* prejudicial to *Augusta's character,* and in my vehemently and indignantly resenting *such* a calumny, I was assured that the report was confirmed by your refusal to assign a reason for your separation. . . .[8]

In effect, Therese was asking Lady Byron to let it be known that she believed in Augusta's loyalty and innocence.

Annabella replied promptly that she regretted the gossip, that she did indeed believe in Augusta's loyalty but that it would be improper for her to make public the reason for the separation. The result of this exchange was that, not long after Byron left England, Annabella paid a call on Mrs. Villiers. As with Pandora, the lure of the forbidden was powerful. It was possible that Mrs. Villiers might know things not known by Annabella, though she deluded herself that she had a worthier motive.

After a certain amount of backing and filling, with Mrs. Villiers feeling that only a public disavowal of the ugly rumors would help Augusta, Annabella finally was compelled to disillusion Therese by saying that, alas, the rumors were true. She had heard everything from Byron's own lips on more than one occasion.

Therese Villiers was not so much shocked as angry at Augusta for her want of honesty. Augusta had represented herself as entirely guiltless—Therese had believed her—and now she felt like a dupe. Off she went to Augusta and demanded the truth. Augusta, an artful dodger, evaded the issue. The more Therese tried to force some admission of guilt, the more transparent were Augusta's evasions. What was even more reprehensible, she seemed to feel no repentance. In comparison, Lady Byron seemed a tower of integrity; Augusta lost and Annabella acquired a champion.

The ladies agreed that Augusta had to be taught the error of her ways, but they decided to wait until after her approaching confinement. The convolutions of Annabella's thinking were more obscure than Therese's, but they shared the same idea: Augusta did not appreciate Annabella's long forbearance, and it was time that she did. In May, after Augusta gave birth to Frederick, Annabella wrote to her, saying among other things: ". . . circumstances in your conduct—indispensably impose on me the duty of *limiting* my correspondence with you. . . ." After enumerating the circumstances in vague terms, she added:

> I shall still not regret having loved and trusted you so entirely—I am truly interested in the welfare of your children, and should your present unhappy dispositions be seriously changed, you will not then be deceived in considering me as one who will afford every service and consolation of your faithful friend.

In spite of this Annabellish ambiguity, Augusta got the point. Her answer is too long to quote in full but one part is important in regard to Libby's future:

I have been assured that the tide of public opinion has been
so turned against my Brother that the least appearance of
coolness on your part towards me would injure me most
seriously—and I am therefor for the sake of my children compelled to accept from your compassion the "limited intercourse" which is all you can grant to one whom you pro-
nounce no longer worthy of your esteem or affection.[9]

That should have been the end of it. Augusta had responded with proper humility, but reading between the lines
it was easy to see that Augusta was frightened. Annabella had
suffered cruelly because of this woman and the desire for revenge is an all too human frailty. Not that she could admit to
revenge; that was not Christian. She found her answer. She had
not been able to save Byron from the abyss; so she would redeem Augusta. Augusta must be induced to confess in order to
save her soul. Strangely enough, Mrs. Villiers agreed. Why this
sophisticated, sympathetic woman allowed herself to become involved in a campaign of spiritual blackmail is one of the mys-
teries which make the human race an endless enigma, but she
condoned her action by feeling that she was protecting Augusta
from herself.

Exacting confession was no problem. Poor Guss, always
willing to do what others wanted if it made them happy, did
the wrong thing. The next time Augusta saw Therese was just
prior to an important social occasion; she had been "ordered to
come up for the Regent's fete," and had written her friend to
"prepare her dress for her." [10] This in itself was not wrong, for
the commands of the Prince Regent were not to be ignored,
especially by a lady-in-waiting. But when the "sinner" arrived
from Six Mile Bottom, Therese found no humble penitent
waiting on her doorstep. As Therese wrote later to Annabella:
". . . our whole conversation was on Gauzes and Sattins—but
I was foolishly disatisfied—I thought her looking quite stout
and well (which by the by she still does), and perfectly cool and
easy, having apparently nothing on her mind. . . ." [11]

As if this cavalier attitude were not enough, Augusta was

still corresponding with her brother; Therese had seen fat letters on the desk. Annabella was quick to agree that this would never do, but she had to find some logical reason for stopping it. Again she fell back on Duty. Byron's influence was negating whatever good had been accomplished, and it was her Duty, as well as Therese's, to put an end to it.

At first Augusta was counseled not to answer his letters except when absolutely necessary, and then in a formal way. The unfortunate woman was torn, for he *had* been good to her most of the time—because of her he was an exile—the least she could do was to answer his letters. There was a hectic time when Byron suddenly announced that he was coming back to England for the sole purpose of persuading Augusta to return to Europe with him. The arrival of the Spanish Armada could not have aroused more excitement or trepidation. Letters flew back and forth between Lady Byron and Mrs. Villiers, along with stern warnings to Augusta to nip this idea in the bud. Augusta obeyed, and Byron irritably replied, "Very well—I *won't* come —." Everyone breathed a bit easier, but after Byron got over his anger, he continued to write affectionately, and presumably Augusta answered warmly. There was nothing left to do but have a heart-to-heart talk with the recalcitrant sinner. Augusta assented to a meeting; she would have done anything to have them leave her in peace. And she was more than willing to explain the "state of her feelings"; in fact, she gave them more than they bargained for.

Her brother had been a bad boy and all that, but she hadn't wanted to do wrong, and she'd never been disloyal to Annabella. She'd been a good friend when Annabella needed a friend. On and on she rambled as she always did, pushing back her hair from her forehead as she did when she was nervous, but always the conversation was brought back to one point. If the correspondence between her and her brother was innocent, she should have no objection to letting the others read the letters. Augusta was no match for two Torquemadas. She agreed to pass on his letters. She would be circumspect in her replies, and of course, she would never let him know what was going on. Dutifully she handed the letters over as they came to her, including some already in her possession. Here is a quotation from one:

> . . . I have never ceased nor can I cease to feel for you a moment that perfect and boundless attachment which bound and binds me to you—which renders me utterly incapable of real love for any other human being—for what could they be to me after you? My own XXXX we may have been very wrong—but I repent of nothing except that accursed marriage —and your refusing to continue to love me as you had loved me. I can neither forget nor quite forgive you for that precious piece of reformation—but I can't be anything other than I have been—and whenever I love anything it is because it reminds me in some way or other of yourself . . . it is heartbreaking to think of our long Separation—and I am sure more than punishment for all our sins. . . . I . . . have no cause of grief but the reflection that we are not together—. When you write to me speak to me of yourself—and say that you love me—never mind commonplace people and topics—which can be in no degree interesting to me who sees nothing in England but the country which holds *you*—or around it but the sea which divides us. —They say absence destroys weak passions —and confirms strong ones. Alas! *mine* for you is the union of all passions and all affections.[12]

This was written from Venice, May 17, 1819, three years after he left England, but his love was still as strong as death. Shocking as it is to know of Augusta's grand betrayal, it is still true that *he* had betrayed *her* by his wagging tongue and indiscreet pen, and for that she was at the mercy of her two persecutors. Still she must have derived some pleasure in turning over these passionate letters to the implacable Annabella. "They are absolute love letters" was Annabella's indignant reaction expressed to Mrs. Villiers. And how it must have galled her to read the one quoted above in contrast to one *she* received, also from Venice:

> Throughout the whole of this unhappy business, I have done my best to avoid the bitterness, which, however, is yet amongst

us; and it would be as well if even you at times recollected,
that the man who has been sacrificed in fame, in feelings, in
everything, to the convenience of your family, was he whom
you once loved, and who—whatever you may imagine to the
contrary—loved you. . . . If you think to reconcile yourself
to yourself by accumulating harshness against me, you are
again mistaken; you are not happy, nor even tranquil, nor will
you ever be so, even to the very moderate degree which is
permitted to general humanity. . . . You will smile at this
piece of prophecy—do so—, but recollect it: it is justified by
all human experience. No one was ever even the involuntary
cause of great evils to others without a requital: I have paid
and am paying for mine—so will you.[13]

Nevertheless, Annabella could analyze, dissect, judge, write
reams of correspondence to Mrs. Villiers, draw up lines of conduct for Augusta to follow. The worldly Mrs. Villiers must have
enjoyed reading these juicy missives meant only to be seen by
one pair of eyes. Eventually she and Annabella brought the sinner around to the point where Guss went over completely to the
enemy. She wrote to her brother that she had been shocked by
Don Juan and wished he hadn't written it. Byron loved her, but
he was never a man to suffer fools gladly. In a reply he reflected
wryly, "I am delighted to see *you* grown so moral. It is edifying."

He knew she was influenced in some way by that "infamous
fiend" of a wife, but there was little he could do. He had his
own life, and a full life it was despite his bitterness toward the
woman who forced him into it. Far off in lovely Italy, he was
secure in his fame, solaced by the love of the young and beautiful Contessa Teresa Guiccioli. He was now a rich man thanks
to the sale of Newstead and the success of his published works.
His wealth had been further increased at the death of Lady
Noel when he received his share of the marriage settlement. No
gain without some loss; he had to call himself George *Noel*
Gordon, Lord Byron, and signed his formal and business letters
"Noel Byron." This coupling of his name with that of the
"troublesome old busybody" must have made him wince each

time he wrote it. Nevertheless he was as content as a man of his temperament can be, and never forgot Guss. In 1820 he was still so concerned for her welfare that he even wrote to Lady Byron about it. She replied that "the past shall not prevent me from befriending Augusta Leigh and her children in any future circumstances which may call for my assistance. I promise to do so." [14] A year before his death he wrote to Guss, extending an invitation for her and the whole family, including the Colonel, to pay him a visit, and offering to foot the bill. Nothing came of it, but he forgave her. His letters were brotherly these days rather than loverly: "Do you remember when I was 'gentle and juvenile, curly and gay' and was myself in love with a certain silly person?" [15]

He often thought about his daughter Ada, the child he never knew who was now nine years old. He refused to write to Annabella directly about their daughter, but he did write to Guss:

> I wish you would obtain from Lady B some account of Ada's disposition, habits, studies, moral tendencies and temper as well as of her personal appearance. . . . When I am advised on these points I can form some notion of her character and what way her disposition or indisposition ought to be treated. At *her* present age I have an idea that I had many feelings and notions which people would not believe if I stated them *now,* and therefore I may as well keep them to myself. Is she social or solitary, taciturn or talkative, fond of reading or otherwise? And what is her tic—I mean her foible? Is she passionate? I hope that the Gods have made her anything save *poetical*—it is enough to have one such fool in a family.[16]

There is something endearing, almost pathetic, in his concern for Ada—something humorous, too—when he writes sagely: "I had dreadful and almost periodical headaches till I was fourteen—Perhaps she will get quite well when she arrives at womanhood—though if she is of so sanguine a habit * it is

---

* Ada had a tendency toward nosebleeds at this age.

probable that she may attain to that period earlier than is usual in our colder climate."

Did he ever question Augusta about his other daughter? Yes, but less directly, and using Libby's nickname. Sometimes it was "Da," sometimes "Do." In one letter, written not long after he left England, he asked with concern about Libby and told Augusta that he wanted to hear about the child. He also told her, quite sternly, never to write to him about Lady Byron, and indeed never even to use her name in correspondence.[17]

From Venice, in 1816, he wrote: "Pray remember me to the babes and tell me of little Da." Another from Verona: "Remember me to the child (er) and to Georgiana, who I suppose has grown a prodigious penwoman." [18]

In 1818 he had occasion to write to his friend Tom Moore about the death of one of Moore's children:

> I know how to feel with you because I am quite rapped up in my own children. Besides my little legitimate I have made unto myself an illegitimate since, [*] to say nothing of one before.[19]

As for Augusta herself, she muddled along, but constant financial troubles wore her down. She was reduced to begging and borrowing—from Byron, from other relatives, even from Annabella. The loans were lost in an ocean of debts.

Then, that summer of 1824, her life changed for the better. She had lost her "baby Byron" but she was an heiress. Byron had left her twenty-five thousand pounds outright. There was also sixty thousand, already settled on Lady Byron, which would be divided among the Leigh family in the event of Lady Byron's death. It was unlikely, however, that any Leighs would benefit by that for many years to come. Although Annabella was always suffering from obscure afflictions which gained her much sympathy and attention, she outlived almost everyone involved in her youth and middle age. Nevertheless, Augusta now possessed

---

* He refers to Allegra, his natural daughter by Clare Clairmont.

twenty-five thousand, in those days a substantial fortune. And with the expectation of sixty thousand more at some future date, the Leigh children would one day have sizable nest eggs.

A great day in the Leigh household! The children must have been astounded by the change in "Moe." *Now* when she sat at her desk, gone were gloom, the frayed nerves, the trembling hand; she was their old Moe again. One can picture Augusta, ebullient after seventeen years of genteel poverty, promising everybody everything at once. Georgie would have some sort of dowry to insure her making a good match, George and Frederick would have expectations and therefore could marry well, Henry and Emily would be able to have the toys they longed for as well as other needed things. She would put something substantial aside for Libby, too. *He* would have wished that. And there were George's gaming debts—and the butcher, the baker, the candlestickmaker! She had sickened on her diet of humble pie, but now it was all over. Poor Guss!

As soon as the news got around that Mrs. Leigh was an heiress, the creditors descended in a swarm. Debtors she never knew existed came forward—moneylenders she'd put off for years demanded their share plus interest. Down went the bank balance, and down went the brilliant plans. The locusts were everywhere, gobbling voraciously. Within two years they cleaned her out.

The good goose with all her goslings was back to doing what she'd always done—begging and borrowing—and the gander was up to his usual gandering. It was the beginning of the end for Augusta, not in years but in hope. From then on she sank slowly into the morass.

Libby, now twelve, was about to say farewell to childhood and start on her own perilous journey across the treacherous bog.

4

Oh, Love! what is it in this world
Of ours
Which makes it fatal to be loved?
　　　—DON JUAN

WHEN LIBBY WAS STILL ELEVEN, HER SISTER GEORGIANA became engaged to a distant cousin on the Byron side of the family. His name was Henry Trevanion, a young man ten years older than Libby and destined to be her nemesis.

The Trevanions were a Cornish family of ancient lineage which settled at Caerhays in the early fifteenth century. The Trevanion residence, Caerhays Castle, is still well known in Cornwall for the beautiful gardens and surrounding park. The family became related through marriage to the Byrons when Admiral Byron, grandfather to Lord Byron, married one of the two daughters of William Trevanion.

William died in 1767 without male issue, but in 1801 a royal order restored the title and arms to John Trevanion Purnell Bettesworth Trevanion, grandson of William's other daughter. Henry was his second son. Unfortunately Henry's father squandered the family fortune which, though not large, had been more than adequate to maintain the Trevanions in comfort. John tore down the fine old manorial residence, hired the fashionable architect John Nash to erect a castle-like edifice. Papier-mâché was a new invention and all the vogue; Nash induced John Trevanion to roof the castle with that material

56

with predictably disastrous results in an area as damp as Cornwall. For years the place was more of a sieve than a home. The John Trevanion family seemed indeed to have been reckless as well as extravagant; there were rumors that a favorite after-dinner pastime was shooting out the eyes of the family portraits.[1]

Regardless of the family eccentricities, young Henry could legitimately claim noble antecedents which insured him certain privileges, one of which was the right to a life of leisure. If such an individual had no money of his own, he could generally acquire some from the more solvent members of the family, and if he played his cards properly he might catch a solvent wife. Augusta Leigh's sudden access to money may well have had something to do with Trevanion's engagement to Georgiana; the equally sudden dissipation of the fortune must have been a blow, though the engagement was not broken off.

Nobody approved of the match except Augusta who doted on Henry and maintained that it was a true love match between her daughter and fiancé. In view of all that was to come later, one suspects that Augusta was indulging in a lot of wishful thinking. Colonel Leigh detested Henry and for once he was right, though the family had scant respect for his opinions. Even Augusta stood up to the Colonel's wrath.

For such a pliant woman she was amazingly stubborn about the coming marriage, extolling "dear H.T.'s" good qualities to all who would listen. To the Dowager Lady Byron she went into endless detail about first meeting Henry in a reunion with his family who were also her relations. She found him "so far superior to the *common herd,* but without the slightest idea until lately that Georgey was like to attract him or indeed any body—. She is such a *quiet* being—." [2] The paragon was "studying the Law and has the talent to make the most of his Profession." Love match or not, the engagement dragged on interminably, mostly for financial reasons. Henry's spendthrift father had lost his wife and was now contemplating a second marriage, and being a self-centered man *his* marital arrangements came first. H. T. spent a considerable amount of time visiting the Leighs despite the Colonel's dislike, and there is evidence that during the visits he was not solely involved with his fiancée.

It must have been a disturbing period for everyone, but particularly for Libby who never made any secret of her feelings. She made fun of Trevanion, not only about the parlous state of his finances but about his delicate state of health. She had her father's keen sense of the ridiculous, and her mother's constant eulogy of this good-looking but feckless young man struck her as very silly indeed. Much later, after disaster had struck Libby because of Trevanion, she learned things about "dearest Moe" which explained her mother's behavior during the engagement.[3]

At some time prior to this engagement, Henry had been Augusta's lover. Worse than that, Augusta had promised him her daughters one after the other as soon as they were old enough. The story came from Henry and Georgey and could therefore be true. Yet both of them were on the outs with Augusta at the time they told the story to Libby. Eventually Georgiana became thoroughly estranged from her mother, and Henry was certainly not a man whose statements should be accepted as gospel truth. Unfortunately, Augusta's future conduct toward her son-in-law at the expense of Georgey and Libby, plus some of her letters written during a family crisis, plus the Colonel's loathing of the man, together do lend some credence to the shocking allegations.[4]

Disapproval made no difference to Augusta. Henry had no money and Georgey had no dowry; Augusta would take care of it. She had fallen out with a number of her rich relations, who disapproved of Henry, but there was still Annabella. Lady Byron had kept up the "limited intercourse," had been godmother to Emily in 1818, had paid frequent duty calls and had seen the other children. Augusta reminded her in a letter of a former offer of reimbursement connected with a certain transaction which amounted to a thousand pounds. Annabella paid it. She had promised to befriend Augusta and her children and she abided by that promise. Georgiana had her dowry at last.

On February 4, 1826, Georgiana and Henry were married in the Chapel at St. James's. Nobody in either family attended the ceremony but Augusta and Libby, who was the bride's attendant. The Colonel flatly refused to give his eldest daughter away to the abhorrent Trevanion, so Augusta asked a close family friend, Colonel Henry Wyndham, to stand in Colonel Leigh's place. All in all it was a wedding which augured ill for the future!

During the next two and a half years the young couple lived in various places near Six Mile Bottom and were often guests of the Leighs. Libby visited them in their different abodes but not through personal preference. These sojourns were engineered by Henry and Georgiana with Augusta's compliance. Georgiana was glad to have her young sister in the house because it made Henry less difficult.[5] Libby was growing attractive in a long-legged, coltish fashion, but more important than her appearance were her ebullient high spirits. She was too innocent to be fully aware of her brother-in-law's guarded looks and obvious zest for her company. Yet instinct must have warned her that all was not as it should be because she strongly objected to paying visits to the Trevanion household.[6] Her objections were to no avail; Augusta wanted to make things agreeable for Henry more than she wished to indulge Libby's so-called whims. In that two-and-a-half-year period, Georgiana could not have been much fun. She gave birth to two daughters, Bertha (1826) and Agnes (1828). Had she produced a son it might have been better all around, but poor Georgiana was one of those unfortunate individuals who never had any good luck.

At Six Mile Bottom things were also on the downgrade. Once Augusta had got along very well with her husband despite his selfishness and indolence; in his own way, the Colonel had cared for her, as much as he could for anyone. Now he was growing impossible to live with. Perhaps he should not be blamed entirely; his wife's fatuous devotion to Henry would have tried any husband's patience. The Colonel was no Job. He threatened, he tyrannized; he refused to allow the older boys to go to school, encouraged their weaknesses, piled up debts, probably railed constantly against Trevanion. Augusta was beside herself, writing long wailing letters to Annabella about "Il Marito's" (she referred to her husband thus in many letters) treatment of her and the children, and especially about his meanness to Henry. "In all my miseries H. T.'s conduct and character are a great source of consolation—he is QUITE what I expected of him." [7] And always in those letters would be the inevitable request: could Annabella lend a few pounds? Annabella could and did most of the time. One wonders what Byron would have thought if he had been there to see such lack of moral fibre in the woman he had adored with such passion. His mother had been a thrifty Scotswoman, and he inherited her hatred of being beholden to anyone. He was also proud of his name and his title and this pride saved him from the brink many times during his hectic life. Augusta could not afford the luxury of pride.

No one denies that she led a wretched existence, but never would she admit that any of it was her fault. Her frenetic letters to Annabella made every problem loom larger than life, so that it looked as if poor Guss was leaping from one catastrophe to another like a mountain goat. At one point Annabella grew so alarmed that she suggested it might be better for Augusta and the children to live abroad. Augusta was appalled by that notion. It would mean another dreadful row with Il Marito and he would be sure to win out as he always did, and besides—what would become of poor H. T., and Georgiana? The Leigh household was an armed camp and the Trevanions were hopelessly divided. Libby was growing increasingly rebellious about her enforced visits to the Trevanions.

Early in 1829 it looked as if she would be given a reprieve. The Trevanions were growing poorer, and their troubles were soon to be compounded by the birth of a third daughter, Ada, which took place that summer. Fortunately for the benighted family, Lady Byron ("Aunt Annabella") offered them the use of Bifrons, a country house near Canterbury, many miles distant from Newmarket. Annabella had leased the place, installed herself, child and staff, then had taken a dislike to the house and moved elsewhere. Her life would be a long series of removals as she wandered from one part of England to another; the nomadic existence of a frustrated, unhappy widow with an only child, and with more than enough money to indulge her moods. The Trevanions were welcome to live at Bifrons until the lease ran out.

Great was Libby's joy at hearing the news, but it soon turned to despair. It was decided that she was to accompany the Trevanions to Canterbury because of Georgiana's delicate condition which always made her wretched in health and spirits. Libby pleaded, indulged in tantrums, but without success. Before the journey Augusta took her aside and sternly admonished her to behave herself. She must "be nice" to Henry and not make fun of him.[8] If she truly loved her dearest Moe and her sister she would change her ways. Libby was just fourteen, and obedience to parents was the order of the day. Tearfully she promised to obey.

Life at Bifrons could not have been more grim. An engraving of the house shows it to be large and bleak, and the Trevanions had not the money to keep up appearances in proper fashion. Georgiana spent a large portion of her time in bed because of her condition. Henry's society had become so distasteful to her that she encouraged him to seek out Libby as his companion, which, after all, was the reason for bringing her along. Libby was supposed to sit with him in the house, talk to him, have her meals with him. If he were outside she was to walk with him, drive to the village with him. At night after the servants had gone to bed, Georgiana found different pretexts for sending Libby to Henry's bedroom.

There seemed to have been a strange ambivalence in

Libby's attitude toward Henry. In her Autobiography she wrote many times that she always disliked him, but it is clear that he affected her emotionally from the moment she met him. She tried to protect herself *from* herself by ridiculing him; a common gambit. At Bifrons she was at the most vulnerable stage of adolescence, subjected to the constant society of a man who was strongly attracted to her, and a man of considerable sexual experience and prowess, according to what we know of him. He was not compatible with his wife and never had been which was all the more reason for him to lust after his vibrant young sister-in-law.

Libby was ignorant of the facts of life as most well-brought-up girls were in that day; a heart-to-heart talk between mother and daughter on the eve of her wedding was supposed to prepare the bride for the marriage bed. Libby had no such preparation, but she was a Byron, with the sensual appetite and sexual drive which was part of her heritage on both sides. Possibly she did find Henry unlikable when she was thinking objectively, but he exerted a baleful influence, a kind of evil spell upon her which she could not resist. It would not have been too difficult for him to wear down her youthful resistance and arouse her to the point of submission. But when the union had been consummated and she was back in her own bed, the girl must have suffered agonies of fright and guilt. She had been brought up in the strict Calvinist doctrine so that, like her father, her conscience and her appetite were in an endless state of war. It did not, alas, prevent her from returning to Henry's bed; the supposedly secret affair went on for several months until, to quote her, "I was ruined—and likely to become a mother by one I had ever disliked." [9]

Today, what with the pill and sexual emancipation of women, those words seem archaic, but to Libby the outlook was shattering. An unmarried mother was the most bitter disgrace to a family, and such a girl seldom found a man willing to marry her in Libby's stratum of society.

When she informed Trevanion of her condition, his reaction was incredible. He implored her to "tell the truth to
Georgiana and throw myself—and him—upon her mercy." [10]
He can be excused for giving in to temptation; his wife had all
but flung the girl into his bed. But to ask the girl to beg forgiveness for *him* as well as for herself is unforgivable.

The confession was an orgy of emotion, with Libby in
abject tears and Georgiana taking the entire blame upon herself. She admitted that she had been so jealous of her young
sister's superior attractions that she had deliberately exposed
her to a temptation she would be unable to resist.[11] Libby was
good-hearted and loved her sister; she forgave Georgey. They
had a good cry, but after it was over and tears were dried the
husband and wife had to face some unpleasant facts.

Something would have to be done, and quickly, before
the neighboring gentry found out that Libby was in the family
way by her brother-in-law. The Trevanions and Leighs must
not find out either. Moe would forgive, being Moe, but the
Colonel would *not* forgive, and his rage would be formidable.
The panicky couple wrote to Moe that they were going abroad
and wanted permission to take Libby with them.

Permission was given without a second thought. Augusta
hadn't seen them for months and was delighted that everything
had worked out so well at Bifrons. She knew that Libby would
learn to appreciate Henry's sterling qualities, once she made
the effort. She never questioned where the Trevanions were
getting money for the trip; Augusta seldom did question where
money was to come from until she had to dig it up or risk
imprisonment for debt.

The Trevanions could not dismiss the question so easily.
As usual with them, they did not think things through but
trusted in God to come to their aid. Where indeed would they
get the money? They dared not ask their families nor could
they turn to Lady Noel Byron. That austere lady would not
look kindly upon the use to which they had put her hospitality.

Yet through one of those miraculous twists of Fate which were an integral part of Elizabeth Medora Leigh's life, Lady Noel Byron was the one who helped them out.

If the Trevanions had thought they were keeping their secret from the neighbors, they were soon to be disabused. There was not much for the gentry to do in that leisurely era when servants were easy to come by and tenant farmers did the heavy work. The country squires kept benign watch over their tenants, took part in local politics, often made their bids to become M.P.'s. The wives were supposed to take an interest in the doings and welfare of the villagers and to bear numerous children who were given over to their nannies until they were old enough to be handed over to governesses. The Industrial Revolution had created a huge pool of young men and girls whose parents no longer could support them through their special skills nor could they pass on a trade to their sons or daughters. The children had to try their luck in some large city, often with disastrous results, or become servants in the manor houses. A family of the gentry had to be poverty-stricken indeed to do without servants.

A good part of the time the gentry were on the go from one country house to another, paying visits which could last for weeks in the winter and spring when the roads were treacherous. There were endless gatherings—dances, picnics, card games, hunting—and gossip was rampant. But with everybody knowing everybody else and a large proportion of them relations, time was bound to hang heavy. Any newcomers in the local scene were a welcome relief and their comings and goings were under close surveillance. A great deal of gossip came from the servants' hall. In fact, one of the main duties of a lady's maid was to provide her mistress with the latest scandals so that the delicious tidbits could be passed on over the teacups. One could say that the lady's maid was to the nineteenth-century lady what the telephone is to the present-day housewife.

It did not take long to suspect that something was going on at Bifrons, what with Mrs. Trevanion ailing and Mr.

Trevanion always in the company of his wife's young sister. Even in the dress of that period, pregnancy was difficult to hide, particularly with a girl like Libby who had a boyish figure. The gossip livened things up around Canterbury as nothing had done for years. It was a shocking way to repay Lady Byron's generosity and kindness. She would simply have to be informed, but who was going to bell the cat?

It had to be someone of the highest moral character, and this individual would have first to be absolutely certain of the facts. Chosen for the task was the Reverend the Honorable William Eden, a member of Lord Auckland's family and thus on friendly terms with Lady Byron. He paid a surprise visit at Bifrons, took the Trevanions by surprise, and saw young Elizabeth Medora who displayed unmistakable signs of being in the family way. Incredibly, he induced the frightened Trevanions to give dispositions to the effect that the child was not only pregnant by her brother-in-law but *at his wife's full connivance*.[12]

Armed with this explosive document, Eden and a friend, the Baroness Gray, went to call on the seventh Lord Byron and his wife Mary. Of all those who knew Annabella, the former Captain George and his wife were highest on her list of trusted friends. The friendship was mutual. When George Anson Byron succeeded to the title and estates, he assumed that his cousin would leave him something to "maintain himself according to his rank." They had once been on excellent terms; Captain George had often visited Newstead and had gone to the seashore where Byron and Augusta were together in the summer prior to his marriage.

But he must not have realized that Byron had a long memory.

In 1817 Byron had written to Augusta that he would not "forget him [George] in a hurry," and would never forgive his siding with Annabella at the time of the separation. "Let them look to their bond," he quoted ominously.[13] Annabella must have read this letter inasmuch as she read all of Byron's correspondence, but apparently, she never mentioned this to Captain George. It was therefore a drastic blow to his hopes when he learned that he received nothing in the will of the late Lord Byron. Graciously Annabella turned over her share of the legacy—two thousand pounds per annum—since she was already amply provided for. George and his wife never wavered in their gratitude and loyalty to Annabella.

Oddly enough, in spite of all Annabella had suffered at the hands of Byron and Augusta, she never allowed it to color her feelings toward Elizabeth Medora. Back in the days when she was still calling on the Leighs she could never look at the little child without a feeling of tenderness. "I wonder why?" she wrote in her Journal, and for once she didn't analyze her reaction. Now this winsome little creature with the shining eyes and pouting mouth, so like the husband she could not forget, was no longer an innocent child but a young girl in desperate straits. Annabella learned, moreover, that the Trevanions wanted to withhold the story of their guilt from Augusta. Recalling Augusta's persistent loyalty to the unworthy Henry, Annabella could well understand why; his conduct would not be "a source of great consolation" if Augusta were to learn the truth. Again Annabella found herself involved in the tangled web of Augusta's children whom she had promised to befriend.

She had no reason to help the wretched Trevanions—she had already done more than she should have—but she could not ignore the fact that they had three small children on their hands, and if the unfortunate Libby did not miscarry, they would have another infant to look after. She could not, in all conscience, throw them out of Bifrons as punishment for Henry's sins, though Georgiana seemed equally guilty. To a woman of Lady Byron's rectitude it was appalling that a woman could be so wicked in her attitude toward her young sister, whom she had always professed to love.

As a result of the deposition, Annabella dropped all communication with the Trevanions, although the Honorable and

Reverend Eden did not give her leave to use this deposition for any purpose except in her dealings with the new Lord Byron. After discussing the matter with him and Mary she decided to provide the necessary funds for the Trevanion ménage— and Libby—to leave the country long enough to allow her to have her child. She did not give the funds directly; all arrangements were made through George and Mary Byron who, in turn, used an intermediary. It was stipulated that Lady Noel Byron's name was never to be mentioned in any transactions forthcoming.

In January, 1830, the Trevanions and Libby embarked from Dover across the Channel to Calais.

5

And lovelier things have mercy shown
To every failing but their own;
And every woe a tear can claim,
Except an erring sister's shame.

      —THE GIAOUR

In MIDWINTER THE CHANNEL CROSSING WAS ALWAYS A dismal experience. The boat pitched and rolled, the sea swept over the side scattering the few hardy souls who preferred to be on deck rather than face worse unpleasantness below. *Mal de mer* was no respecter of rank or nationality; ladies and gentlemen, both French and English, stretched out on the floor beside their servants amidst a cacaphony of squalling babies, weeping children, and groaning adults. After the trip came the ordeal of the customs house; the *douaniers* enjoyed bedeviling the English passengers. Often it took hours in a cold, draughty hall before their neighbors from across the Channel were permitted to go to their hotels and lodgings.

Unlike most English towns Calais had few houses to let for those with moderate means. Being a port of entry it was crowded with well-fed, well-clothed English trippers and commercial travelers who jammed the hotels and waited impatiently for spaces on some *diligence* which would take them somewhere else, preferably Paris. For the few who planned to stay awhile there were accommodations but not attractive ones, mostly ancient buildings catering to "foreigners"—one

68

family to a floor; their owners made little effort to see that the apartments were cleaned between tenants.

Ordinarily a girl of Libby's lively perception would have been intrigued by her first experience on foreign soil, but she was in no condition for sightseeing nor was Calais on most sightseers' lists. The town was encompassed by ancient fortifications of some historic value, but in other respects it was not an unusually attractive city, and the surrounding countryside was flat and bleak. Most of the townspeople were no more kindly disposed toward the English than the customs inspectors were; it was not easy for them to forget that they had been waging war with their hereditary enemy on and off for centuries. The recent war against the English had left a definite imprint everywhere in Calais. The houses and inns needed paint inside and out; the few carriages were inclined to be shabby; many horses wore harness made of rope rather than leather.[1]

England, on the other hand, had been in the midst of an industrial boom after 1815, building canals, improving roads, erecting factories. By 1830 she would also be engaged in building railways, an innovation which would make it possible to travel through towns and villages hitherto off the turnpikes and coach roads. All in all the Napoleonic Wars had not affected daily life in England to the degree that they had ravaged Europe. In France there was much hidden resentment against English people for that reason, although the French, being realistic, put up with the British passion for making the Grand Tour in return for pounds.

The bustling, noisy seaport of Calais was a far cry from the rustic quiet of Canterbury, but Libby could not enjoy the change. She had to remain in seclusion until after her accouchement which was due in April. It would have been unwise to risk being seen by friends or acquaintances of the Leighs and Trevanions who just *might* be passing through on their way to Paris. After the debacle of Bifrons Henry and Georgey could not afford any more gossip which might possibly find its way to their Aunt Annabella. Since all their financial transactions were handled through the present Lord Byron, they had no proof that their aunt knew what had happened, but it was reasonable to suspect that the money came from her, inasmuch as the present Lord and family were in no financial position to help anyone. True, Lady Noel Byron had not answered any of their letters, but there could be other reasons for her silence.

Libby was so worn down by pregnancy and the rigors of the Channel crossing that she fell ill of "a chest condition" which would plague her on and off for years to come. Out of alarm that she might be "falling into the consumption" a "medical man" was called in.[2] In that day there was no way to determine whether a bronchial condition was phthisis, pleurisy, or some other equally dangerous respiratory ailment, and since little was understood about the principle of contagion, no attempt was made to isolate someone with suspected tuberculosis. As for treatment there were various noxious cough remedies, mustard plasters, prolonged bed rest on a feather mattress under mounds of blankets, as much food as one could stuff down, and an occasional glass of wine or porter to build up the blood. It was scarcely the proper regimen for a girl who was seven months pregnant, but consumption was more to be feared than childbirth. A good percentage of women survived that ordeal; people seldom recovered from consumption.

It must have been a depressing household, with the Trevanions and their brood forced to live in an alien land under the same roof with the victim of their marital problems. It would have been a special hell for Henry to see the change in the young girl he had seduced, once so slender and full of verve and now so bloated and sickly. As for Libby herself, racked by a cough and heavy with child, she must often have longed to die.

On February 19 she went into premature labor. The doctor was called in but there wasn't much he could do for the mother until after she gave birth, and it was likely that the child would be stillborn. When the infant did make its entry into the world it proved to be a boy—miraculously alive—and showed promise of remaining so. There was no thought of Libby's keeping the baby; other arrangements had been made—but for April, not February. Thus the doctor had to scurry about to find a wet nurse and a place equipped to take care of a premature infant. He would also have to call in a priest to baptize the babe as quickly as possible in case it did not live. The mother's condition had also to be considered. That could become grave in Libby's case.

Miscarriages often caused "flooding" which could ultimately lead to shock, and when the patient was already debilitated shock could be fatal. All that a doctor could do was to keep the patient warm and see to it that the head was slightly lower than the feet. Ergot was sometimes given to stop the bleeding, but it was still touch and go. Left to his own devices, Libby's doctor would doubtless have asked a priest to stand by—France being a Catholic country—but the Trevanions were staunch Anglicans who would have resented a priest in the sickroom.

Fortunately Libby had youth on her side, and after a few days she was pronounced out of danger although it would be weeks before she would be well enough to travel. Before she returned to England it was important that she regain her full strength and look as if nothing had ever been wrong with her.

There were reasons, however, why the Trevanions were anxious to leave France as soon as possible. One was political unrest which indicated that a new revolution was in the making. There was also the omnipresent problem of finances. Once in England they and their family could live with some relation temporarily and Libby could be dumped on Moe at St. James's. Moe, being so myopic, would not notice any marked change in her daughter's appearance after fourteen months of separation.

While Libby was convalescing she thought much about her child. She had been told he was alive and in good hands, but that it would be best for her to forget his existence. She had agreed to do so before the child was born, but as often happens, she was beginning to regret giving up her baby. There was, of course, nothing she could do about it, but that did not prevent heartache. It would be interesting to know what went on in Henry's mind. So far his wife had given him three daughters, but Libby had borne a son. And a son, ironically, whom Henry could not bring up as his own. One wonders if he would have been so willing to give over the child to strangers, sight unseen, had he been prescient enough to know it would be a boy. As for Georgiana, the birth of a boy was another grievance against her young sister whose "superior attractions" appeared to be limitless.

On April 15, Libby became sixteen. It was decided that she could undertake the channel crossing without danger. The Trevanions arranged to stay with "an old aunt" who lived in London at 38 Cadogan Place.[3] For Libby it would be wonderful to be with Moe again. On May 2, 1830, they set sail and that night they were again on British soil.

6

'Tis strange—but true, for truth is always strange;
Stranger than fiction; if it could be told,
How much would novels gain by the exchange!
How differently the world would men behold!
How oft would vice and virtue places change!
The new world would be nothing to the old,
If some Columbus of the moral seas
Would show mankind their souls' antipodes.

—DON JUAN

THE REUNION OF MOTHER AND DAUGHTER WAS CERTAIN
to have been highly emotional, for both were inclined to express themselves in a volatile way, full of exclamations and sentimental phrases. One has only to read Augusta's letters—and
some of Libby's—with their underlinings and exclamation
points to imagine the words translated into speech. This is not
to say that they were insincere in their protestations, a mistake often made by introverts of which Annabella was a prime
example. She was forever criticizing Augusta, and later Libby,
for their tendency toward hyperbole which she felt to be sheer
affectation. Yet there is no doubt that Libby and Augusta
had a deep affection for each other until a conspiracy of misfortunes caused their tragic estrangement.

Nevertheless, after fourteen months away from her mother,
it must have been a difficult adjustment for Libby. To Augusta,
Libby was still an adolescent, sometimes moody and rebellious
but with the "best of hearts," and of course, of virginal inno-

cence. It wasn't easy for Libby to enact the role of unworldly young girl which was expected of her.

For Augusta there had been some alterations in her life style, but at the age of forty-six an individual's personality and habits have become too set to allow for much change. As always she was occupied by her own troubles, and if she noted any difference in her daughter's looks or manner there is no record of it. In fairness to her, she did have a multitude of problems, which will be dealt with now because they have a direct influence on the course of Libby's life.

Since George III's time old St. James's Palace, dating back to Henry VIII, wasn't used often as a royal residence. The King had acquired Buckingham House which he and Queen Charlotte preferred to live in, but St. James's was still used for many Court functions and all those living there through "grace and favour" were supposed to take an active part. Queen Charlotte had died in 1819—her insane, blind husband had followed her into death a year later. Augusta had lost her position as lady-in-waiting but was allowed to retain her apartments rent free and the pension of three hundred pounds a year.

She had kept up her longtime friendship, if one could call it that, with the Prince Regent, now George IV. In 1809 he had been a sponsor at Georgiana's christening, and despite Colonel Leigh's fall from grace, Augusta had not aroused the royal displeasure. Yet her position was highly vulnerable, for she was dependent on the favor of a monarch noted for his instability. The only constant factor in his character was his consuming and selfish pursuit of pleasure.

Clearly His Majesty was not the safest person to count on in a crisis. Fortunately Augusta's half-brother, the Duke of Leeds, had kept his influence at Court while many of his contemporaries had lost royal favor. The famous diarist of the period, Charles Greville notes, for example, that the Duke of Leeds sat at the head of the table with the King in the middle at a dinner in the Great Supper Room.[1] The Duke was also given the ticklish job of making out the invitation list for various Court functions, subject, of course, to the King's approval.

This does not mean that Augusta could not have maneuvered herself through the labyrinth of palace intrigue if she had to do it on her own. From early childhood she had been forced by circumstance to fit herself into the pattern of other people's lives. Her step-mother, Mrs. Jack Byron, had assumed the responsibility of bringing up her husband's motherless little daughter, but after the birth of her own son and the death of her husband she was financially unable to support two small children and had turned over Augusta to Lady Holdernesse, Augusta's maternal grandmother. That kindly, long suffering lady was already bringing up the children abandoned by her wayward daughter Amelia when that reckless beauty had eloped with "Mad Jack" Byron. So, from the age of four on, Augusta grew up with the Osborne family which consisted of two half-brothers, George (later the Duke of Leeds) and Francis (later Earl of Godolphin) 2 and a half-sister Mary (later Countess of Chichester).

Augusta was not exactly a poor relation for she had a small income, but the scandal of her mother's adultery could not be entirely forgiven or forgotten, and she was the fruit of that disastrous alliance. Still Augusta was lovable by nature despite her innate shyness. The Osbornes were all fond of her and considered her part of the family. Augusta had learned through experience that the easy way was generally the best way to handle difficult situations. One should recognize this in order to have a proper perspective on her relationship with Libby.

It was ironic that Libby's arrival coincided with one of the most difficult periods in Augusta's muddled life, when a number of longstanding problems came to a head at the same time. Her friend George IV was not long for this world. Years of dissolute living had turned the once floridly handsome Prince into a creature crippled by gout and liver trouble and so enormously fat that he seldom appeared in public. Impatiently waiting in the wings for his demise was his brother William, Duke of Clarence, who had lived in the shadow of his showy eldest brother for sixty-four years. In 1818 he married Adelaide of Saxe-Meiningen, a not too attractive girl half his age but with a strong will and even stronger opinions. William was a hearty, easygoing man who loved to walk in the park and hobnob with the hoi polloi, but he was growing more and more influenced by his wife who took a dim view of George's profligate life and gamey associates. It could augur ill for those who owed their Court positions to the dying king. Augusta could only hope that she would survive the change-over once it came.

There had also been a recent death in the Leigh family. In March the second daughter Augusta, the one with "weak intellect," had died at nineteen in a nursing home at Kensington. Her death was a release for all concerned, but Augusta had a special place in her heart for the girl. Colonel Leigh took it very hard, though it didn't prevent him from leaving the welfare of the family to his harassed wife. Besides Georgey and Libby she had four others to bring up. Emily, twelve, was a quiet, well-mannered girl, and Henry at ten was still too young to cause too much trouble, but George and Frederick were growing more like their father each day. Augusta was forever having to extricate Frederick from some scrape.

Not surprisingly her looks and disposition had not improved with age. She had never been able to afford to dress in the height of fashion, but now she was dowdy and her figure could have done with tighter stays. Her airy charm had given way to bursts of self-pity and her letters were full of grievances.

For several months prior to Libby's arrival, Augusta had been enmeshed in a web of altercation and misunderstanding which put the quietus to her association with the woman she once called "dearest Sis," Lady Noel Byron. It began late in 1829 with an embroilment over a mortgage between Augusta and the Honorable Douglas Kinnaird, one of the two trustees of Byron's estate. Kinnaird had been well disposed toward Augusta and her financial woes, but now he was suffering from terminal cancer and in no mood to put up with her muddleheadedness. Exasperated beyond endurance he resigned his trusteeship. Lady Byron wanted Dr. Stephen Lushington, her longtime ally and adviser, to take Kinnaird's place. Augusta did *not* want Dr. Lushington who had always been on Annabella's side and would continue to be. Annabella was extremely highhanded about the matter, paying scant heed to Augusta's wishes. She didn't feel Augusta had any rights in the selection, but she took care to write to various people, including Mrs. Villiers, in an effort to justify her position. Without consulting Augusta she saw to it that Dr. Lushington was appointed. This decision was relayed to St. James's through Annabella's solicitors.

Augusta's amour propre was deeply wounded, and for once she made no secret of her indignation. The ensuing correspondence between her and Annabella was still going strong in February of 1830, with each woman feeling she had right on her side. Finally Augusta reached a point where she wrote to Lady Byron to say that, despite her feeling of bitter anger and her almost broken state, she was willing to forgive everything.[3] To Annabella it was outrageous for Augusta Leigh, of all people, to "forgive" her for anything; forgiveness was Annabella's province. Augusta had also the insolence to point out that though Annabella might think her behavior justified, this didn't necessarily make it just.[4]

Augusta claimed that she was now completely heartbroken; nevertheless this time she refused to abase herself as she had been doing for sixteen years in order to retain Annabella's friendship.[5] By now Augusta had faced up to the unpleasant truth that Annabella had not wished her well for many years. Annabella was indeed full of rancor and needed only a valid excuse to reveal her true feelings. That same February the opportunity presented itself.

Byron's close friend Tom Moore published the first volume

of his biography of Byron. He had gone to considerable effort to show Byron's widow in a favorable light, but he also expressed admiration for Byron's sister. To compound his mistakes Moore dwelt at some length on the separation proceedings in which Byron's side of the story was revealed publicly for the first time. Annabella's mother emerged as a typically interfering mother-in-law mostly responsible for the collapse of the marriage. Annabella's furious reaction was to write and privately publish a pamphlet in which she denigrated Moore's biography in contemptuous terms while at the same time maintaining that she was forced to publish her "Remarks" in order to correct Moore's distortions of fact. Abandoning her former discretion she quoted a letter from Dr. Lushington which referred to "additional information" about the separation which mentioned Augusta's part in the marital breakup. Annabella asked various important personages and friends, including Lushington, to advise her on the content of her manuscript. Several felt she should not publish the material; Lushington suggested that Augusta should be permitted to read the manuscript before it went to the printers.

Predictably none of the advice was taken. It seems clear that Annabella intended that the references to Augusta would undermine her former friend's position at Court and in Society, both of which would be disastrous. Having broken her "policy of silence" she went all out. Hundreds of people, important and otherwise, many not known to her personally, received copies of her "Remarks." One was sent to George IV, but he was too ill to read it. He was scarcely the one to sit in moral judgment on anyone, but if he had read it in the wrong mood he might have turned against Mrs. Leigh. A copy was sent to Moore, also one to Augusta. No immediate response came from St. James's, and Annabella finally reached the point of asking Mrs. Villiers to call on Augusta, who would surely express an opinion to her childhood friend. Therese agreed to call but after being informed three times in one week that Mrs. Leigh was "not at home," Therese lost her taste for espionage.

Augusta, naturally, responded to the pamphlet with distress and dismay. One reaction was to refuse to meet with Therese Villiers, who was evidently an emissary from Annabella. Another response was outrage at the lack of feeling shown by Annabella to both Augusta and her brother. Augusta claimed to be more concerned about the effect of the pamphlet on the reputation of her late brother than she was on her own. Naturally, she denied that she had played a part in the breakup of Byron's marriage. In a letter which she wrote to her friend, Reverend Hodgson (who had also received a copy of the pamphlet and who was properly appalled), Augusta piously and self-righteously called down God's forgiveness on her former sister-in-law.[6]

As it turned out the pamphlet caused repercussions against the author more than against Augusta, though it did increase her tension.

This, then, was the state of affairs in the Leigh ménage when Libby arrived on the scene. Except for her sister's death she seemed unaware of the other harassments. In her Autobiography she states: "My mother, at this time, endeavoured to force me much against my wish, into society and balls, though I endeavoured to excuse myself on account of my extreme youth, and by the fact that I was in mourning for another sister whom we had recently lost."[7]

Augusta could not have objected to the second excuse, although the first should have puzzled her. Libby had always been a gregarious child who loved going to children's balls and public amusements. Undoubtedly her reasons were sincere enough, but there must also have been an element of self-protection in her desire to avoid the social swim.

She had a large number of maternal relations who were generally in London during the season, and most of them had known her when she was "a happy child."[8] No longer could she think of this conglomeration of uncles, aunts, and cousins as the kindly people she had known since babyhood, who dandled her on knees and laughed at her antics. Now she had to be on guard every moment of the time. Her uncle, the

Honorable Francis Osborne, for example, was married to the former Elizabeth Charlotte Eden, daughter of Lord Auckland and therefore related to the Reverend the Honorable William Eden, involved in the disaster at Bifrons. He seems to have handled his part with admirable discretion, but in that tight little group of interrelated families one word dropped by mistake could set off a chain reaction of gossip. Libby also had to be careful around her Aunt Mary, Lady Chichester. Aunt Mary had been fond of her and it was mutual, but she was closest of all the family to "dearest Moe." And Henry and Georgey had warned her that Moe was the one person who *had* to be kept in ignorance of the Bifrons debacle.

One person who could prove highly dangerous was her mother's friend Mrs. Villiers, whom Libby had known from the time she was a baby, but she was not aware of the ramifications existing in the relationship between her mother and Mrs. Villiers. It was probably a good thing that she didn't know; she had enough to worry about. No sooner was she ensconced at St. James's than she had a visitor. "Mr. Trevanion came very often—almost daily—to visit me," she wrote, "and his visits were not in any way discouraged by my mother." [9]

Libby feared this man, knowing him for what he was, but she could not discuss his visits with her mother, nor was it likely that Augusta would have listened. On the subject of Henry she had a closed mind, nor was she concerned that he was paying daily visits without his wife. She alone clung to the notion that the marriage was sound—as sound as any marriage could be—when it had been wretched from the beginning.

Libby's tragedy was that everything conspired to make her vulnerable to the spell which Henry once cast upon her and intended to do again. She was left to her own resources most of the time, without enough to occupy her thoughts. There was really very little for young ladies of good families to do, outside of needlework, reading, taking walks or drives accompanied by chaperones. Ladies of all ages spent more than half their time changing their clothes to fit the particular social event on their daily schedule. A girl wearing a morning dress in the afternoon was certain to cause lifted eyebrows. Nineteenth-century England, with all its grace and beauty, was perhaps the most money-conscious, snobbish era to be found anywhere, and no one knew it better than Augusta—or her daughter.

Not for Libby, alas, were the feminine companions of her childhood who were now making their "entrance into the world" on a restricted basis under the watchful eyes of their mamas. Poor Libby must have felt miserably ill at ease in that circle of palpitating virgins. All their education—hers too— was for one purpose: to make them desirable enough to catch eligible husbands. Their conversation was composed of gossip, the latest fashions, and the popular novels of the day which dealt exclusively with romantic love. If a girl had a bent toward the intellectual it was best not to show it or risk being labeled as a blue-stocking which was a big strike against her with most men. Annabella Milbanke was one of the rare exceptions, but the man she married was exceptional.

Although Libby had nothing in common with girls her age, she must have envied them their prospects for the future. Most of them would make advantageous marriages and they would follow the one strict rule laid down by Society: to come to their bridegrooms with hymens intact. Once they had done their duty and produced an heir or heirs, they could indulge in extramarital dalliance, *but not before*. They could take their places in the only world that counted to a girl of Libby's background, a world which was hers by right of birth and family connections.

If she had been the amoral, scheming vixen she was later accused of being, she would not have allowed her fall from grace to exert such a powerful influence on her thinking. She could never be an heiress but she was attractive enough to catch masculine eyes. Her mother and maternal relations would have been delighted to help her snare a husband. But in common with nineteenth-century heroines, Libby truly believed that she was "ruined" and had no right to expect the privileges of girls who were not tarnished. Perhaps it was one reason why she did not do more to discourage Henry Trevanion's daily visits. With him she would feel none of that gnawing unworthiness; no one but her mother had respect for *his* moral character. Inasmuch as Augusta was willing to let Henry take over the responsibility of Libby's welfare, it was inevitable that she would find herself falling under Henry's influence.

Augusta, going about her daily affairs, "did not appear to have a suspicion of any kind." [10] The young couple did behave with the greatest decorum in the presence of others. One of their occupations was to read the Bible together each morning, a singular amusement but one which was bound to please Moe. She delighted in giving Bibles as gifts. She had given one to Byron which he took with him on his travels. After he died it was found on the table by his bed.

On good days, when piety lost its charm, Libby and Henry could take walks in St. James's Park where many of the nabobs took their daily constitutionals. Or they could go further afield, to Hyde Park, and watch the flashing beauties passing by in their fine carriages. In bad weather, if time hung too heavy, they could stroll about the palace. Not much was left of the original palace built by Henry VIII except the Tapestry Room, Presence Chamber, and Chapel. In the Presence Chamber was some carving on the chimney piece: the initials H and A entwined—Henry Tudor and Anne Boleyn. Libby's fate was in the hands of another H. T., not so violent a man perhaps but a man almost as selfish.

During her first weeks with her mother, a number of happenings occurred which fully occupied Augusta's time and energy. On June 26 George IV breathed his last; William IV ascended the throne. The former king's passing caused little grief. After the funeral ceremony all the guests gathered at St. George's Hall where they were "as merry as grigs." [11] Luckily the new regime did not hurt Augusta's position after all, and her half-brother the Duke of Leeds was still solidly entrenched.

On July 24 the King held his first levee at the palace. It was very crowded and a number of people fainted from the crush. In fact, all the new King's social functions were overrun with people. He was having the time of his life being King, had immense dinner parties every night, often with the same guests, but fortunately for those in Court circles he didn't insist on keeping everyone up too late. Around eleven he would say goodnight and off to bed he would go with his young bride in tow. Augusta's duties must have been onerous in those hectic weeks, but at least she had no worry about Libby who was being watched over so well by that paragon of manly virtue, dear H. T.

One day early in July he arrived with a letter just received from a friend in Calais.[12] He took care to hide it from Moe but Libby was apprised of its contents. The gist of it was that recently an Englishman who claimed to be the tutor of the present Lord Byron's children had turned up in Calais. His purpose was to make inquiries about Libby's confinement. He had called at the former Trevanion residence and made an offer of twelve hundred pounds for the child, saying that he was acting for Lord Byron. Nobody would give him any information except that the child had died of convulsions around the age of two months.

This news was a dreadful shock to Libby. She had never lost hope that one day she might see her child again. If the letter was true he had died while she was still in Calais, but nobody had told her. Henry insisted that it was news to him also, but Libby could be certain of nothing. The more she thought about that strange letter, the more she wondered if it told the real truth. Was her son really dead?—"he had shown promise of living." And that business of Lord Byron offering twelve hundred pounds! His income from the jointure turned over to him by Lady Noel Byron amounted to only twelve hundred a year, and with four young children of his own, why would he saddle himself with another? But Lady Noel Byron could easily part with twelve hundred, and Libby jumped to the conclusion that the child was hidden off somewhere in England under her Aunt's care. Nobody in France could verify the truth or falsity of the letter. The people of Calais were occupied with more important matters.

The revolutionary volcano had erupted in July, resulting in the *coup d'état* which put Louis Philippe on the throne of France. The fate of a bastard infant was of small concern to people engaged in guerrilla warfare through the streets of Calais, but to Libby it was all-important. Thirteen years later she was still unconvinced that her son had died at two months, although she eventually admitted that he could have died in the interim.

Was there any truth to this bizarre story? Or was it the distortion of an all too active sense of grievance against those who Libby felt had persecuted her? In her autobiography Libby maintained that correspondence relative to the matter was kept in her strongbox, but the contents of her strongbox were burned after Libby's death.

During the rest of the year Henry continued to spend a large part of his time at St. James's, often late into the evening while Augusta was going about her social duties. If she ever gave a thought to Georgiana, languishing at 38 Cadogan Place, there is no evidence of it. She continued to be blissfully unaware of the turbulent undercurrents swirling around her. At a later date Therese Villiers wrote to Lady Byron that she had heard whisperings about the Bifrons-Calais disaster, but she withheld it from Augusta. She admitted, however, that she had deliberately made veiled allusions and asked leading questions, hoping to trap Augusta into saying something which would prove that she *did* know. Apparently Augusta's reactions convinced Therese that her friend knew nothing about Libby's seduction.

In spite of the daily proximity of Henry, and Augusta's permissive attitude, Libby seems to have kept her former lover at arm's length for a time. Had she been older, Trevanion might not have been able to exert such an effect upon her mind, but the ten years' difference in their ages and his experience were all to his advantage. Inevitably, propinquity, idleness, and a strong sexual need were triumphant. Once Libby succumbed to Henry's blandishment, she abandoned herself just as she had done at Bifrons.

Considering the host of servants employed in the palace and the large number of friends, relations, and members of the immediate family who were likely to put in an appearance, it is miraculous that the lovers were not caught *in flagrante delicto*. If anyone did suspect or winked an eye, the information was not relayed to Augusta. This does not mean that all went without a hitch. Both of them had to live with their individual guilts and contend with their religious and social upbringing. One of Henry's uncles was Vicar of Whitby, and his family publicly observed all the rules of moral behavior whatever they may have done in private. All the Osborne family were devout Anglicans, and as previously noted, Augusta was given to pious utterances.

Although Henry could indulge in the most callous and ruthless activities on occasion, he was not by nature an insensitive boor. He loved poetry, was a great admirer of Byron's works, even published a book of his own verse in 1827. All his life he was strongly attracted to the austere beauty of ecclesiastical literature.

His marriage was an unqualified disaster, but divorce was difficult and greatly deplored, so he and Georgiana had to make the best of a very bad bargain. In time they might have drifted into a partnership based on mutual interests, as thousands of other ill-matched couples were doing, but they had such an abrasive effect upon each other that it was impossible for them to adjust. There is no doubt that Georgey was in a pitiable state, but it was one she helped to bring about. Thus she was denied the one dubious satisfaction left to a neglected wife: she could not berate her husband for infidelity.

That Henry did suffer the pain of a guilty conscience is evidenced by a note he wrote to Augusta [13] not long after he returned to London and renewed his relationship with Libby.

> My dearest Moe,
> I owe some explanation for the pain I gave you by my wild note—I took laudanum—I promise not to do so again—would God that had been all. Your affectionate kindness distracted me with hopes which are now no more—and Nell [a nickname he used sometimes for Libby] had half my consent yesterday to have disclosed the fatal cause of my misery—it shall now and ever be a secret. She cannot speak without the consent I have revoked in my note last night, and you are too dear and good to ask of her a confidence the breach of which involves—my life. Never again allude to the subject if you have love or pity for your unhappy
>
> H. T.

He must have still been under the influence of laudanum to write such a senseless letter, but it was no more improbable than Augusta's reaction to it. She glanced through it calmly and handed it back to Libby without a word of comment. Obviously her daughter was involved in a serious predicament, but Henry had written that she must never allude to it—and Henry's word was law.

Early in January, 1831, Libby discovered that she was "likely to become a mother" for the second time. When she told her lover the bad news he reacted as he had done at Bifrons. He begged her "to confide the truth to my mother," substituting Augusta for Georgey, and as before, fobbing off the confession on Libby. Then he had a change of heart and told her not to tell—to which the bewildered girl agreed. But by February Libby could no longer be silent; the time was rapidly approaching when her condition could not be hidden.

Instead of going directly to Augusta and making a clean breast of the affair, Henry composed a letter which explained about the past in sordid detail and described the dismal expectations for the future, all of which he blamed on Augusta. A clever stratagem—some of it *was* her fault—but Henry Trevanion was not the one to sit in judgment. After completing the letter he ordered Libby to copy it and sign it with her name. The girl was in such a daze that she meekly obeyed all his instructions. Again Henry asked her not to hand over the letter, but after withholding it for a few days she suddenly gave it to her mother.

Augusta burned it, but her own words explain her reactions. As seemed to be the custom with these people, she could not bring herself to talk things out in a sane and sensible manner. She wrote letters—three of them—and the first two were to Henry despite the fact that the "confession" was in Libby's writing. These letters are ambiguous and convoluted, but they should be read if only to disprove the accepted belief that Libby was the heartless, ungrateful child of a devoted, long-suffering mother.

To Trevanion Augusta wrote:

> It would be impossible in the first instance to speak to you my dearest—without such emotion as would be painful to us both—and I therefore take up my pen, but only to break the ice—for I feel equal (and in some respects greater) difficulty than I should in speaking. You know how I have loved and regarded you as my own Child—I can never cease to do so. To the last moment of my existence you will find in me the tenderness, the indulgence of a Mother. . . . Show me only how I can comfort and support you—confide in me, dearest. . . . What might not have been prevented could I have known, guessed, even most REMOTELY suspected. . . . Much do I blame myself! but as He who knows our hearts knows our trials, and the circumstances in which I have been placed, for the welfare and happiness of others, I trust I shall find pardon. . . .
>
> I am convinced, dearest, that as I have opened my heart and feelings to you, you will comfort me! . . . Heaven bless, comfort and guide you.[14]

Trevanion must have taken an exceedingly dim view of this letter judging by what followed. He had hoped for some plan to unravel the net he had woven about himself, not an orgy of sentiment and a request to comfort his dearest Moe in her hour of darkness. In anger he dashed off a second accusatory note which Augusta answered with an even longer letter which said in part:

> Your note just received is to me inexplicable. When and how have you "witnessed me acting upon a system of distrust"? When you answer this, I may be able to meet your accusation —certainly a most unjust one.

Augusta went on to say that, while with him and Libby on the night before receiving Henry's second letter, she had tried her best "to subdue my feelings and to appear cheerful," until Henry had gone. She spent a sleepless night and arose early so that she could call on "dearest G." (Georgiana). She went on at some length about her understanding of his predicament and her sympathy with his feelings, then she reverted again to her meeting with Georgey:

> I have explained to her my ideas on some minor points of prudence, which are perhaps more essential than you think . . . for where the ruin of so many may be the alternative of its observance, it becomes a serious consideration.
> Now Dearest—let me implore of you to be comforted—to do your utmost to make the best of circumstances—to trust in my affection. . . .
> Do not accuse yourself, dearest, and make yourself out what you are NOT.
> Remember I do "depend on your Love"—and oh, how I *have* loved you—how I will always love you and God bless you, dearest.[15]

Then, at long last, Augusta turned her attention to her daughter:

> As in conversation upon painful subjects one is apt to express oneself strongly, and lest you might misinterpret such expressions and mistake *that* for unkindness which would be but the

effects of agitation, I must write to you, my dearest, what the fullness of my heart and my anxiety would dictate every moment to you.

I cannot describe with what pain I observe much that is passing before me, and my beloved and unhappy child, I implore you—on my knees I implore you! to use every effort of your soul to cope with those temptations which assault you. You have the greatest good sense—the best of hearts—you know NOW what is your duty and on what terms alone you can hope for mercy.

Reflect that you are—no, not now—Great God avert it! that (how shall I write it?) you have committed *two* of the most deadly crimes! recollect who you have injured!—and whom you are injuring—not only your own Soul, but that of another you think more dear than yourself. Think of *whom* you have deprived of his affection. Think of others upon whom shame and disgrace must fall, if even now you are not *outwardly circumspect* in your demeanor. Think of his family—of yours—of your unmarried and innocent sister [Emily]—of that broken heart of your Father—for that—THAT would be the result I am convinced—you know not his agonies for the loss of that poor Angel [sister Augusta] who was from cruel circumstance comparatively an alien to him—think of what *this* would be! —and more still more, of the DREADFUL consequences to HIM— to another still more—that no time or place would shield him from their vengeance! think of what might and almost undoubtedly WOULD be the consequences even in THIS world and think of those more important interests, the eternal ones of all those Beings dear to you! Pardon me if I inflict pain on you—I must in this case "be cruel to be kind"—nor could I forgive myself, did I neglect to rouse you to the consideration of such consequences! I implore my dearest child therefore, as regards these fears, to be prudent and circumspect to the last degree, and I still more implore her and her knees to pray to God for His assistance to enable her to forsake her sins and to repent of them. That He will always do to those who in sincerity ask, we are assured.

To repeat my ardent desire to be of comfort to ALL is needless. Heaven guide me, in its mercy, aright—in the labyrinth in which I am involved. I earnestly pray for such guidance—I would not say a reproachful or unkind word to anyone—*but*—Dearest, listen to one thing—which is certain and inevitable—a continuance (by which you must not understand that I require impossibilities, or do not and will not allow for the weakness of human nature and the strength of its temptation)—but an obstinate continuance in this DREADFUL affair—or the least deception, will either upset my reason or break my heart. You imagine perhaps that this is a way of speaking and feeling—that my disposition is such that no *lasting* impression can be made upon my feelings—that I have lived through so much I am like flint or steel at bottom, with only a light surface—but—do not *flatter* yourself that I should survive, or that my senses would THAT blow. I have suffered much—long (neither you or ANY human being knows how much) but—I never knew sorrow like this—it was fit perhaps my pride of heart should be humbled—I looked to YOU as the hope and pride of my life. I felt you might be taken from me by Death, but I was not prepared for this wretchedness—Spare, oh, spare me, Dearest. Spare yourself and all you hold most dear! Depend on it, your efforts will be rewarded and in your mother's heart, surely you might find comfort.

You know that I confidently hoped and intended you to be confirmed this Easter. I suppose it is *now* hopeless—consult your own heart and wishes. There is at any rate one thing I would ask—which would be a comfort to me. I hoped to be able to prepare you sufficiently myself with the help of reading —but now I feel it would be a great satisfaction to me if some Clergyman were to assist in this. Of course his instructions would bear soley upon the preparation and information til you felt your mind and heart disposed for it. I pray that the Almighty may so dispose it! Dearest Darling! speak to me, confide in me—and be assured you will meet with all the affection, sympathy, kindness, indulgence that you need and wish from your most affectionate though wretched mother.

Can I say more? If I can—tell me what—and let me comfort you if I could do so! God bless you! [16]

This letter, though written in bitter anguish by the despairing Augusta, was one of the turning points in Libby's life. In spite of certain puzzling actions on Augusta's part, Libby had continued to love her mother. But reading this letter, with its obscure rancor couched in mawkish sentimentality, must have been a cruel revelation of Moe's tragic weakness. The "dearests" scattered here and there amidst threats of eternal damnation and accusations of terrible selfishness could not hide the fact that there was no willingness on her mother's part to assume any of the responsibility. And as Augusta did in the letters to Henry, she spent much time and thought on the wretched state of her own feelings; a very human failing in times of stress, but not admirable. What makes this letter so painful to read is the contrast between it and those written to Trevanion, in which she sought so desperately to assure him that he was more sinned against than sinning. There was scarcely a word of blame for *his* part in the "dreadful affair"; Libby was the instigator. The crowning touch—and unintentionally humorous afterthought—was Augusta's impassioned desire for Libby to learn her catechism so that she could be confirmed at Easter.

The girl was quite disillusioned by all this. "At first she was very kind to me," Libby wrote, "Though afterwards she became very cruel, though to H, the only difference she made was to increase her kindness." [17] It would be interesting to know what went on in the belated meeting between Augusta and Georgiana. It is unlikely that Georgey confessed to starting the liaison at Bifrons by throwing her sister at her husband's head.

Now that Augusta knew the dismal truth, she was terrified of the possible consequences. A scandal could have serious repercussions in Court circles, but far more to be feared was the reaction of Il Marito. Her husband would be apoplectic with rage against the son-in-law he loathed, and that rage would also include *her*. What kind of mother would leave her young daughter alone day and night in the company of a man, no matter who he was? And to make matters worse, Augusta was aware that Libby was the Colonel's favorite. She cast about frantically for some way out of the inevitable disgrace. In her fright she tried to induce Libby to take a medicine to bring on an abortion, but the girl refused.[18] Having failed in this endeavor, Augusta discussed the matter further with Georgey.

The Trevanions were planning to go to live in a country house outside of Bath, and Georgey was willing to take Libby with them. She and Henry were on worse terms than usual; she needed Libby as a buffer between her and his harsh temper. This time Libby did not object to the idea. Apart from her mother's veiled hostility there were practical reasons to consider. She could not have a baby in St. James's Palace, and the other alternative was to be packed off to some sinister place where girls in her condition could give birth in secret. Anything was better than *that*.

Nevertheless, allowing Libby to go a second time with the Trevanions did present problems for Augusta. She had sworn to her family that she had no inkling of the Bifrons affair until Libby gave her the letter of confession. Most of Augusta's confidantes were willing to accept her plea of innocence, but from now on she was expected to deal firmly with the situation. Dealing firmly, alas, was not Augusta's metier. She was in a dreadful dilemma. If she did permit Libby to go, she could be accused of becoming an accessory after the fact. But time was passing, and what could she do with the wretched mother-to-be? She did have more than her share of crosses to bear and was under constant nervous strain, but her attitude toward Libby in contrast to Henry, even to Georgey, during this entire interlude is not easy to understand.

Her statements about Libby were accepted as facts and reported as such to others. Lord Godolphin, for example, told Mrs. Villiers the following melodramatic story (which had been told him by Augusta). Libby was so determined to go with the Trevanions to Bath that the hysterical girl stood before her mother, a bottle of laudanum or some other poison clenched in her hand, and threatened to swallow the contents unless permission was forthcoming. This so alarmed Augusta that she then discussed the problem with Georgiana, after which permission was wrung from her.[19] In other words, Libby was made out to be the chief aggressor who would stop at nothing to break up her sister's marriage. Yet on the subject of Georgey's willing connivance in the first seduction there is a vast silence. The suicide threat *may* have taken place—lovesick girls have made such threats through the ages—but Augusta was shrewd enough to seize upon it as a reason for acquiescence. True or false, in March Libby left for Bath with the Trevanions, a move which would have the most far-reaching consequences for everyone concerned.

7

And if I laugh at any mortal thing,
'Tis that I may not weep.

—DON JUAN

LONDON SOCIETY STILL TOOK THE WATERS IN THE SALU-
brious mineral springs of Bath, but since the Prince Regent
had made Brighton the "in" place, Bath was not quite as fashionable as it had been under the aegis of Beau Nash. Some
important figures, social and otherwise, did maintain homes
there and at certain seasons the town was full of visitors. Byron,
who believed in Fate and was intrigued by coincidence, would
have been grimly amused by the turn of events which found
"poor, dear little Do" in a house near Bath under the "protection" of Georgiana and her husband. When Mad Jack Byron
was looking for a second wife, he chose Bath during the season
as the ideal spot to meet a woman with enough money to keep
him in the style he preferred. It was good thinking, for there
he met Catherine Gordon.

Not that the Trevanions went to Bath for social reasons.
They went because a relation offered them the use of the country house. The Trevanions may have had financial and emotional problems but they seemed never to lack for relations
with real estate. Except for a different locale, the sojourn at
Bath was a repeat performance of Bifrons with the same cast
and similar plot. Neither was there much change in the Trevanion life style. A year before the threesome had been holed

94

up in Calais, awaiting the clandestine birth of an illegitimate child, the only difference being that they were now on English soil with the beneficent permission of "dearest Moe." Henry's attempt to foist all the blame on Augusta had not hardened her heart toward him. She was keeping in touch through letters couched in the most affectionate terms, as if nothing untoward had happened.

The Trevanion household could never be a happy one, but things went from bad to worse in this new abode. Henry was behaving abominably to the woebegone Georgey. All that stood between them was Libby, just as fifteen years before a "certain silly person" had stood between Annabella and *her* husband. Libby had her faults, but she was loyal to those she loved. She still felt a bond of affection for her sister in spite of the betrayal at Bifrons. Georgey was a more complex personality, neurotic to an extraordinary degree even for that day. Her ambivalence toward Libby was matched only by her mixed feelings toward her mother. She was better at hiding her emotions than Libby but inwardly she seemed to have seethed with hostility toward mother and sister alike, a burning resentment which made her do things she was bound to regret after the damage was done.

The constant simmering warfare between Henry and Georgey must have driven Libby to distraction, and when she was tried too far she had tantrums. There is no way of knowing what precipitated Georgey's telling Libby that her birth was "the result of adultery and incest." [1] It is likely that this disclosure followed one of Libby's scenes, for she could be very scathing and vitriolic in anger, as her father used to be when aroused. Whatever provoked Georgiana, it must have been doubly painful for Libby to hear such appalling statements at this particular time. And for added shock value, Henry told her about *his* affair with her mother, including the alleged promise to let him have her daughters one after the other, as soon as they were old enough.

It would not have been impossible for Georgey to know

about the liaison between her mother and Uncle By. It started in the summer of 1813 when she was five, and for several months thereafter her uncle paid extended visits to Six Mile Bottom. After Libby was born young Georgey and brother George spent those exciting weeks at the seashore and later at Newstead. A child of five sees and hears far more than adults realize, although it may not fully comprehend what it sees and hears until years later. Neither Byron nor Augusta would have deliberately flaunted their passion in front of the children or behaved indiscreetly before the servants. But a look, a gesture, a hand which lingers too long upon another hand, the tingling awareness of each other which cannot be disguised; these manifestations of desire are universal. So are the raised eyebrows, the head shakings, the whispered comments which children are not supposed to notice. And Byron's behavior on his honeymoon visit was so shocking that Georgey could not have failed to be startled by the change in her beloved Uncle By.

At first Libby had the normal reactions of shock and disbelief. "I then believed, though I had been told the contrary by my sister and her husband, that Colonel Leigh was my father," she wrote. "I wished to spare him the knowledge of my shame. We were all taught to dislike and deceive him. But I pitied him—and would have done anything to hide his faults or expose him." [2] Reading between these sparse lines, one can feel the anguish of the girl and her reluctance to believe what she'd been told. Yet there did seem to be evidence that it could be true. She had always been different from her brothers and sisters in various and subtle ways.

One of the reasons given by those who do not subscribe to her belief that Byron was her father is that she was said to resemble Colonel Leigh. But she also resembled Byron, particularly the lower half of her face. Later she wrote that she resembled Henry Trevanion enough so that they were able to pass for brother and sister.[3] These resemblances could be due to the fact that the Trevanion genes were the dominant strain.

Byron, Augusta, and Colonel Leigh all had grandparents in common.*

It was indeed a shock for Libby, but for a girl of her temperament, who had been rejected by mother and sister when she most needed their love, it was not altogether displeasing to think that she could be the daughter of her famous uncle; that she was, in effect, a being set apart. It would have been too much to expect her to be completely objective about her mother's share of the guilt. That letter absolving Henry of all responsibility while taxing *her* with "deadly crimes"—was it fair and just? Was not her sin pale indeed compared to the sin her mother committed? Everything which had happened in the past two years seemed to bear out Henry's accusations against dearest Moe. The Trevanions had given Libby a powerful weapon, and one day she would not hesitate to use it.

At St. James's Palace things were about the same. With Libby a hundred miles away Augusta could breathe easier, but there must have been moments when she would have given anything for a strong shoulder to lean on. Il Marito was off on one of his protracted trips, and if all went well Libby's child would be born and arrangements made for its care before he returned to London. The relationship between the Leighs had not improved with the passing of the years, but they were not separated in the usual sense of the word, nor did Augusta want so drastic a move to take place. Better to muddle along—make the best of things—hope that somehow or other it would all work out according to plan.

But in the first week of June Augusta received a letter which put an end to this dream. Georgiana could no longer endure Henry's cruelty and was planning to leave him. Augusta was shattered. If Georgiana made good her threat she would have nowhere to go but St. James's, bringing her three little girls, and Libby would have to accompany her. It would

---

* See Genealogy chart at front of book.

be mad to allow the girl to stay with Henry. Now she would have to inform her husband, but she was too frightened to do it herself. Instead she begged the Leigh family friend, Colonel Wyndham, to tell the bad news, but she implored him to make it clear that she had known nothing of the Bifrons affair nor had she been told of Libby's second pregnancy until too late.

The scene of this melodrama changes now to Bath. A few days later, on a morning, a coach pulled up outside the door of the Trevanion residence. Out stepped two men who proved to be a constable and an attorney, both hired by Colonel Leigh to arrest Henry for abduction.[4] According to law this was a criminal offense for which Henry could be thrown into prison. Before the dismayed Trevanions could think of some way out of the predicament a traveling carriage arrived, and out stepped Colonel Leigh. Libby described the happenings with an eye for detail which does her credit. "The Colonel's old coachman was on the box and a woman, intended to represent a lady's maid, sat inside."[5] The Trevanions must have been quaking with fear, knowing that Colonel Leigh loathed the sight of his son-in-law.

Yet he did not behave as harshly as everyone expected, as indeed the father of a girl had the legal right to behave toward his young daughter's abductor and seducer. It may have been due to his fondness for Libby that he acted with such restraint, or it could have been that his years of consorting with loose women and hobnobbing with libertines had made him tolerant of human frailty. He did not go ahead with the arrest and gave Libby ten minutes alone with Henry before she packed up her possessions.

Henry repaid the Colonel's forbearance in typical manner. "He extracted a promise from me [Libby] that I would escape as soon as possible from my mother and run away with him."[6] The ten minutes up, the Colonel ordered her to go to her room and prepare for her journey. In the bedroom she found Georgey in what appeared to be great distress of mind. "She begged forgiveness of me and entreated me never to abandon Henry. She assured me that she would immediately procure a divorce and that then I could even marry Henry if disposed to do so. Colonel Leigh showed much emotion, as did everyone present."

Such was Libby's way of describing what must have been an orgy of tears and lamentations in true nineteenth-century tradition. The scene, however, was almost a replica of Georgey's actions toward Libby at Bifrons. The parting over, the Colonel escorted Libby to the traveling carriage and off they headed toward London.

It was grueling for Libby to be riding in the carriage with a strange woman and the uncommunicative man she knew as her father. It is interesting to note that she generally refers to him as Colonel Leigh rather than "my father," but that may be due to the fact that she wrote her autobiography many years later. The Colonel was "distressed" on first leaving the country house, but when they arrived at the first turnpike toll-house, he was able to palm off some "crooked farthings" on the unsuspecting tollkeeper.[7] That cheered up the Colonel considerably. Libby was not in a cheery mood, however; the carriage was comfortable enough but there were no really smooth roads in that day. Even the best of them were full of ruts, dusty in hot weather, filthy with manure; in bad weather they were slippery as quagmires.

The trip from Bath to London was over a hundred miles. They must not have tarried a moment longer at a wayside inn than was necessary to change horses because they reached the city at midnight of the same day. In all that time nothing was said about Libby's destination but she assumed it would be the palace. To her bewilderment they stopped in the neighborhood of Oxford Street where the Colonel dismissed his own carriage. Inasmuch as Libby makes no further mention of the so-called lady's maid, this mysterious female seems to have been dismissed along with the carriage. The Colonel then called a hackney coach from a stand and he and Libby drove off, but not in the direction of St. James's. By this time she was growing apprehensive; she did not know the neighborhood they were passing through, and the streets were dark and becoming sparsely settled.

Finally they arrived at a gloomy-looking house which seemed to be in a rural area. There Libby was turned over to another "strange woman." Her father departed and she was taken to a room where the windows were nailed shut, with bolts and chains on the door. To the panic-stricken girl the place had "every show and ostentation of a prison." [8] In her terror she could well have thought that the thing she most dreaded had come to pass: she had been "put away" in some asylum never to be seen again as had happened with her dead sister.

By today's standards it is a heartless way to treat a girl of sixteen approaching her confinement, but the Leighs did not consider themselves inhumane. They were acting in the time-honored tradition of parents with wayward girls who had disgraced the family by getting themselves in the family way. The house was not an asylum but a hideaway for pregnant girls of good families, in a section of London known as Lisson Grove. The barred windows of Libby's room looked out on the recently developed Regent's Park. The woman in charge was named Mrs. Pollen; she seems to have treated her unfortunate boarders with reasonable kindness.

During Libby's first days of incarceration her mother came to see her once. Knowing the emotional temperament of both parties it must have been so painful that the experience was not repeated. The Colonel came to see Libby three times, but apparently these visits were even more difficult because Libby refused to see him again. Some religious books were sent her by one of her aunts, "I forget which." After that she was left to sweat out her last days of confinement alone except for the ministrations of Mrs. Pollen.

This family crisis did bring Augusta and her husband together, at least for a time, because the two of them discussed the matter with John Hobhouse. In his Journal, dated July 1, 1831, he mentions being told a sad story from Colonel Leigh and his wife [about Libby's predicament]. Strange to say, the poor wife still clings to her husband and says she will follow him to prison—and stranger still Mrs Leigh seemed to me to be afraid of using harsh measures. . . . The poor girl is very fond of the man—she is hid in London. . . . The man is wandering about London trying to find her, with a pistol in his pocket.

Libby's version of what was happening to her surely would have appalled the honest and upright Hobhouse and would have given him further reason to be puzzled by Augusta's unwillingness to deal sternly with her son-in-law.

Early in Libby's stay with Mrs. Pollen, the latter hinted that she could make it easy for the girl to escape, ostensibly to go with Trevanion, but Libby refused. She had no reason to trust the word of Mrs. Pollen or Henry Trevanion. Without money and in the last stages of pregnancy with no place to go, it would have been foolhardy to venture into the streets of London, particularly in a section unknown to her. It was not until the following year that the city had its first police force; she would have been fair game for any evildoer lurking in the noisome lanes and alleyways. On refusing Mrs. Pollen's offer, she was then told that she'd be safer away than remaining in the house because Mrs. Leigh's servants could be bribed to put something in Libby's food to bring on an abortion, a suggestion not new to Libby.[9]

This warning was not altruistic on Mrs. Pollen's part. She might not attempt such a risky business, but servants could be bribed. If one of her unfortunate charges died, as the victims of such powerful poisons often did, she, not the mother, would be held responsible. Even if the girl did not die but became violently ill, it would go hard with Mrs. Pollen, for the law of the land permitted no margin for error. Once the mother showed signs of quickening, a person guilty of inducing abortion was summarily given the death penalty and hanged at Tyburn.

Shortly thereafter Libby gave birth to a stillborn child.

For the second time in her brief life she had gone through the ordeal of childbirth, and had been treated as a criminal, while those responsible for her misfortune went free. She had no idea what was going on in the Trevanion household or at St. James's—whether or not anyone knew she'd given birth or cared if she lived or died. For all she knew she might remain behind these bars indefinitely.

Two weeks went by. One day she was looking through the window and saw a carriage passing by. In it were Georgey and Henry. Libby did not know if it were by accident or design, or if either of them had seen her. She learned next day that they did know her whereabouts; for in the next fortnight Henry drove by every day—alone. He made certain signs to her which she did not understand, but soon she found notes in Georgey's handwriting sewn into her linen when it came from the wash. *Plans were being made for her escape.* She must be in readiness at all times. When the opportunity presented itself she was to do as she was told and ask no questions.

> One day the lady to whose care I had been entrusted told me that if I liked to walk out of the house nobody would stop me, and showed me how to remove the chains affixed to my door. I did not hesitate in any choice between two evils, but at once put on my bonnet, followed her instructions and found Trevanion waiting to receive me. We left the street with all possible haste and secrecy, which we might have spared ourselves, as nobody attempted to follow us.[10]

How her escape was made possible she cared not; that she was under the dubious protection of a man who had brought her nothing but tragedy concerned her even less. She was out of the gloomy prison cell—it was July, the sun was warm, she was free. In that moment of relief, Henry seemed a veritable Galahad, and she would have been glad to go with him to the ends of the earth.

By hook or crook they made their way to the Channel and embarked for France. The second chapter of her life was finished.

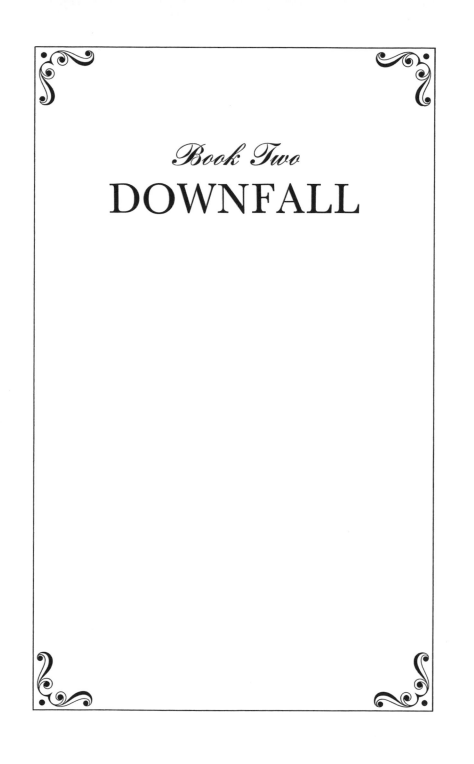

Book Two

DOWNFALL

8

There is a very life in our despair,
Vitality of poison—a quick root
Which feeds those deadly branches; for it were
As nothing did we die; but Life will suit
Itself to Sorrow's most detested fruit,
Like to the apples on the Dead Sea's shore,
All ashes to the taste.

—CHILDE HAROLD'S PILGRIMAGE

W E MADE OUR WAY TO THE CONTINENT AND FOR TWO years after this time we lived together on the coast of Normandy under the assumed name of Monsieur and Madame Aubin." [1]

Since Waterloo the travel-minded English had been attracted to the beauty of the Normandy and Brittany coastline. By 1831 there were hotels in many coastal towns and villages which catered especially to English people. Most of the Norman peasants understood and spoke a smattering of English; many units of the British Army of Occupation after Waterloo were stationed there, until France paid off her war indemnity. The presence of M. and Mme. Aubin, English despite their French name, would not have aroused undue curiosity in a village by the sea as they might have done a few miles inland.* Small inns in resort areas looked upon "foreigners" as good business, and as long as they spent money and obeyed the laws they could be

---

* The name of the village in which they stayed is not given in any source material. Libby may have omitted it deliberately, for reasons of her own.

sure of a friendly smile or welcome from every cottage door-
way. If, however, the foreigners were not overly generous with
tips or were obviously transients, the smiles would fade.

But regardless of his station in life, no Frenchman worthy
of the name was ever averse to eyeing an attractive woman,
which Mme. Elizabeth Aubin was proving to be. She was not
beautiful in the fair classic style so admired in England, but she
was tall and slender and carried herself with the grace of a
lady, as any well-brought-up girl was taught from childhood.
Moreover, both she and Henry could speak the language well
enough to be at home on French soil, and they were also more
Celtic in appearance than Anglo-Saxon, a legacy from their
Cornish forebears.

It would be a relief to be able to state that at long last
Libby experienced some happiness with Henry, now that they
had freed themselves from the restrictions imposed by convention and responsibility. There is no doubt that Henry was
sexually obsessed by her and that she responded with equal
passion, at first certainly; but there were difficulties inherent
in the relationship which militated against lasting happiness.

First, there was Libby's health. She was never a robust girl;
in letters between Augusta and various friends there are frequent mentions of childhood illnesses suffered by Libby, and
she was always subject to respiratory ailments. Probably some
of these health problems were psychosomatic in origin, and
the same could be said of Henry's "delicate health" which was
the reason given for his inability to take up a professional
career suitable for one of his rank in life. Lack of financial
security causes anxiety, and this lack must have contributed to
the nervous tension which beset Henry and Libby throughout
their liaison. Libby was also plagued by miscarriages which
are known to be detrimental to the mental and physical well-
being of any woman. She made it clear that Henry wanted children by her, and a child would have given her an emotional
outlet.

Another problem was the question of Henry's divorce.

Georgiana did apply for one; there was correspondence between her and Henry on the subject. Lord Chichester (the son
of Augusta's half-sister Mary, now the Dowager Lady Chichester) also wrote to Henry, "urging his separation from me," to
quote Libby, "though I never read their letters, I was told
by Trevanion what they were about, and that he and Lord
Chichester could not agree." [2] Libby may have been misin-
formed about the contents of some of the letters. In all Henry's
dealings he proved himself a skillful liar and character assassin
many times over. Although Georgey did try to keep her
promise to Libby, the plan came to nothing. Who can know
if Henry cooperated fully to bring it about? He was by nature
so self-indulgent that he may have made little or no effort to
exert himself. Probably Lord Chichester did write to Henry at
this time, for Libby would have seen the envelopes if not the
contents of the letters. But whatever passed between Chichester
and Henry, Augusta was not involved.

In a statement to Lady Byron written several years later,
she says, "From July 1831 to June 1833—I was left in ignorance of Elizabeth's abode—and almost of her existence." [3] In
that two-year period Augusta was on close terms with her sister
and nephew, and it seems odd that she was ignorant of her
daughter's whereabouts. It is understandable, though, that the
Chichester family and Augusta were prejudiced against Libby
inasmuch as Georgey and her three little girls were living
with Augusta at St. James's Palace, utterly dependent upon
what Augusta could eke out of her meager income. The thought
of Henry and Libby living a carefree life of sin in France
was a painful reminder that the wicked flourish "like a green
bay tree."

The sinners, alas for them, were not flourishing too well.
All too soon Libby realized that Henry had not changed. He
was as irascible to her as he had been to Georgey and just as
irresponsible, the difference being that she had no legal claim
on his protection and could be left high and dry whenever it
suited him. Not that Libby was faultless, for she was never

easy to live with if her temper were aroused; nor did she knuckle under to harsh treatment as Georgey did. Violent quarrels were followed by passionate reconciliations, which were followed in turn by more scenes. Probably each of them was guilty of provoking anger in the other; still, endless conflict was an added drain on Libby's health.

It was during that first summer abroad that Libby began to think about joining the Church of Rome. It has been suggested that she was motivated by defiance of her family; that, in effect, she thought of herself as a Byron rather than a Leigh.[4] Byron, though brought up in the religion of Scotland, was attracted to the Catholic Church during his years in Italy. He placed his natural daughter Allegra in a convent to be brought up by nuns, against the strong objections of her mother (Clare Clairmont). Libby's interest in Catholicism did not meet with Augusta's approval at all; she had been brought up to think of the Church as "the Scarlet Woman," and Libby was aware of this. Yet defiance could not have been her sole reason for contemplating conversion.

She was not an intellectual or given to abstract thinking, but from her subsequent actions it is clear that she felt the need for an inner security which she never received from her family and would never find in Henry. Now she was in daily contact with the people of a land which for centuries had been dominated by the Church. Until the Revolution forced the separation of church and state, half the land in Normandy and Brittany was under the jurisdiction of various abbeys and cathedrals. Libby could not fail to notice that the Church was as much a part of the daily life of the community as eating and sleeping. Religious celebrations in any Norman parish were eagerly awaited and thoroughly enjoyed by the entire populace.

The *Fête Nationale* (Bastille Day) was a time of great rejoicing, but the inhabitants of a village or small town had a special fondness for the *Fête du village,* in honor of the local patron saint. A band concert, a torchlight procession, street

dancing to the tune of the fiddle and concertina, the flow of
fine Norman cider and Calvados; it was a day of days. And what
onlooker was not moved by the sight of eager young girls on
their way to their first communion, in their long white muslin
dresses, white cotton gloves, and veils topped with little crowns
of flowers?

Libby was brought up in an agrarian community; she
knew that the life of the tenant farmers in England was hard
and drab, with most of the rewards for their unremitting labor
going to the gentry who owned the land and cottages. The
French peasants, from the very young to the aged, worked
from dawn to dusk, but most of them owned their little parcels of land. The village was self-contained, made up of a few
families who had been there for centuries and had no desire
to move elsewhere. The only outsiders welcomed as part of
the group were the parish priest and the schoolteacher, though
they were not considered to be true villagers. The peasants
had neither time nor inclination to meet strangers except on
market day in the nearest town. Then the whole village set
forth in their carts or on foot, to buy and sell, argue politics,
find out what was going on in the country.

All this hustle and bustle was interesting to watch. There
was always something for Libby and Henry to see from their
windows: in a seaside village there were fishing boats, children
bent double carrying baskets loaded with freshly caught fish,
men hauling in their nets or mending them on the beach. But
M. and Mme. Aubin were not part of this restless activity.
Everything known about Libby reveals her intense need to be
loved, to be admired, to give of herself, to participate. Moreover, Libby was, in some ways, a product of convention. She
may not have been happy with Henry, but having put herself
beyond the pale morally and socially she wanted the security
of marriage. Much was forgiven, or at least condoned, if a
woman succeeded in marrying the man who had seduced her,
even if divorce made the marriage possible. When it was clear
that Henry was not going to be free to marry her, Libby

knew she had placed herself in an untenable position. In this
community, unlike an English one, there was no provision
made for charity cases, no work available for needy families who
weren't villagers. Each family took care of its own and if extra
help was needed the job was given to the daughter or son of
another peasant.[5] So, if Libby were foolhardy enough to break
with Henry she would have no place to go, no way to earn
a respectable living. She could not return to her family and
expect to be greeted with cordiality, if indeed she was greeted
at all. She had, moreover, to contend with Henry who did not
want a separation and would have made trouble for her if she
left his bed and board.

In her desperation she cast about for some kind of solace
to help her make the best of a bad bargain. The simple faith
of the people around her seemed to give them peace of mind—
spiritual strength—or courage to endure their unrewarding
lives. What she could not know as an outsider was that the
average peasant was not in the least concerned with things of
the spirit, though he might give lip service to piety by going to
mass and confession and observing the religious holidays. Birth,
marriage, and death were occasions when the curé was necessary,
but most of the men in his parish made fun of him behind his
back. The real power in the village was the justice of the peace.
A Norman peasant always had a lawsuit going, sometimes with
a brother or sister, about grievances which could have been
settled over a glass of cider or Calvados.[6]

Seldom was a village curé fortunate enough to know,
much less to make a convert of, someone like Mme. Aubin
who was a member of the Anglican Church, and more especially a young woman of obvious breeding and education.
This particular curé must have attacked the project of instruct-
ing this potential convert with true Gallic enthusiasm. In
December, 1831, Libby was baptized into the Roman Catholic
Church.

This move precluded any possibility of marriage to Henry
whether or not he got his divorce, but Libby continued to live

with him. Having been baptized she was starting life anew, shorn of all past transgressions, but the curé seems to have accepted her *liaison coupable* with a man who was not her husband. He was, after all, the spiritual father of a parish composed of down-to-earth peasants, and it was prudent to take a realistic attitude toward human frailty. At some time or other most of his flock must have confessed to most, if not all, of the seven deadly sins and been given absolution. There were also mitigating circumstances to be considered in the case of his new convert. A woman, be she wife or mistress, who was dependent absolutely on a man for the basic necessities of life could not be expected to deny that man his "rights" to her body, nor would he be expected to abstain. Neither would the curé wish to place a woman in a position where she might be abandoned by her protector.

Yet there was a change in Libby after her conversion, a gradual drawing away from all that had formerly been essential to her happiness. As with all converts she was anxious to abide by the teachings of the Church and was greatly influenced in her thinking by this desire to conform. Confession, followed by absolution and penance being one of the sacraments, she began to regret the ill will between herself and her mother and the damage she had done to Georgey and her children. She began to contemplate the future and what she would do with it. Yet repentance was not the whole reason for her wish to escape the thralldom of Henry Trevanion.

Frequent miscarriages wore her down so that she had to rest a great deal, which gave her time to brood. Whether or not she and Henry still read the Bible every morning is not recorded, but it is reasonable to assume that religious books were in evidence about the ménage. She became imbued with the idea of entering a convent as a lay boarder, and by spring of 1833 the idea had taken firm root. It is hard to imagine lively, gregarious Libby making such an alteration in her way of life, but it is the kind of move which often does exert a powerful appeal to young men and women who have suffered disillusionment, broken hearts, and the like. It was especially prevalent in the romantic literature of the nineteenth century which might have had indirect effect upon an impressionable, frail young woman with too much time on her hands. Unfortunately Henry did not take kindly to this idea and without funds of her own she could not pay the sum required for her maintenance as a boarder in any convent. But at last, in early June, 1833,

> owing to the delicacy of my health and Henry having no hope that his favorite wish could never [sic] be accomplished, that I should bear a living child, he agreed to my wish that we should separate. He took his real name, I mine with the exception of a letter [*], and we went to Lower Brittany. I wrote to my mother to inform her of such and my desire and intention of entering as a Boarder in a convent.[7]

The letter was written in June, from Pontivy, saying that she was ill and penitent and requesting funds to enable her to go through with her plan.[8]

Pontivy was a fair-sized town, about fifty or so miles from Quimper, in the heart of a region dominated by religious fervor. Its church festivals were known throughout France (as they still are). One of them, *Le Pardon de Folgoët,* celebrated in September, brought pilgrims from all over Brittany, many of whom, in that day, elected to make the entire journey on their knees.[9] On every road one was likely to pass a Calvary atop a hill; wood carvings representing the Crucifixion, the figures often life-sized and many of them intricately carved. These wayside shrines were placed there in bygone times by local priests to serve as reminders to passers-by that they must resist the lures of the devil, that life on earth was but a fleeting interlude on the way to Heaven—or Hell.

This atmosphere of devout Christianity, almost pagan in its preoccupation with idols and rituals, was bound to

---

* The name Medora and the initial M were not used by either Libby or Augusta at this period.

An 1829 engraving of Medora Leigh.
Pierpont Morgan Library.

Portrait of Byron, by Thomas Phillips, 1814.
Newstead Abbey Collections. Courtesy City Librarian of Nottingham.

Augusta Leigh.
Drawing by Sir George Hayter.
Trustees of the British Museum.

Six Mile Bottom, Medora Leigh's birthplace.
Courtesy, Peter Quennell.

Newstead Abbey.
Newstead Abbey Collections. Courtesy City Librarian of Nottingham.

Lady Byron.
Pierpont Morgan Library.

A cartoon by Cruikshank, commenting on the separation of Lord and Lady Byron.

St. James Palace, London, where Augusta Leigh maintained residence.
Picture Collection, New York Public Library.

Caerhays Castle, Cornwall, home of the Trevanion family.
Courtesy Cornwall County Council, Truro, and Christine Hawkridge North.

A portrait, often said to represent Augusta Leigh, but more likely
to be of Medora Leigh.
Newstead Abbey Collections. Courtesy City Librarian of Nottingham.

8.

August 13th 1843
3 Church Road
H Panero

My Mother

Letter from Libby to her
mother, quoted on
page 245
Pierpont Morgan Library.

Stephen Lushington.
Pierpont Morgan Library.

Charles Babbage.
Illustrated London News,
November 4, 1871

Ada, Countess of Lovelace, by Margaret Carpenter,
a portrait at Ockham Park.
Department of the Environment, London

To The Editor of the Times.

Sir,

About five and twenty years ago, circumstances, not necessary to be here stated, put me in the position of a negotiator with Lady Byron for the means of subsistence to the fourth of the Seven Children of the Honble. Augusta Leigh, named Medora, who was then in London in absolute & abject destitution. I did not see Her Ladyship but I had more than one interview with Dr Lushington her adviser & representative on the occasion. In our conferences the paternity of Lord Byron to the above mentioned Medora was as thoroughly understood and recognized as the maternity of Mrs Leigh: in fact it was the sole basis on which we raised our positions; without it neither of us had a standing or could have had a case. I did not succeed in my endeavours, and my failure is seen: what contradictory with Mrs Beecher Stowe's statement that Lady Byron never faltered never gave over in motherly tenderness towards 'the child of sin': I ascertained at the same time that the damning secret was known to very many persons, of whom for your private information I append the names of some of the most distinguished, and I should be glad to learn how their knowledge can be reconciled with the dignified and magnanimous silence claimed as a merit for Lady Byron, as assuredly it cannot be imagined to have been imparted by the guilty pair, and who else than her Ladyship could have imparted it! It was known also to a rogue of a French valet, who threatened publicity by committing an assault, for which he would be taken to Bow street, and have an opportunity of telling his tale. He also threatened a civil action against Lady Byron, which Dr Lushington told me he would certainly advise her to defend. As nothing came of his threats, I must conclude he was bought at his own price, but I have no information on the subject.

I enclose my card in compliance with your notice as a guarantee of my good faith, certainly not for publication and I remain Your...

H.B. M.M.

Marylebone
24 September 1869

T. Smith

The Duke of Leeds
The Honble. R. Osborne
The Honble. ...
The Earl of ...
Sir John ...
Sir George Stephen...
...

An 1869 letter to the London *Times* from Thomas Smith, telling Medora Leigh's story to the public.
Pierpont Morgan Library.

have impact upon Libby who already felt drawn to the religious life. About thirty miles east of Pontivy was the even more ancient town of Carhaix, situated between the hills of Brittany and the sea. Near the town stood the old Cistercian Abbey of Relecq which had been abandoned by the Church during the Reign of Terror when all religious orders had to leave their monasteries and convents. After peace was restored to the Church of France, the various orders gradually reassembled and returned to their old buildings. Before the Revolution the Congregation of the Daughters of the Cross, a Cistercian order, had three flourishing convents in Brittany.[10] One of them, in 1833, had been restored at Tréguier and another was established temporarily in the old, dilapidated abbey near Carhaix.

Libby had selected this convent because it had accommodations for lay boarders. Then as now the Daughters of the Cross devoted themselves to the education of young girls though they encouraged older women to come there for spiritual retreats.[11] The French equivalent of sixty pounds was the sum required for a year of maintenance, and this is what she asked her mother to send her.

There was no immediate answer to Libby's letter, and during that time she had her usual difficulties with Henry. He had "agreed" to a separation, but as will be discovered later, he was having second thoughts about letting her go. It was not easy for Libby to resist his importunings—he could be disturbingly effective if he chose to be—but she tried to fend him off. At long last came the letter from her mother, "engaging to allow" Libby the sixty pounds per annum. She did not send the full amount; it came in dribs and drabs, amidst endless delays. Augusta's promises were always well meant, but she did herself and others a great disservice by promising what she could not possibly fulfill. In July Libby left Trevanion and entered the convent with the full expectation of renouncing the world of the flesh for that of the spirit. Henry remained in Pontivy, refusing to accept this move as a *fait accompli*.

Among the boarders were the usual number of girls who

hoped to be admitted into the novitiate, intending to become nuns. Others, like Libby, had not yet made up their minds about the future. All of them were to discover that life within the four walls of the abbey was a totally different experience, far more than anyone on the outside could imagine. Some could adjust to the strict austerity; others found it too difficult. A lay boarder was expected to conform to the principle of self-abnegation, to do her share of labor, to be disciplined if she didn't measure up. Could "Elizabeth Leigh" have weathered the adjustment and found the tranquility she wanted? It is a question which must always remain unanswered. She had been in the convent barely a month when she discovered that she was again with child!

"And now my greatest hope," she wrote, "was that I might in some way be able to conceal the delicate state of my health, which forbad the hope that the child would live." [12] Right or wrong, the unfortunate girl was in a dilemma that would have taxed the wisdom of Solomon. To tell the truth would nullify all hope of remaining in the convent. If she returned to the outside world there was no guarantee that her mother would continue to send the money. Without that security—and in a parlous state of health—there would be no choice but to go back to Trevanion and admit defeat for good. She decided to say nothing to anyone, hoping to miscarry quickly and keep it a secret. It would have taken a bit of doing, privacy being all but nonexistent, but she was not in a condition to think things through.

Unfortunately, or so it seemed at the time, the miscarriage did not take place. It may be that the spartan regimen of the convent and freedom from the constant turmoil with Henry had improved her health enough for her to avoid losing the child. Abortion was out of the question for a devout Catholic, nor would Libby have countenanced that alternative. She had already proven that. There was nothing else to do but tell the truth to the abbess. The abbess proved to be compassionate although she could not permit Mlle. Leigh to stay on as a boarder. Libby did have to find lodgings nearby, but the abbess permitted her to go on using the convent as a mailing address. Libby maintained that she "had hope of entering another convent at a later time when I should have no reason to leave it." [13] Apparently the abbess believed her, and doubtless Libby was quite sincere at the time, although life had other plans for her.

Libby settled in lodgings in Carhaix, using the sums sent by her mother for the supposed maintenance in the convent. Henry found lodgings there also, but not with her. "I did not feel that I was doing wrong," she wrote in self-justification. "Trevanion was not under the same roof with me and from the time I entered the convent I never was but as a sister to him." [14]

Her conscience was pricking her, but in this instance it may have been best for all concerned that she withheld the truth from her mother. They did, however, keep up a correspondence, with Augusta entreating her "to return to England under my own eye and protection." [15] By this time Libby had little faith in her mother's protection or the motherly eye which seemed always to be looking elsewhere when Libby needed help.

As time progressed and it looked as though she might carry the child to full term, Henry persuaded her to leave Carhaix with him. He, too, had been receiving letters from his father urging him to return and give up the Jezebel responsible for his downfall. There was a risk that steps might be taken to force the issue, and Henry was no more anxious to go back to England—and a forced reconciliation with Georgiana—than Libby was to risk being clapped behind bars as had happened before.

They went north to Morlaix, a good-sized Breton town situated about five miles from the English Channel on the estuary of a river. Outside the town they found a place to live. It was the Chateau Penhoët, an ancient manor house dating back to the thirteenth century, located at the confluence of a river and a brook off the main road.[16] The exterior may have been picturesque, but like all ancient houses which have fallen into neglect, it was damp and infested with rats and other vermin. But in their precarious financial condition, they could not afford to be choosy.

Were it not for the scanty sums sent sporadically by Augusta, forwarded to Morlaix, they would have been hard put to subsist on Henry's minuscule allowance. By now the name Aubin had been dropped entirely; they were passing themselves off as brother and sister. Henry used his real name while Libby was Mme. Elizabeth Leigh, supposedly the wife of a Henry Leigh. They occupied separate quarters in the gloomy old house and continued to live on a platonic basis. A short time after they took up residence there, Libby's nine months of waiting were over.

On May 19, 1834, at eight in the morning, she gave birth to a daughter—and to her joy and Henry's—the baby seemed strong enough to survive. Two days later Henry appeared before the mayor of the Commune of Plouneur-Menez to sign the birth certificate. He gave the names of the parents as Henry and Elizabeth Leigh, but the baby's name was put down as Marie Violette Trevanion. To add to the resultant confusion about Marie's birth which would cause so much trouble later, the baptismal record certifies that:

> Anne Violette *Leigh,* legitimate daughter of M. Henry Leigh and Mad. Elizabeth Leigh (nee Trevanion) was born at the Chateau Penhoat, baptized on 11 of December by M. Lejac, curate. The godfather was Yves Pouliguen, the godmother Annette Pouliguen, both farmers. The document was signed by Henry Trevanion, *acting for the absent father.*[17]

In spite of the change in her name, she was called Marie by her mother and by that name she was known throughout her life.

While all this was going on in Morlaix, something was happening in Carhaix which would have a disastrous effect upon the future of Libby and Henry. Soon after they left Carhaix, Henry's uncle George Bettesworth arrived in the town expressly to "seek his nephew and induce him to leave that country which was most desirable while Elizabeth remained in it." [18] To his amazement and indignation he discovered the birds had flown elsewhere. After making a few more inquiries he dashed off this information to Henry's father who was living in London at the time, at 10 Chester Square. The elder Trevanion, equally indignant, went directly to St. James's to confront Augusta with the latest proofs of her daughter's perfidy.

In fairness to Augusta, the facts as presented in the letter would have aroused anyone to anger. Libby had spent but a short time in the convent (no reason given for her leaving), had rejoined Henry, and the two had then decamped to Morlaix. Prior to this unpleasant news Augusta had written to the abbess to inquire about her daughter and had received no answer, giving the impression that the whole story about entering a convent was trumped up by Libby. For years Augusta had protected herself by evasions, sometimes deliberate untruths, but she was outraged at finding herself a dupe.

"Under such circumstances," she stated virtuously, "I could not continue her allowance without considering myself accessory to her misconduct." [19] Letters flew back and forth across the Channel, full of reproaches, recriminations, self-justifications on both sides. Augusta turned to her nephew Lord Chichester for help in this new crisis; she had Henry's irate father to contend with as well as her daughter and son-in-law. Lord Chichester tried to straighten out matters by writing to Henry, to Libby, to the elder Trevanion, and read all Augusta's letters before she sent them. Libby's letters to her mother were "cold and in many other respects most painful." [20]

Augusta could not know that these "painful" letters were the brain children of her Mr. H. Trevanion.[21] He was up to his old tricks again, interfering and making mischief between mother and daughter by telling Libby what to write. Had she been left to her own devices she might have come to terms with her mother. She proved that she wished to atone for her mistakes, and she remained, except for occasional backsliding, a sincere Catholic all her life. And there are endless manifestations of a real and abiding affection for her mother which she was never able to eradicate completely. Augusta was hopelessly muddle-headed but her impulses were kind, and she did manage to scrape up some funds for Libby at a time when she was sorely pressed on all sides.

But Libby, alas, was living under the same roof with Henry Trevanion, and though she did not share his bed, he had a Svengali-like influence on her mind. There is a streak of sadism in all his dealings with Augusta, ironically one of the few people who wished him well. So, as he had done in the past, he masterminded Libby's correspondence, dictating responses to Augusta's letters; in effect, her cold and painful letters were not necessarily expressions of her true feelings.[22] The result was that communication ceased between mother and daughter, and Libby and her child were now dependent upon the protection of Henry, which could have been his motive for causing the rift. He was, in every way, Libby's bad angel, but in one respect she was happier than she had been since she was "a happy child." [23] She had borne a child which lived.

9

The hope, the fear, the jealous care,
The exalted portion of the pain
And power of love, I cannot share,
But wear the chain.

—"ON THIS DAY I COMPLETE
MY THIRTY-SIXTH YEAR"

WE CONTINUED TO LIVE IN A SECRET AND UNFREQUENTED spot," Libby wrote. "Henry at this time gave himself up wholly to religion and shooting; I to my child." [1]

It boggles the mind that anyone could fill up his waking hours in two such diametrically opposite pursuits, but Henry had an infinite capacity for genteel ennui second only to his ability to scrounge money out of his family. Difficult as it is today, or any time, to have empathy for this lily-of-the-field, he was only following the accepted pattern of living for men in his station of life. Shooting was a favorite pastime of the country gentry in England, and the peasant farmers of France could often be seen wandering the countryside with their hunting dogs.

It was a Gothic-novel kind of existence for Henry and Libby in the smelly old manor house by the side of a stream. One would be hard put to find a milieu less appropriate for a nervous, not too robust girl, with a little child to bring up and barely enough money for the necessities of life. The environs of the chateau were undeniably beautiful—the whole landscape of

Finistère is unique in its beauty—but there was something disquieting about that particular locale. "Penhoët" means "end of the woods" in the Breton language, and the forests of Brittany in that day covered vast areas. The peasants were afraid of losing their way in those dense, dark woods, to be set upon by wolves and other predators which lurked at night in the thickets and caves. Many a hunter had gone into the forest and was never seen again unless, by accident, some other hunter came upon his ravaged body.

The Bretons, though deeply religious, were intensely superstitious and clung to their pagan legends and beliefs. They believed in the *korrigans,* the Breton name for fairies, but these woodland creatures were not the gay sprites of England who danced at night and made rings in the grass. The *korrigan* midnight revels did not include dancing, but they lurked in churchyards where they unwound the shrouds from the dead. Even the dress of the peasants suited the Gothic background. Their broadbrimmed hats, long hair, and trunk hose (rather than trousers) dated back to the sixteenth century. In winter they enveloped themselves in goatskins, as their pagan ancestors had done.[2] Brittany was indeed a century removed from the rest of the country. She had been cut off from France by mountains and forests, from the rest of the world by the English Channel and the Atlantic. The Bretons were fiercely insular, each village or commune speaking its own patois which was not always understandable to travelers from a village a few miles distant.

Although many of the Breton nobility and large land owners led cultivated, graceful lives with frequent journeys to Paris, the peasants were in the main a hard race, cruel in their dealings with each other, harsh to their old people. In Libby's day, the old women were often seen wandering along the roads begging food and money from passersby.[3] The one exception was the treatment of horses; the Bretons couldn't do enough for them. At St. Eloi (near Plougastel) they had a curious ceremony called *le baptême de chevaux* where horses from all over the countryside were brought to the church and led around it seven times.

The curé stood at the entrance, holy water sprinkler in hand, and sprinkled the horses as they passed by. In that day the animals were then led into the church to the christening font where the curé made the sign of the cross on their foreheads. Their flowing tails were then trimmed and sold for the benefit of the church.[4]

Finistère was indeed a strange and fascinating place, full of beauty and mystery, but certainly not hospitable to strangers, and the interior of the Chateau Penhoët was not likely to perk up the spirits. "We never met alone and seldom met at all," Libby wrote. Yet she was not unhappy in her loneliness. At twenty, motherhood had fulfilled her as nothing else could have done. With all the criticism and blame heaped upon her in the years ahead, no one ever accused her of being a bad mother. She adored Marie to the exclusion of everything else, but she did not spoil her or allow her to become selfish and undisciplined.

In the fall of 1835, after a year and four months of poverty, Henry was forced to go to England for more money. For a man who was chronically on the edge of financial disaster he always seemed able to procure funds for his own use if not for his wife and children. It might be well here to set matters straight about his financial situation inasmuch as it played such an important role in his relationship with Libby. At the time of his engagement to Georgiana and the ensuing marriage settlement, an accounting of Henry's expectations revealed that he would receive an income from a substantial trust fund on the death of his father. Also, on the death of an uncle and aunt he was entitled to the sum of four thousand pounds and income from a reversionary trust.[5] This did not put him in the category of young gentlemen with great expectations, that breed so admired by nineteenth-century novelists, but it would have provided him with an adequate income. Yet from all that is known of John Trevanion Purnell Bettesworth Trevanion's spendthrift habits, which included borrowing against his estate to pay for refurbishing Caerhay's Castle, it was not likely that his children would receive much of an inheritance after all the creditors were satisfied.

Prior to Henry's going to England for money, his father and Augusta were engaged in veiled hostilities in connection with the Henry-Libby-Georgiana triangle. On May 10 Augusta wrote to apologize for not replying to Mr. Trevanion's letters because she had been so upset by news from the continent. She assured him that she would not agree to an arrangement between Henry Trevanion and Elizabeth that did not have Mr. Trevanion's approval. She went on to say that her chief concern was for her daughter Georgiana and Georgiana's children, and she urged Mr. Trevanion to maintain his interest in them regardless of the circumstances, no matter what Henry and Libby had been so foolish as to do.[6]

Clearly the elder Trevanion set the pattern of behavior followed by his son Henry: fobbing off the unsavory mess on Augusta. Alas for her, it was true that she had been the one who moved heaven and earth to push through her daughter's marriage although Henry's father had wanted it postponed until after his own nuptials. There had been a money problem which could have been straightened out satisfactorily, given enough time, but Augusta wanted to go ahead against everyone's advice and judgment. Because of this unseemly haste the elder Trevanion could only allow Henry four hundred and fifty pounds a year instead of the nine hundred per annum which he had promised.

No longer did Augusta fly to the defense of dear Henry. On the contrary, she pointed out to the elder Trevanion that his son's appalling behavior had brought anguish to her family, and had thrown her finances into disarray. She reminded him too, that when she first met Henry, she had no idea of this side of his character.[7] She also reminded Mr. Trevanion that it was she who prevented Georgiana and her children from having to beg for their food.[8]

At this time she and Georgiana were on agreeable terms and going about together socially. As Lord Byron's sister, Augusta was enough of a celebrity to insure invitations from hostesses who recognized the asset of an interesting guest. In one of Augusta's letters, for example, she asks if she can bring her daughter Mrs. Trevanion to a certain function.[9] She was still shy by nature—as was Georgey—and preferred the society of those she had known for a long time, but in her own way she was doing what she could to bring a little lightness into Georgey's life, though it would have been impossible for mother and daughter to have an easy rapport. Too much had gone wrong, too many dismal memories shared which no amount of shrugging off could dispel. And there were the omnipresent Trevanion daughters, now nine, seven, and six, who had to be clothed, fed, and educated, with little chance of their finding future husbands. It did not assuage Georgey's bitterness to know that Libby had presented Henry with a daughter whom he seemed to prefer to his legitimate offspring. This was the status quo in England when Henry returned that fall to get more money to support his extramarital ménage. The fatted calf may not have been slaughtered and roasted as a welcome to the prodigal, but he succeeded in his mission.

Six weeks later he returned to the Chateau Penhoët with money, and certain expectations which had nothing to do with finances. From the time that Libby entered the convent, in the summer of 1833, she had no sexual intimacy with Henry and in the ensuing year and a half they had drifted even further apart. Now to Libby's dismay: "I saw remains of what I had thought wholly extinguished—his passionate attachment to me. But I was no longer a child—I was twenty-one; and two years experience had enabled me to know how to resist." [10]

From Henry's point of view it is understandable that his amour propre was affronted by this show of independence. At first it may have struck him as a temporary whim which could be overcome by the usual flattery and endearments. Twice before she had fended him off for a time before succumbing; she would do it again. From his viewpoint she had no right to reproach him. He took her back after she had to leave the convent; he stood by her through her confinement and made no demands upon her afterward. And despite all attempts by his family to induce him to give her up, he had gone back to her. But she did not want to go back to him, not in the way he wanted, and it galled his ego.

Libby may have been one of the legion of women who lose interest in sex for a while after giving birth, especially when they must give their full time and attention to the needs of the baby. Even if there had been ample funds, Libby would probably not have wanted to turn over Marie to the care of some peasant girl or old woman hired as a nurse. The peasants were scrupulous about the whiteness of their head coverings, some of which were truly magnificent, but their heads crawled with lice, and seldom did any peasant, man or woman, wash face, hands, or body. As for using soap and water on a baby, it was anathema. No child's head was subject to the rigors of brushing or cleansing until the age of two at least. It was considered bad for the hair, and water might addle the infant's brain by seeping into the skull.[11] In order to insure complete protection a babe wore a bonnet or cap day and night. It is true that by present-day standards nobody was antiseptically clean in that day, whether living in a palace or a thatched hut, but a girl of Libby's upbringing did observe certain rules of personal cleanliness which would have been incomprehensible to a peasant. Byron, in fact, bathed so frequently even in his last months in Greece that some of his comrades considered it thoroughly effeminate.[12]

Regardless of Libby's reasons for rejecting Henry's advances, she paid dearly for it: "I pass over three years of misery, but I am willing to give every detail of what I was made to suffer, though I do not think it is absolutely necessary to do so." [13]

Later, however, she confided the painful details to a friend who revealed, among other things that: She was made to act as servant to another member of the household, Henry's mistress.* This and other hardships wrecked her health after some years, and she fell "dangerously ill." [14]

---

* In no available source material is the name of Henry's mistress mentioned.

Just as Byron turned the screws on Augusta when she refused him after his marriage, so did Trevanion revenge himself
upon Augusta's daughter. Now she knew what Georgey had suffered, what it was like to be subjected to the humiliation of
another woman's ascendency in the household. Her small store
of strength was depleted by overwork, but far more damaging
was the effect upon her morale. It is forgivable for Henry to
take another woman to share his bed; sex was important to him
and Libby had refused to go back on the old basis. Inasmuch
as they were known as brother and sister and occupied separate
quarters, Henry would have been expected to satisfy his needs
elsewhere. The best of men would eventually tire of a steady
diet of religion and shooting. And having found a woman who
attracted him enough to make her his mistress *en titre,* he could
be excused for bringing her into the chateau.

But to crush Libby's spirit by treating her as a servant and
encouraging his mistress to do the same was unpardonable.
Libby may have exaggerated Henry's harsh treatment in talking
to her confidante; it is a common failing when lovers become
enemies. But from all that is known of Henry's temperament he
was capable of the meanest kind of behavior toward those who
were close to him, whether or not it was deserved. Libby's plight
was made all the more unbearable because she could not escape.
Thanks partly to Henry's machinations she had alienated her
mother and relations and could expect no assistance from that
quarter. Without a sou she could not leave the chateau, for
Brittany was as intolerant of indigent females as Normandy,
perhaps more so. Now that she had a child to care for she could
not risk arrest or imprisonment; the authorities often deported
such women to far off colonies.* If that were to happen to her,
what would become of Marie? There was simply no way for
Libby to survive except to remain in the chateau and be treated
as a chattel, which indeed she had become.

---

* The novel *Histoire du Chevalier Des Grieux et de Manon Lescaut* by the
Abbé Prévost published 1731, is based on this practice.

Libby to survive except to remain in the chateau and be treated as a chattel, which indeed she had become.

In the spring of 1838, after three years of privation and unhealthy living conditions, she fell gravely ill. So ill, in fact, that it alarmed Trevanion enough to call in a "medical man." (All classes of society seem to have referred to doctors as "medical men" or "medical gentlemen.") In this case the gentleman was named M. Carrel, and he proved to be not only capable in his job but a man of great perception and compassion. She was "declared to be in a consumption," but she appears to have been suffering from pneumonia or some equally virulent chest infection.[15] Dwellings in Brittany, whether peasant huts or manor houses, were dismally cold in the winter and early spring. To offset this, the simplest cottage consisting of one main room had an enormous fireplace large enough to accommodate chairs ranged around the blazing logs in the center. Often several generations, including servants, slept in the main room, a family to a bed. The sleeping arrangements in a manor house were not quite so communal, but the only heat in any room was still the fireplace, with perhaps a warming pan to take the chill off the sheets in the bed.[16]

To take care of a patient with a serious chest condition under these circumstances was a full time job which M. Carrel seems to have undertaken himself. Marie must have been a frightened little girl, bewildered by the stranger sitting at the bedside of her mother day and night. Luckily for mother and child, M. Carrel nursed his patient through the worst of her illness, but the disease left her so emaciated that it would be weeks before she could be up and around. It also left her a prey to melancholy, not unusual in convalescing from a wasting illness. For a time Libby felt she had but a few months to live, but Marie gave her the will to fight.

While she was recuperating Carrel still spent much time with her, and during those long days he became increasingly curious about the occupants of the Chateau Penhoët. It could not have taken long to conclude that things were not what they were reputed to be in the ménage. Who were these English people, obviously of good family and education, and why were they living a hand-to-mouth existence in this lonely spot? Apart from normal curiosity, M. Carrel was also interested in his patient as an individual; this was not necessarily a romantic interest, though he could not have been entirely indifferent to her as a woman. Libby inspired strong emotions in men and women alike— sometimes hate, sometimes love, never indifference. Carrel questioned her, diffidently at first, until he saw that she was eager to confide in him. Libby admitted that she trusted him because he was kind and did not want to exploit her as so many had done; she told him the truth about her birth, background, and association with Henry in all its lurid detail.[17]

Carrel could not fail to be impressed by her references to her aristocratic relations, her mother who lived at St. James's Palace and was also the sister of the renowned poet Lord Byron. Byron had never been welcomed in France during his self-imposed exile; he had been considered too radical by the Bourbons who returned to the throne after Napoleon's downfall. Byron had never made any secret of his admiration for the little Corsican. There was a Bourbon on the throne in 1838, Louis-Philippe, but he was a constitutional monarch and dared not impose his will too forcibly on his subjects. Byron had become a hero of the revolutionary movement seething throughout Europe. There was no doubt in Carrel's mind that Mlle. Leigh was a swan among geese and should not be made to suffer at the hands of Trevanion.

Libby concurred heartily. She stated frankly that she implored Carrel to help her free herself from the cruelty of a man "whom I had never really loved and who by his conduct every day convinced me more and more of his worthlessness." [18] Yet she and Marie could not leave until she was strong enough nor could she make a move without funds to maintain herself and child elsewhere. Carrel felt that her only chance was to make her peace with her mother and well-to-do relations, one of whom would surely come to her aid. Libby knew it would not be practical to write to her mother after a four-year estrangement, part of which was her own fault. So, in July, she wrote to her Aunt Mary, Lady Chichester, begging her to intercede for her with her mother. Her letter was a heart-rending account of what she'd endured and her conviction that she had but a few months to live. Her one desire was to die, away from Trevanion's persecution.

Lady Chichester showed the letter to Augusta and both were appalled by its contents. Yet with the normal reaction of concern and pity, a residue of doubt remained. It was not easy to forget Libby's protestations of penitence and wish to atone for her sins which contrasted so completely with her subsequent behavior and unfilial letters to her mother. At this time Augusta had not learned that most of those letters were the handiwork of Henry Trevanion. She could not therefore avoid a certain skepticism about the new crisis, and the same was true of Lady Chichester, but still—Libby had once been dear to them and her letters could not be dismissed with a shrug.

When Libby's letters did not bring a quick response, M. Carrel wrote to Augusta, corroborating his patient's statements and adding some of his own. By this time he had been subjected to Henry's diabolic skill in distorting facts and making mischief; he had been told not to believe a word of Libby's story. The assertions of congenital liars are so plausible and apparently sincere that great damage can be done before they are found out. This time, however, Henry was not dealing with a credulous girl or a gullible older woman. Carrel was a hardheaded Breton not easily bemused, and his brother was also a lawyer. And lawyers have a decided preference for facts backed up by written records and affidavits. This was (and is) especially true of French lawyers who may not feel that a man's word is as good as his bond, but his *signature* on a document is sacrosanct.

Carrel wanted to make sure of his ground before he took direct action on Libby's behalf so he decided to check on the truth or falsity of Trevanion's allegations. The result of Carrel's correspondence with Augusta and Lady Chichester was to prove that Trevanion, not Libby, was the liar. After Augusta consulted with her legal adviser, she sent Carrel Libby's certificate of baptism and certificates of Georgiana's baptism and marriage. She also communicated with Carrel's brother on the legal aspects of the case. Lady Chichester sent five pounds.[19]

The money enabled Libby and Marie to quit the chateau in August, accompanied by Carrel; they returned to Pontivy where they settled in a cheap but decent section among respectable neighbors.[20] As usual, Augusta agreed to see that funds would be forthcoming so that Libby and daughter would not be in want. Libby was still weak from her near-fatal illness and would need nourishing food and bed rest.

Although Henry could now enjoy the delights of his new paramour without the troublesome presence of his former mistress and child—and the necessity of providing for their sustenance—he showed himself to be a true dog in the manger. In no time he was writing to Georgiana that her sister was in the hands of a charlatan out to exploit her for financial gain. In view of the minuscule sums sent by Augusta from time to time, Trevanion's accusations would be laughable were it not for the precarious state of Libby's finances and health. An occasional five pounds from Lady Chichester was often all that kept Libby and Marie from actual want.

At last Carrel took matters into his own hands and wrote to Augusta that it was vitally important for Mlle. Leigh to have a fixed income, otherwise the nervous tension would prevent her from ever getting well. In his opinion the sum of a hundred and twenty pounds a year would insure modest but adequate lodgings and food for mother and child.[21] Again Augusta agreed to the arrangement, though by now it should have been clear that she could not possibly live up to it. Libby should have known it, too, but a realistic attitude about money was something her mother never learned and could not pass on to any of her children. She did continue to correspond with Libby on a most affectionate basis, and without Henry's interference, Libby's replies were all that a mother would wish. The following is an excerpt from a letter written in December, 1838, revealing clearly—at times painfully—the depth of Libby's feelings toward her mother:

> My own dearest kindest Mamma,
>   Your dear kind letter has made me so happy—but has given me the certainty of how far too good you are. . . . If, when under the influence of other feelings, my conduct toward you may have led you to suppose you seemed harsh or anything but what you are, and always were—the best—the kindest and most devoted of mothers, forgive me . . . God Almighty be merciful to those who betrayed my confidence in you, my own dear Moe—*that* confidence existing, my own ruin *could* not have been affected. . . . Only remember My Own *Dearest* Mamma, you have never erred but by too great kindness. . . . I who know more in this sad misery than anyone, know only how innocent you are—how good and kind you have been to all concerned—pray for me—do—do—pray for me as you alone can do. Keep my letter—and if ever at a future period your kind heart fears having occasioned a pang to your own unfortunate Libby, read this over and believe we *have* been cruelly deceived toward each other.[22]

Unhappily, letters, no matter how loving, do not pay for food and lodging, and by the beginning of 1839 Libby had reached a point where she was dependent upon the charity of her neighbors. Such kindness toward an outsider from people noted for their suspicion of strangers speaks well for Libby's ability to make friends, but it was at great cost to her amour propre. Neither was her tension lessened by the decision of Trevanion to leave the Chateau Penhoët and return to lodgings four miles away from Libby's residence.[23] Henry seemed unable to cut the tie which bound him to his sister-in-law; it was a genuine case of human bondage which might have aroused sympathy except that his behavior during this entire period was full of malicious intent to make as much trouble as possible.

Early in 1839 Libby was again flat on her back with an

illness severe enough to demand the services of a nurse. Her letters to England, and those of Carrel, were so heartrending and alarming that Augusta thought she should make the trip to Pontivy so she could take charge of her daughter and incidentally meet M. Carrell.[24] He and Libby, however, did not take kindly to the idea. It was bound to do more harm than good. With Trevanion in the area, who would be certain to make trouble between mother, daughter and doctor, it would only add to the nervous tension which was largely responsible for the deplorable state of Libby's health.[25]

One can certainly appreciate Libby's reluctance to have her dearest Moe descending upon the ménage, full of motherly concern and well-meant advice—and the intention of transporting mother and child back to England. One marvels that she could have entertained the notion, with her apartments at the palace already overflowing with dependents of all ages and sizes, but Augusta seldom did have second thoughts until confronted by the disastrous aftermaths of foolhardy decisions.

By spring Libby's small store of hope for better days had reached the vanishing point. Even her compassionate friend Carrel began to have grave doubts about her future. To Libby, the thought that she might actually die and leave Marie penniless in a foreign contry was a terrifying prospect. She wrote to her mother, begging her to arrange some sort of provision for her child's welfare and education. She knew that by the terms of Byron's will she would share in the sixty thousand pounds reverting to her mother on the death of Lady Noel Byron. Her aunt seemed always to be gravely worried about her health, so it was not inconceivable that she might die within a few years.

Augusta decided to discuss the matter with Sir Robert Wilmot-Horton before making a decision. Sir Robert was her cousin, formerly Robert Wilmot, who took the name of Horton on his marriage to Anne Horton, an heiress, who also happened to be so good-looking that she inspired one of Byron's most famous poems: [26]

She walks in beauty, like the night
Of cloudless climes and starry skies;
And all that's best of dark and bright
Meet in her aspect and her eyes:

This fortunate lady was Libby's godmother and thus on
close terms with the Leighs, especially Augusta who consulted
her husband on many legal matters. His advice, however, was
not always practical or wise. When Libby was asking to be freed
from Trevanion's "tyranny and persecution," Sir Robert proposed that Henry be thrown into debtors' prison for money received from Lady Byron which had made possible his marriage
to Georgiana. This had not been repaid and Libby's understanding was that it was not supposed to be repaid. Horton assured
her that Lady Byron consented willingly to this action, though
there is no actual evidence that she was ever consulted on the
matter. In spite of Trevanion's brutality Libby warned Henry
to be on his guard against "what was neither honorable or
just." [27] It was a curious reaction under the circumstances, but
the Leighs were notorious for being creatures ruled by impulse
rather than by reason.[28]

In the case of providing for Marie, Augusta was, for once,
both sensible and reasonable. She could make over the sum she
planned to bequeath to Libby by a deed of Appointment (also
called a Reversion), insuring provision for Marie's future
though no immediate funds would be forthcoming. Still, it was
a guaranteed asset on the order of an expected legacy, as compared to promises which were never fulfilled. Byron's estate
was administered by prudent trustees who would prevent its
being frittered away by poor, misguided Augusta, if she outlived Lady Byron. Augusta consulted Sir Robert to find out
how much money would be required to underwrite Marie's
education.[29] After deliberation and inquiries he told her that
twenty-five thousand pounds would be enough, but Augusta,
not wanting to be niggardly, raised the figure to three thousand. A fully attested copy of the Deed was sent to Pontivy;

Augusta retained the original. It is necessary to explain all this, because the Deed became a *cause célèbre* and assumed an importance out of all proportion to the amount, involving any number of people and creating hard feelings which were never straightened out.

Relieved and grateful as Libby was to have the copy in her possession, there still remained the persistent problem: what to do about the present. Carrel was fully cognizant of all her financial transactions because the sums from England were sent to him, as Libby's guardian. In the period from August, 1838, to September, 1839, less than ninety pounds had been sent by Augusta and Lady Chichester.[30] The only banker in Pontivy was unusually cooperative about arranging and extending credit to Mlle. Leigh, but Carrel was well thought of, and that was in Libby's favor. Without him she would have had a grim time of it. In the nineteenth century and well into the twentieth, a married woman in France had to have written authority from her husband to open a bank account, take out insurance, accept employment. If she did not have a properly attested marriage contract, arranged before her marriage, and her spouse died suddenly without making provision, she was entitled to nothing. Without the security of marriage or private income a woman was in trouble in almost every aspect of daily life unless she had a protector.[31]

Trevanion, lurking in the background, was busy at his writing desk regaling his estranged wife with slanders about Carrel, calculated to arouse doubt about the man's character. In one of Augusta's letters to Libby she wrote that H.T. was clearly jealous of the doctor. Certainly he behaved like a disgruntled ex-lover, accusing Carrel of wanting to have an affair with Libby so that he could get possession of her money. Georgey ran to her mother with this bit of gossip, but either she garbled the facts or was misunderstood, because Augusta thought that Carrel wanted to marry Libby for her nonexistent fortune. Off went a letter from Augusta, begging Libby to clarify this situation, which seemed so dubious and unpalatable.[32]

At a later date, Therese Villiers commented wryly that she could not believe Augusta. This was doubly ludicrous because Carrel, the supposed fortune-hunter was only too well aware of the severe pecuniary problems of the Leighs, particularly those of Mlle. Leigh. Moreover, Augusta must have known this, inasmuch as she had made Carrel the custodian of Libby's welfare. The oddest part of this typical Leigh imbroglio was that Augusta would give a moment's credence to any statement made by Henry Trevanion. Henry also slandered his longtime lawyer, Sir George Stephen (later to be of great legal service to Libby).* Trevanion constantly denigrated Stephen to such a degree that Libby warned her mother to beware of the gentleman. Eventually she turned to Stephen for help when all else failed and, as shall be seen shortly, he came through for her magnificently.

Though Libby was very ill during the summer of 1839, she was nursed through the worst of it by Carrel, but her financial situation worsened with every passing day. On September 5 she wrote to her mother in a desperate effort to get a little help. Ten days later Augusta replied to the effect that she would do her best to abide by her agreement because she hoped for "an improvement in my own pecuniary position, the delays of which have proceeded from causes entirely beyond my control." Although one becomes exasperated beyond endurance at times with Augusta's inability to handle financial transactions, none of which can bear close inspection, it would be uncharitable to fault her for lack of human kindness. It is painfully evident that she was genuinely upset by Libby's illnesses, enough to make her ill too. And she did care for her child in spite of the Trevanion scandal. Still, it would have been better to admit flatly that she could not help Libby at this time or in the foreseeable future. At least Libby would have known the grim facts.[33]

---

* According to Henry, Stephen was carrying on an extramarital romance with his wife's sister, a respected spinster of forty-two who kept a young ladies' finishing school at Brighton.

Augusta was indeed having problems to contend with at home. One of Georgiana's daughters had a long and serious illness, and as usual, Augusta had to foot the bills. But to Libby, hundreds of miles away, her own troubles seemed so overwhelming that she could think of nothing else. Carrel looked at her situation realistically. There was only one sure way to solve her financial stalemate: borrow on the Deed. The attested copy was presented to the bank where it ran headlong into the banking laws of France which would not permit a *copy* of any document to be used as collateral. Libby wrote to her mother, explaining the problem and asking for the original.

Augusta was aghast. The Deed was for Marie's welfare and education, not to be sold for *present use*. She asked the Chichester what she should do and they advised her not to send it.[34] Undoubtedly they gave her the right advice, but from Libby's viewpoint it was catastrophic. The distracted girl could not understand why the Deed was withheld when she was in dire need. This is not to suggest that the Chichesters were indifferent to her misfortune, but those who have never experienced acute financial hardship cannot fully understand the frightening prospect of destitution.

The year 1839 came to a close and 1840 loomed ahead bleakly. "During some months," Libby wrote, "the correspondence between myself and my mother continued as affectionate as ever, I endeavouring all the while to obtain from her the means of existence, and she retaining the Deed." [35] Whether Augusta should be judged critically or approvingly is a moot question, but the fact remains that from the start of the new year, no more funds were sent by her to Pontivy. On March 8 Henry's father died at Brussels.[36] By the terms of Georgiana's marriage settlement she was entitled to a hundred pounds a year from the elder Trevanion, but she had never received a farthing in his lifetime and nothing was immediately forthcoming after his death.[37] Georgey was thus still dependent upon her mother which was one of the reasons advanced for sending no funds to Libby.

Libby gave up all hope of persuading her mother to give up the Deed; she wrote instead to Lady Chichester asking *her* to intercede in her behalf, not aware that it had been the Chichesters who advised against sending the original. Libby also wrote to Sir George Stephen, Trevanion's lawyer, requesting him to get in touch with Lady Noel Byron. Libby was hopeful that her aunt would use "any influence she might possess with my mother, to induce her to give up that which was my right." [38]

Stephen was magnanimous enough to overlook any slurring remarks she had made about him; he even sent her a few pounds. It was not until July that he sent Libby's letter to Lady Byron with a covering letter of his own in explanation. He did not know Lady Byron personally and had never had any business dealings with her, but he knew her reputation for rectitude and interest in charitable projects. Had he been aware of the bitter estrangement between Lady Byron and Augusta Leigh, it is possible that he would not have thought it wise to heed Libby's request. But he did have more than enough knowledge of the Trevanion family problems, especially Henry's. He could see no harm in sending poor Libby's letter to her esteemed aunt; it might even do some good. And thus it was that Annabella Byron was confronted once again with the seemingly endless tribulations of Augusta Leigh's daughter.

10

There is a tide in the affairs of women,
Which taken at the flood, leads God
Knows where!

—DON JUAN

SINCE THE BIFRONS DEBACLE AND ITS AFTERMATH, ANNA-
bella had avoided any involvement with Elizabeth Leigh. (She
never called her Libby.) Since 1830 she had severed all connection with Augusta, though she had been kept informed of
Libby's activities by various people, one of them being Therese
Villiers. Annabella knew about Libby's second pregnancy, the
sojourn at Bath followed by the interlude in the home for wayward girls, and the elopement to France with Trevanion. She
felt pity for the unfortunate girl but the less she had to do with
any of the Leighs the better. In the winter of 1838 Sir Robert
and Lady Wilmot-Horton had a discussion with Annabella
about Libby's problems, particularly her financial difficulties,
but it seemed to have been a conversation *en passant* inasmuch
as nothing came of it.[1] Now, out of the blue, arrived Sir George
Stephen's letter with the enclosure from Elizabeth Medora.

On May 17 Annabella turned forty-eight. For twenty-four
of those years she had lived a life without delight. Except for
her brief year of marriage, sexual love had been nonexistent
nor did she want to risk another intimate relationship with a
man. In childhood and girlhood she had established a number
of close friendships with the daughters of her mother's friends.

137

In later life she became attached to certain strong-minded women who, like herself, embraced causes or made their mark in other fields, such as authorship or the stage, to name two. Significantly, most of these friends had been or were still unhappily married.

"With me, they are passions," she wrote in her Journal with commendable insight, but she did not mean it in a physical sense. The act of love between women was known to exist— it was even mentioned in some of the racier French novels—but women of Annabella's upbringing would have been shocked beyond recall at the suggestion that it might take place among women in their social stratum. It is true that there was a lot of kissing and embracing when best friends greeted one another or said good-bye; nineteenth-century novels are full of effusive and sentimental conversations between women which reflect the speech and thinking of the period. From the viewpoint of modern knowledge about homosexuality in both sexes, Annabella may have had latent Lesbian tendencies, but it would be a grave error to suggest, even to think, that these tendencies ever became overt. All her words and actions reveal her to have been inhibited to an extraordinary degree even for that era of feminine repression. There were, of course, certain ladies of high degree who were anything but repressed in their sexual life, but they were the exceptions.

Annabella did have one absorbing emotional outlet: the upbringing of her daughter. So far, Ada had fulfilled her mother's fondest hopes, and her father, had he lived, would have been proud of his one legitimate daughter. He would have been a little puzzled, however, by certain aspects of her thought processes. At fifteen she had already displayed extraordinary talent for higher mathematics which later earned her the friendship of Charles Babbage, the mathematical genius and inventor of the first calculating machine. At seventeen she was presented at Court and became a popular belle of the season. She had a brilliant mind but was no bluestocking; she loved to dance, had more than her share of eligible beaux and enjoyed flirting as much as any other seventeen-year-old. She was graceful and pretty, and one of her charms was her lovely speaking voice inherited from Byron. Most people described her as dainty, with the exception of Hobhouse who met her first on February 24, 1834, at one of the Queen's Drawing Rooms. He described her in his Diary as "a large, coarse-skinned young woman but with something of my friend's features, particularly the mouth." [2] He may have been miffed because, at that meeting, she told him she disliked him. This dislike had been instilled in her from childhood by her mother who resented all of Byron's former cronies, particularly Hobhouse whom she never forgave for taking Byron's and Augusta's side in the separation. Later, when Ada was not so much under this influence, she and Hobhouse became good friends.

On July 8, 1835, at age nineteen, Ada married William, the eighth Lord King, aged thirty, who was created Earl of Lovelace in 1838. It was a good match. The Kings were an old, noble family, the family seat being Ockham Park, near Weybridge in Surrey. It was a large mansion situated in the midst of a beautiful park about two and half miles in circumference. Besides this estate he had another, Ashley Coombe, in Somerset, and a London town house in St. James's Square. Not only was William well fixed financially, and well born, he was also an agreeable, kindly man, devoted to his young wife. In the first years of his marriage he and Ada were very much under Lady Noel Byron's domination; still, Lord Lovelace was on the most cordial terms with his mother-in-law and remained so for several years.

It was in all ways a happy marriage, and by 1840 Ada had given birth to three children: Byron, in 1836; Anne Isabella (called Annabella), in 1838; and Ralph, in 1839. After the birth of her daughter, Ada had "a tedious and suffering illness which took months to cure," [3] and from then on she was subject to spells of poor health, but she never gave in to illness and made light of it in letters.

Besides bringing up Ada, Annabella filled her life with

charitable projects, many of them dealing with the education of working people. She traveled, visited her friends, attended as many social events as she chose to do, and frequently changed her residence, preferably to a new country house near friends of long standing with whom she felt at ease. She had grown used to being an object of curiosity whenever she appeared in a public place, and she did not find it entirely displeasing though she shrank from ostentation. All things considered, she had a better time of it than most single women, but no amount of travel and visiting back and forth with the Lovelaces and friends could fill the emptiness of her life. She needed a *raison d'être;* as with many lonely people, she sublimated her normal emotional needs by living other people's lives.

Libby's letter, for that reason, presented a dilemma. It must have aroused painful memories of places and events long past: Kirkby Mallory, Halnaby Hall, Six Mile Bottom, Piccadilly Terrace. Of Augusta, the lovable scatterbrain whom Byron had yearned for until death, to whom he had written those haunting love letters. How unworthy of his devotion Augusta had been, but to Annabella the most shameful thing Augusta had done in a lifetime of mistakes was her treatment of Elizabeth Medora. Augusta had sacrificed her daughter's good name in order to keep on the good side of Trevanion,[4] and now that the inevitable happened and the girl was abandoned with a bastard child, Augusta had washed her hands of responsibility, even refusing to send the original copy of the Deed. Annabella had hastened to make certain through "high legal authority" that Augusta had no right to withhold the document. Apparently her daughter and grandchild could perish for all *she* cared. Annabella's first impulse was to extend a helping hand, but past experience with the Trevanion-Georgiana-Elizabeth Medora triangle, with the whole Leigh household in fact, had taught her to proceed with caution.

She was not consciously aware of the dichotomy in her reaction to Libby's letter. She answered it carefully because she was under the impression that the girl had been abandoned by a man to whom she might return if ever he wanted her.[5]

Too well did she recall her own anguish as she paced the floor at Kirkby Mallory, after reading Byron's tender, loving letters begging her to patch it up. She had stood firm in her refusal because she had the moral strength to withstand his pleas, but how could the daughter of Augusta Leigh be expected to have the stamina to resist temptation? Much rested upon Libby's response to that first letter.

Libby had no previous experience in dealing with her aunt. She remembered dimly a sweet-faced woman who paid an occasional call on Moe in connection with a family celebration, such as Emily's christening. From all Libby had learned subsequently, Lady Byron was generous but one had to be careful not to offend her or she could be difficult. Libby was therefore surprised to receive her aunt's kind letter, which expressed genuine concern although it could not be construed as a direct offer of help. Libby was shrewd enough to realize that a reply couched in the right terms might make the difference between financial assistance and starvation. Fortunately she was no longer under the baleful influence of Trevanion and answered her aunt's guarded letter in a simple, succinct fashion. Annabella was vastly relieved by the letter which seemed without the slightest tinge of that sort of piety to which Augusta was prone and which filled Annabella with the most profound scorn.[6]

The result of Libby's second letter was another careful step forward on Annabella's part. She wrote that she planned to arrive in France on July 14 and if Libby wished to see her, she would set up a meeting between them, proposing they meet at some half-way point.[7] This suggestion must have seemed like manna from heaven to Libby, also to M. Carrel who had despaired of finding a solution to his patient's problem. This time Libby did not equivocate in her answer. The tone of the letter convinced Annabella "that her one desire was to be placed anywhere out of Trevanion's reach." The fellow was also living in Pontivy, but the girl was steadfast in her determination to stay clear of him. As far as

Annabella was concerned, at least, that clinched the decision.[8]

In August Lady Byron sent money for immediate needs to Pontivy and arranged for a traveling carriage to accommodate Libby and Marie, also an English doctor of her own choosing to care for the patient en route. Annabella then proceeded to the west of France—Tours—where she planned to meet the travelers and at this time she intended to leave Libby and Marie with some friends who would take proper care of them.[9]

The parting between Libby and her good friend Carrel was sad, but along with the sadness there must have been relief on both sides. For more than two years Carrel had done what he could to protect Libby's interests, and in return he was suspected in certain quarters of deliberate fraud when he advised his patient to insist on possession of the Deed. He had put up with all this for a young woman who had never been more to him than a sick patient in deep trouble. Libby could not fail to recognize the inequity of the relationship, but there was literally nothing she could do in return for his kindness but offer herself to him. The state of her health—the whole nature of the association—precluded such a thing, but there was no doubt of her gratitude.

The traveling carriage made its way toward Tours and the Loire Valley, through some of the loveliest countryside of France, the famed "chateau country." Libby was far too exhausted to enjoy the journey—at the best of times she was not much of a sightseer—but she could derive satisfaction in knowing that each turn of the wheels took her that much farther from the man who had spoiled her life for thirteen years.

Lady Byron had this to say about her first meeting with Libby, on August 21, 1840.

> I found her altered beyond the possibility of recognition—and in a sort of confused and stupified state of mind, attended at times with great excitement.[10]

The medical man who accompanied Libby and Marie from Pontivy did not give too promising a report of Libby's state of health, especially her pulmonary symptoms. Annabella considered herself highly qualified as a diagnostician and general practitioner; many of her letters describe her treatment of various illnesses and her advice on certain nostrums. One of her maids, Ann Rood, who later married Byron's valet, Fletcher, was one of Annabella's captive patients. "I believe I saved her life," Annabella wrote to her mother, "by a timely dose of Castor Oil when she was in danger of an inflammation in her bowels." [11] The poor girl could have been afflicted with a badly inflamed appendix and died of peritonitis as a result of this rugged treatment, but luck was on both their sides.

This is not meant to denigrate Lady Byron's concern for the health of her niece, but unfortunately her preoccupation with the physical aspects of Libby's illness, and her insistence on believing that she was not long for this world, did more harm than good in the months to come. At the moment, however, her handling of the problem was all that could be desired. It must have been a shock to come face to face with Elizabeth Medora. The last time Lady Byron had seen her was in 1818 when she attended the baptism of Augusta's sixth child, Emily, and was one of the sponsors. "Do" was then going on five. In 1820 Annabella could still write that she "felt the most tender affection" for the pretty little creature. Neither could she forget her "treacle moon" at Six Mile Bottom, watching her husband's expression whenever he looked at baby Medora. Once, when the subject of portraits came up, Annabella told Byron that she would like to have him painted when he was looking at Medora; his tenderness of expression was quite lovely.[12]

How sadly altered was that child, now a tall, haggard woman of twenty-six, so emaciated that her clothes hung on her like a scarecrow, her dark skin dry and sallow from long illness, her dark eyes bright with fever and excitement. The solemn little girl Marie clung to her mother's hand, more

French than English in speech and deportment, and about the same age as her mother when last seen by Annabella. The child was six years old, and during those years she had nothing to count on but her mother. There had been times when she was in grave danger of losing even that rock in the last perilous years at the Chateau Penhoët. Only a heart of granite could remain unmoved by the desolation of mother and child, and Annabella's heart was not of stone.

Though she had made a point of stressing that she planned to install Libby and Marie in a pension at Tours, with no intention of taking them into her own ménage, she was not being honest with herself. On the day she wrote to Libby and asked her to entrust herself to her (Annabella's) care, she had already reached the decision to take over Libby's life and that of her child, thereby filling the void in her own life. Probably she was not consciously·aware of it, self-delusion being one of the commonest of human frailities. Nevertheless, she was unable to leave a helpless girl, afflicted with consumption, desperately concerned about her own and her child's future, in the hands of others. *She* would take charge.[13]

And what did Libby see—and what were her reactions—when she came face to face with her benefactress? She saw a slight, fragile-looking woman with a high forehead, gray hair, and skin of wraith-like paleness and delicacy. There was a sweetness, a wistfulness in her gray-blue eyes which belied the firm set of her lips. The tone of her voice was rather brittle because of her excellent diction, and she had a way of emphasizing her words by rapping on something with her small fist.[14] Since Byron's death she had worn widow's weeds and seldom appeared in public without a widow's cap. Very occasionally she wore lavender rather than black; her clothes were always simple. Yet in spite of her small stature she was quite a formidable little woman. Height has nothing to do with strength and determination, as the new young Queen of England was to prove conclusively.

In Libby's condition she could not have given much

thought to her aunt's appearance or what might happen in the future. After five years of harsh privation and almost constant illness it was wonderful to have made the trip in a capacious traveling carriage, with all arrangements made for her and Marie's comfort when they put up at a wayside inn for the night. The medical man was in charge of everything, and with no expense spared, the travelers were given top priority. The miraculous part of this new security was that it would continue; it was no sweet dream with the inevitable rude awakening. Lady Byron had said to entrust herself to her, Lady Byron was a woman of her word, the days of poverty were over. It is not surprising that Libby was in a confused and incoherent state; she must have been hysterical from sheer relief.

It had been Lady Byron's plan to continue on to Paris for the winter and spring after establishing Libby and Marie in comfortable circumstances. But having decided that "Elizabeth" was too ill to be left on her own, Lady Byron proposed that: "I should accompany her to Paris and remain with her for a time. I did so, being desirous of attending to the least wishes of one toward whom I had reason to feel so grateful." [15]

At Lady Byron's request, Libby called herself Madame Aubin, and this would be the name she used for the rest of her life in France. Ostensibly she was a widow traveling with her child in the entourage of Lady Noel Byron. It is odd that Libby chose that name, for it must have been her choice, but it suited Lady Byron's purposes better than Mlle. Elizabeth Leigh. Apart from its being more respectable for a woman with a child to be Madame rather than Mademoiselle, Annabella did not wish the name Leigh to become involved with hers. Aside from a few close and trusted friends—and Lord and Lady Lovelace—her protection of Libby and Marie was to be kept secret for the time being.

A few days after their arrival at Tours, the entourage started on the journey to Paris. Lady Byron, though avoiding display, could afford the best and was accustomed from girlhood to the deference accorded those with rank and money.

Now that Libby was part of the ménage she, too, was treated with obsequious respect by innkeepers, servants, and tradesmen. It was not difficult for her to adapt herself to luxury; the Leighs always moved in the best circles in spite of their financial trouble. Libby had spent many happy times in her childhood with her cousins who lived in spacious country houses, whenever the Leighs made the customary visits to Augusta's well-to-do relations. From the standpoint of rank in life, Libby's connections were as good as, if not rather better in some cases than, those of her benefactress. It had always rankled Annabella a little that the impecunious Augusta had somehow made her feel a bit like a country cousin, though it had been unintentional. Libby could fit in very well indeed with her aunt's mode of living.

When they reached Fontainebleau, Lady Byron had an attack of her "heart condition" from which she always suffered intense pain, and they had to remain there until she could continue the journey. This illness of hers was never described in clear medical terms and between spells she led an active life. Some of her trouble was undoubtedly psychosomatic, but she did have a condition which laid her low on occasion. She was not in low spirits, however, and some indication of her mood is revealed in an extract from a letter she wrote to a friend while convalescing at Fontainebleau:

> I am particularly happy just now, Feelings that have long lain, like buried forests, beneath the moss of years, are called forth and seem to give happiness to one for whom I feel something like a Mother's affection. This is a little gleam in my life— it will not last, but its memory will be sweet. The object of my affection is marked for an early grave. Show this to your Mother, who will understand it better than you.[16]

The recipient of this euphoric epistle was Lady Olivia Acheson, daughter of Mary, Countess of Gosford, who had been one of Annabella's best loved childhood friends. Lady Olivia was many years younger than Annabella and Lady

Gosford considerably older, but this was not unusual for Annabella. As a girl she sought out friendships with women of her
mother's generation, but as she grew older she was drawn
toward girls who could have been her daughters.

There is something poignant about the depth of her feelings towards Libby which come through in this letter. At first
glance those overly sentimental phrases seem unlike Lady
Byron; they could have been written by Augusta Leigh. The
sad part is that Annabella's feeling transcended a mother's
affection. Once again she was in the grip of the Byron charm,
that strange amalgam of gaiety, sensuality, sweetness, and dour
moodiness which had bedeviled her from the moment she first
encountered a Byron. She seems to have tried, unconsciously,
to relive the happy moments with her husband; she called her
niece "Medora" for a time although she disliked the name, and
asked Libby to call her "Pip." Only one person had called her
that: "a good Pip, a kind Pip, the best wife in the world for
Byron," he used to tell her when he made her sit on his knee
in one of his moods of tenderness. The daughter was like him
in so many ways. She had the Byron quirk of turning abruptly
to look at someone entering a room, head lowered, glancing
uneasily from beneath her brows. Now that her cheeks were
no longer gaunt and skin no longer dry and sallow, she bore a
marked resemblance to Byron, except for the color of her hair
and eyes. In fact, the lower half of her face with the intriguing
pouting mouth was very much like Ada's. Annabella could
see no sign of the dark side of Byron's proud and willful spirit,
though "Medora" did have his childlike gaiety.

In her way, Libby was as happy as Annabella, and though
little is mentioned about Marie at this period, she must also
have found life as exciting as a fairy tale. A pretty, well-behaved
little girl of six seldom has trouble getting on with people.
During the convalescence of the two invalids there were many
long conversations. Libby was encouraged to confide freely
all the tribulations she had endured at the hands of Trevanion.
The Deed was discussed, too; it was, after all, what had in-

stigated the correspondence between Libby and Lady Byron. Annabella promised to help in the recovery of the document from Augusta even if it necessitated taking the affair to Chancery Court as a last resort.

There was one subject, however, which was never discussed though it was uppermost in both their minds. Annabella wondered if "Medora" knew the truth about her paternity, and Libby wondered if her aunt knew. At some point in their stay at Fontainebleau the subject was finally broached. Libby stated that "Lady Byron informed me of the cause of the deep interest she must ever feel for me. *Her husband had been my father.*" [17] Lady Byron's version of this conversation was as follows: "She was unfortunately in possession of that fact before she was connected with me, and after much embarrassment from her allusions to it, I determined on admitting it, as it materially influenced the course to be pursued in the suit." [18]

In her lifetime, Lady Byron was criticized for making such a disclosure to her niece; this was her reason for justifying herself. Self-justification was one of Annabella's main occupations; she often belabored a point when it would have been better to leave well enough alone. In the age of Victoria, just beginning in 1840, it was doubtless a breach of good taste to inform a young woman that her birth was the result of adultery and incest, though it was quite understandable under the circumstances. These two people, with entirely disparate backgrounds and an age difference of twenty-two years, were trying to find a common bond to carry them through the first period of adjustment. As it turned out, it was ill-advised on Annabella's part, not because it "wasn't done" but because it eventually caused both of them bitterness and heartache.

Until that moment Libby had only Georgey's and Henry's words to go on, and she had good reason not to accept them as positive facts. The word of Lady Byron, however, was not to be taken lightly. If *she* corroborated their allegations it would have to be true, but how could Libby bring up the subject without offending her kind but starchy aunt? She used the oblique approach, something she had learned from her mother and Trevanion; a veiled allusion, a casual innuendo, being careful not to force the issue, allowing the other person to open the subject. She could not have realized that it would not have been necessary to go about it in this roundabout fashion. In spite of Lady Byron's self-righteous explanation, she had shown a number of times that she was only too eager to discuss the matter, and for a woman who was often didactic and obtuse in handling situations she was singularly adroit in dealing with her well-known "policy of silence." Her confidantes all believed themselves to be unique when, after much soul-searching, she concluded it was necessary to unseal her lips. Of all these confidantes Elizabeth Medora was the one with the most at stake, also the most titillating; she wrote later:

> She implored and sought my affection by every means, and almost exacted my confidence to the most unlimited extent. I was willing and anxious, in any and every way I could to prove my gratitude and the desire I so sincerely felt to repay by my affection and devotion any pain she must have felt for the circumstances connected with my birth and her separation from Lord Byron. Her only wish, she said, was to provide for me, according to Lord Byron's intentions respecting me, and according to my rank in life. She evinced much anxiety for my health and comfort, expressed indignation for all I had suffered, spoke of the comfort I would be to her, and of the necessity that I should be a devoted child to her.[19]

Judging by this summary, Annabella went all out to insure Libby's unswerving loyalty, and it seems clear that Libby tried her best to accede to all her aunt's wishes in the first months of their association. It was in this mood of mutual good will that they continued on to Paris.

I I

I stood
Among them, but not of them, in a shroud
Of thoughts which were not their thoughts.
—CHILDE HAROLD'S PILGRIMAGE

WHENEVER A COACH, TRAVELING CARRIAGE, OR DILIGENCE approached the outskirts of Paris, the postillions, jouncing along on their mounts, heralded their arrival by loud blowing of horns and much ear-splitting cracking of whips by the coach-man.[1] It was a testament to the exuberance everyone felt at the prospect of entering Paris. All main roads across France were laid out to have their ending in the city. To a Frenchman, Paris was the greatest city in the universe, and indeed it was becoming the favorite of Europe and England. German princes, English noblemen, grand dukes from Russia; all came, saw, and were conquered.

Lady Noel Byron's entourage settled down at 24 Rue de Rivoli, a comparatively new section, the building of which had commenced in 1810 by order of Napoleon I. In some respects, though, the Paris of 1840 had not changed greatly from medieval times. It was still surrounded by the old wall, but the present monarch, Louis Philippe, was building new ones. These were heavily equipped with cannon, making the city an impregnable fortress. Outside this bastion were the villages such as Neuilly and Passy, which were becoming suburbs of the city. The populace had not wanted these inconvenient walls, but the King rammed through the project in the Chamber of Deputies, and the walls did not come down until after World War One.

To Libby, Paris was all she had ever imagined it to be. For nine years she had lived in France, and Paris seemed as far away and unattainable as the moon, but now she was there, and under the most favorable circumstances. She fell in love with the city at first sight and would gladly have spent the rest of her life there. It did have drawbacks; the streets were mostly unpaved or cobblestoned with no sidewalks for pedestrians. Coachmen drove close to all doors and one had to be nimble to reach the safety of a porte cochère or risk being run down. The poorer streets were still filthy, dark, narrow, as they had been for centuries.

But whether one was rich or poor, the Paris of that fall and winter was an exciting and stimulating place. Victor Hugo would be elected to the French Academy in January, 1841. His play *Ruy Blas* was having a good but not highly successful run. Alexandre Dumas, père, on the other hand, had a hit at the *Comédie Française, Mademoiselle de Belle-Isle.* George Sand was at the height of her romance with Chopin before they left for Majorca. Madame Récamier, the lovely reclining creature immortalized by David, was now a half-blind woman of sixty-three who had lost most of her fortune, but she was still beautiful and had a salon of sorts in the old Paris convent where she had retreated. Her longtime friend Chateaubriand, now an ailing seventy-two, was still coming to see her every day. Heine was in Paris as were Lamartine, St. Beuve, and Balzac who was longing to be elected to the Academy. Delacroix was the leading portrait painter, along with Ingres.

Young artists and writers were flocking to Paris, most of them poor, but all starved together with a gaiety peculiar to the city. One of them, a journalist named Henri Murger, was jotting down his impressions of the delights and sorrows of his friends, and in 1848 he found a publisher. The book was titled *Scènes de la vie de Bohème;* the Rodolphos, Mimis, Marcellos,

Musettas, and Collines of the day little realized they would later achieve immortality on the operatic stage. And the fabled young beauty Marie Duplessis, the beloved of the youthful Alexandre Dumas, fils, could not know that she, too, would achieve a certain fame in her young lover's semiautobiographical *La dame aux camélias*. The elegant world of Paris lunched at Tortoni's and the Café de Paris, and so did the *"grandes horizontales,"* one of them being Marie, always with her corsage of camellias. For twenty-seven days of the month they were all white; the other three days they were red, which was her delicate way of letting her lovers know she was not available. It was a wonderful era in a wonderful city, with many brilliant social events, and Lady Noel Byron was present at some of them.

On December 30, 1840, for example, she attended a reception in honor of Louis Mathieu, le Comte de Molé, held at the French Academy. The Comte de Molé's father had been guillotined during the Reign of Terror, but the young count and his mother had been sent to England to escape the holocaust. A number of refugees of the *ancien régime* had been given asylum in England, even Louis Philippe had lived there from 1815 to 1817 while exiled for his liberal views by Louis XVIII. It was quite natural, therefore, that the widow of the great English poet and liberal, Lord Byron, would be well received by certain members of the French nobility who had been treated so hospitably by their English counterparts. At this particular reception, Lady Byron met Chateaubriand. The elderly but still fascinating old firebrand had been as famous a lover in his day as was Byron, but he possessed a much more irascible and contentious character. Unlike Byron he was imperious in his attitude toward women and expected them to listen to his words with breathless awe. His reaction on meeting Lady Byron is amusing: "Any argument founded on expediency causes her to take a decidedly opposite course." [2] It would seem that Annabella was as dogmatic in public as she often was in private; it was a foregone conclusion that she would clash head-on with a man like Chateaubriand.

Had certain hostesses known the real identity of Madame Aubin they would surely have been intrigued by the oddity of the alliance between the two English ladies, for though Libby had a French name there was no doubt of her nationality. Some of them would have sought an introduction, but overtures of that sort were discouraged by Lady Byron. Madame Aubin was not well enough to go about socially.

It is true that she had been extremely ill,[3] but not with consumption. From what is known of her symptoms, her siege of bronchial trouble must have left her with some form of pleurisy or chronic bronchitis, which would cause much coughing and discomfort, even pus and blood. Had it been tuberculosis she would probably never have fully recovered.

Annabella was committed to the gloomy prognosis that Libby was living on borrowed time, whereas, from all evidence, she was responding well to proper food, rest, and freedom from anxiety. As with all convalescents, once she was on the mend she began to take some interest in the life around her and grew a bit restive under the indulgent but ever watchful eye of her protectress. She had been led to believe by her aunt that, once she was recuperating satisfactorily, she would be given a set allowance to do with as she pleased, not a large sum but enough to give her a feeling of independence. Instead she was given "small sums and presents" from time to time, but at the whim of the giver.[4] Libby was beginning to realize, as everyone else did eventually, that to get along pleasantly with her aunt, it was better to do things Lady Byron's way.

There were times when Annabella's conviction that she alone knew the answers to all questions must have struck a jarring note. Libby had been exposed to the harsh world from the time she was fourteen. At fourteen Annabella was a precocious girl, sheltered from life and spoiled by doting parents. It was difficult to find a meeting ground either in taste or conversation. Libby was no more interested in abstract discussion than her father had been; her aunt liked nothing better. Libby controlled her irritation better than Byron had done; she was, after all, completely beholden to Lady Byron and was eager to please. She had learned to use her charm as all charming people do; she had learned, moreover, that this priceless gift was more to be desired than untold wealth or the highest place in society. It did not take her long to see that her benefactress was susceptible to the Byronic magnetism, that Lady Byron could be handled, or cajoled, by tenderness, gaiety, and flattery. The only trouble in this method of getting around her aunt was that Lady Byron was far more astute than Libby believed her to be. Unfortunately for Annabella's own happiness, she could not accept impulsive manifestations of warmth in the spirit with which they were given; every word, every gesture, every emotion was subjected to analysis. At times she seemed to be looking for flaws, and they are always easy to find.

Around the end of the year Olivia Acheson was the recipient of another letter, quoted in part below, which shows all too clearly that the first seeds of disillusionment had started to take root, though the letter was couched in the terms of Annabella's own brand of playfulness.

This is to give you warning that for the year 1841 I shall not want nor wish for you, because I have got a Lanky-Doodle [*] who instead of taking the sugar basin away from me, makes me what she calls "conscientious lumps of sugar". She knows that the throat of my conscience is small, and she adopts the sweet sin to the size of it with wonderful precision. . . .

If you want the contents of your neighbor's pocket, don't steal but borrow them; and add to the first little *lump* a second—the failure of payment.

One more edifying instance—if you can't tell a downright falsehood, tell that half which will convey the other half inaudibly to the mind of the receiver. . . .

Love and all friendly wishes to my three young friends from

Your personified Bon-bon
A.I.N.B.

---

* Olivia Acheson was also nicknamed Lanky-Doodle because of her height and slenderness.

Grave P.S.

I think that illness has much to do with the painful circumstances in which you so kindly sympathize. There are some kinds of illness which are manifested only by their effects on the mind, at least in a certain stage of their progress. We are always expecting our fellow-creatures to be endowed with the discernment of disembodied spirits. I will not say however, that I can reason myself quite out of painful feelings on such subjects.[5]

The "little gleam of light in my life—it will not last—." Prophetic Annabella, but not in the way she meant. Nevertheless, notwithstanding the small cloud on the horizon "no bigger than a man's hand," Libby was still her "very dear child." Since the meeting in August there had been no exchange of letters between any of the Leighs and Lady Byron, or with Libby.

Then, in the middle of January, 1841, after a decade of silence, Annabella received a letter from Augusta. Augusta had kept in touch with M. Carrell about her ailing daughter and had also written to Libby; but suddenly there were no answers from Libby. Augusta became sufficiently worried to write to Carrel asking for information. Carrell replied, in confidence, that Libby had left Pontivy two months before; they had been befriended by Lady Byron and were now under her protection. She sent Libby a letter, in care of Carrel, which he was to forward. He did not forward it out of respect for Lady Byron's wishes.

Augusta's relatives and friends urged her to address herself directly to Lady Byron, whose whereabouts in Paris were not exactly secret, to find out what was going on. Augusta had no great desire to make overtures to her former sister-in-law. In 1835 she had written to Annabella asking what she should do if she ran into young Ada Byron at some court function. Augusta had tried to keep out of Ada's way because of Annabella's high handed attitude toward her, but it went against Augusta's grain to ignore her own niece. One must remember that Augusta's position at court and the importance of her family connections placed her well above Ada Byron, socially, and to snub the girl would be observed and whispered about. Annabella had answered Augusta's letter to say that she would prefer no contact between Ada and Augusta.

Finally under pressure, Augusta wrote reluctantly to Lady Byron, begging for news of Libby. She insisted that she had "unshaken confidence" in her daughter and Carrel, both having assured her that Libby had broken completely with Trevanion, but "I cannot conceal from you . . . that there are those who view them differently and consider me their *dupe*. God knows, I have been too often and too cruelly deceived to be in a position to give a very satisfactory answer to such suspicion." [6] She could not have foreseen just how completely she had played into Lady Byron's hands.

Annabella answered on January 20 and because so much hinged on the contents of both letters, both have been quoted in part:

"Could I have believed that you had a Mother's affection for her, you would not have had to ask for information concerning your child . . . Your affectionate letters to her must appear a cruel mockery to those who knew that you left her, for so long a time, only the alternative of vice or starvation.

"Her malady, the effect of physical and mental suffering combined, can be retarded . . . only by extreme care and by her avoiding all distressing excitement. The former I can secure, but not the latter—I would save you, if it be not too late, from adding the guilt of her death to that of her birth. Leave her in peace! This advice is given in no hostile spirit, but with the firm determination to protect her to the utmost of my power."

Annabella also stated that there was no need to keep the letter confidential. "If it should become known, I am prepared, in justice to Elizabeth and myself, to explain fully the reasons for my thus interesting myself in her welfare." [7] No one knows just how much Libby knew of this exchange or what her thoughts might have been. Certainly she had suffered at the hands of

Trevanion and seemed to have discussed it with her aunt, who had also checked the story with Carell and some of Libby's neighbors in Pontivy. Annabella's English doctor had also learned full details of the neglect and poverty which had wrecked Libby's health. Lady Byron did have some justification for her indignant response to Augusta's letter.

The element of revenge was there; it is a common frailty of human beings everywhere. Some have suggested that, through a neurotic compulsion, Annabella had befriended Libby for the express purpose of ruining her life. First she would make her wholly dependent upon her largesse, next she would delude the girl into believing she was Byron's daughter. When the impressionable young woman was completely indoctrinated with the belief that she was entitled to the perquisities due one of her rank in life, Lady Byron would suddenly withdraw her protection, leaving Augusta's daughter destitute and destined for a bad end. Thus the wheel would come full circle.

It is a plot worthy of Iago, but it does not give with the character of history of Annabella. Rigorous and unforgiving she could be, but malignity for its own sake was not in her nature. At this time she had a number of friends also visiting Paris. One of them, Mary Millicent Montgomery, knew the background story which precipitated the exchange of letters and had met Libby with Annabella on several occasions.

As can be seen, Annabella had a number of friends visiting in Paris. Mary Millicent Montgomery had been her closest friend in girlhood and remained her closest friend until death. She was a semi-invalid with a spinal affliction, and Annabella was constantly referring to her as doomed to an early grave, though she outlived Annabella. Needless to say, she was in hearty accord with Lady Byron on the subject of Augusta's behavior toward her daughter.

To say that Augusta was shocked by the letter is an understatement; she was prostrated. By any standards it was a cruel letter, and despite Annabella's stating that it was written "in no hostile spirit," it seems evident that it was meant to wound the woman who had inflicted deep wounds on Annabella, some of which had never healed. It reveals, too, that she had gone to reliable sources to verify Libby's story, making it impossible for Augusta to accuse her former "Sis" of accepting Libby's version without first checking on its authenticity.

After Augusta was over the first anguish, she turned desperately for advice to, of all people, her old childhood friend Therese Villiers. It had been ten years since the two women had seen each other. Mrs. Villiers had frankly disapproved of Augusta's conduct toward Lady Byron at the time of Anabella's divorce.[8] As if that were not enough, Mrs. Villiers had moreover disapproved of Augusta's handling of the Georgiana-Trevanion-Libby affair, which Augusta resented so deeply that Therese put an end to all personal contact. Great was her surprise when, on February 5, she received a note from Augusta asking to see her as soon as possible. It seemed so urgent that, out of respect for past friendship, Therese called on Augusta at St. James's.

She found her old friend in a lamentable state. Therese Villiers could not help being moved by Augusta's anguish "on receiving this untrue and tendentious account of her actions," [9] although she knew there was some factual basis for Lady Byron's accusations. She felt, however, that Augusta's conduct toward Libby regarding financial matters had been misrepresented to Lady Byron.[10] She knew the Byron tendency to exaggerate and dramatize anything to do with themselves; she had doubtless noticed the trait in Libby during her stay at St. James. Moreover, she knew that Annabella, despite her rigidity, could be swayed emotionally when she was fond of someone. Therese advised Augusta to make a correct statement of all that had happened between herself and her daughter, submit the statement to Lady Chichester and her son for their approval, have them attest to its truth, and send it to Paris. Augusta followed the advice to the letter. The material reached Lady Byron on February 12. To Augusta's dismay the letter was returned unopened, care of Lady Byron's solicitors Wharton and Ford, with a brief note on the envelope that she considered the correspondence terminated by her letter to Augusta.

Annabella had not seen much of Mrs. Villiers in recent years—each had other interests to occupy her—but there was no estrangement. Had she known that Mrs. Villiers had something to do with the unopened letter she might have read it; she had an uneasy respect for Therese's good opinion. As it turned out she did not have to open it to know what it contained. Therese was not above reproach—she indulged in gossip without much compunction and enjoyed being involved in personal affairs which were not her business—but she believed in the responsibility of friendship. Because she had once been a close friend, she undertook gratuitously to clarify certain aspects of the Augusta-Libby controversy in the hope that it would soften Lady Byron's harsh opinion.

Her letter of explanation, dated February 19, 1841, was the beginning of an extraordinary correspondence between the two ladies. There were twenty letters, roughly ten apiece, written from February through June, all having to do with Augusta's connection with the Libby-Trevanion misalliance in which she went to exhaustive lengths to put Augusta in a good light. In every instance, Lady Byron went to equally thorough lengths to refute Mrs. Villiers' statements; the result being as complete a collection of data, relevant and irrelevant, as one could hope to find. A number of the letters dealt with Libby's suit against her mother in Chancery Court to force the return of the Deed of Appointment, the costs assumed by Lady Byron.

Annabella's spate of letter writing was not confined to Mrs. Villiers. On February 23 she wrote to her son-in-law, Lord Lovelace, informing him of the suit and what precipitated it, including details about E. L.'s birth and paternity. (She frequently referred to Libby as E. L. in correspondence.) She also hinted to her son-in-law that she would take certain steps toward making known Augusta's (dreadful) secret if, Augusta, in deference to Annabella's wishes, persisted in withholding the deed.[11] Lord Lovelace felt it quite in order to reveal what he

believed to have been a well-kept secret, considering the nature
of the lawsuit. He did not know at this time that his mother-in-
law had been imparting facts about Augusta since 1816. Not
only did she write to Lord Lovelace, she wrote to Ada, and for
the first time acquainted her daughter with her reasons for
taking charge of Elizabeth Medora and Marie.

On February 27 Ada answered, enclosing a note from her
husband. Her letter is quoted in part:

> St. James's Square, *Saturday, February 27th,* 1841
>
> Dearest Mama,
>   . . . I am not in the least *astonished.* In fact you merely
> *confirm* what I have for *years and years* felt scarcely a doubt
> about, but should have considered it most improper in me to
> hint to you that I in any way suspected. . . .

She mentioned having discussed her suspicions with her
husband, then felt ashamed of herself for even thinking of anything so "monstrous and hideous" when he asked what could
have put such an extraordinary idea into her head. "I fear *she*
is *more inherently* wicked than *he* ever was." [12]

Annabella reacted to the last sentence as she always did
when anyone sought to absolve Byron of the least modicum
of guilt. Her answer is perhaps the most revealing testament
of her capacity for self-delusion and self-justification that she
ever composed. It is too long to be quoted in its entirety.

> . . . I have been told by some that it was a weakness—almost
> a want of truth on my part—to wish, as I have done, to leave
> your Father's aberrations sufficiently indistinct to enable you
> still to contemplate his memory with a sort of gratification.
> . . . It is indeed consolatory to me that I can make you the
> friend of my past as well as of my present life, *without reserve.*
> . . . Strange to say I have been led to acquit *him* of some por-
> tion of the guilt by recent disclosures respecting her conduct
> to her child—for one who could, *as she clearly did,* connive at
> the ruin of a daughter, must have been capable of injuring a
> brother in the same way. I had believed her to have been
> wholly a victim. . . .[13]

Recalling the inquisition of Augusta in 1816, with Lady Byron and Mrs. Villiers twice forcing a confession of guilt from the accused, it is difficult to accept that final sentence. Ada replied on March 3 (quoted in part):

> . . . I should like some time to know how you came ever to suspect anything so monstrous. The natural intimacy and familiarity of a Brother and Sister certainly could not suggest it to any but a very depraved and vicious mind, which *yours* assuredly was not. I cannot help fancying that *he* himself must have given you some very clear hints of it. He too well liked to taunt you with his crimes. Alas! [14]

It was perspicacious of Ada to have hit the mark so closely about Byron's "hints." Apparently Annabella had discussed her husband's "aberrations" with her daughter though she seemed to think she had left them "indistinct" in order to protect the father image in Ada's youthful mind. The trouble was that, at heart, Annabella did not want Ada to revere her father or to love his memory. She wanted all the love and loyalty a child customarily gives to both parents.

From the time Ada was a child, her mother had done all that was possible to turn the girl into an extension of herself, suppressing what might be Byronic tendencies in her character. In May, 1833, after Ada's second season was over, Lady Byron hastened to overcome what could develop into a taste for frivolity, which she deplored, by taking Ada on a tour around the country, visiting various factories. Ostensibly it was to be educational for mother and child: to see the new machines in order to have a better understanding of the problems of the working class, and to show Ada that honest toil was more admirable than dancing until dawn at balls and masquerades. The fact that the largest problem of the workers was the danger of being supplanted by these machines probably did not occur to Lady Byron—or her daughter. Then, as a contrast, Lady Byron took the girl to Doncaster for the races, hoping that Ada could see the folly of most worldly amusements. Annabella hated horse racing—"the desperate gambling among the spectators, the futility of the object." [15]

As for the workers, Ada was far more absorbed in the machinery than the people; she had an instinctive comprehension of the inner workings of engines and other mechanical contrivances which eventually became an obsession. Her mother could find no fault with that, for science and mathematics had been a girlhood hobby with her, too. But Ada's reaction to horse racing was something else again. She adored every aspect of it, from the sheer excitement of the sport itself to the betting, especially the latter though she made no great issue out of it at the time. It would have dismayed her mother but it could surely not have been called a trait inherited from her father. Byron had too much of his thrifty Scots mother in him to go in for much gambling. There was also the unedifying example of Colonel Leigh to serve as a warning; far too often had Byron bailed him out of debt and never been repaid. It would be a few years, however, before Ada's fascination with the sport of kings became a serious threat to Annabella's peace of mind.

In the winter of 1840–41 Annabella's thoughts were fully occupied with her new "daughter." The possessive nature and jealousy which affected her relationship with her real daughter were becoming evident in her alliance with the daughter of Augusta Leigh. Throughout her correspondence with Mrs. Villiers during this period, as well as with other people, there are many references to E. L.'s fondness for her mother which was inexplicable to Lady Byron. Having ascertained Libby's whereabouts Augusta had renewed her letterwriting to her daughter in Paris; Libby responded, which distressed Annabella, though she could scarcely object to it openly inasmuch as she maintained the fiction that she wanted Elizabeth Medora to be a free agent. Lady Byron knew all too well how effective Augusta was at inspiring love and was not surprised that she was successful with her daughter having seen how successful she had been with Libby's father.[16]

Libby was not utterly dominated by filial devotion to the point of stupidity. Once she broke away from her childhood dependence upon her mother and could view things objectively she was only too aware of her mother's weaknesses. She knew, too, that she was greatly indebted to her benefactress and respected Lady Byron's intelligence, but she simply could not love her aunt in the same way she had loved her "dearest Mamma." That was the crux of Lady Byron's problem in regard to Elizabeth Medora. In fact, Libby reacted to her in much the same way as Byron had done. He had honestly tried to love the girl he married, not only because he considered her worthy of love but because she so desperately loved him. Tragically for Annabella there was a quality in her love which put people off; it was too overwhelming, too rarefied. All her life she was hoping to find someone "who was able to love her," [17] but she set her sights so impossibly high and demanded so much more than could be given by mortal beings that each "passion" carried within it the seeds of disenchantment. As she grew older and experienced one disillusioning association after another, she became increasingly quixotic in her demands and moods. Other people could escape when things got out of hand, but Libby was a captive. It is true that one has to give up a certain amount of freedom of action in return for security, and it is likewise true that some of the hardships endured by Libby were of her own making. Yet there must have been moments, after six months of daily contact with her high-principled but often querulous aunt, when she looked back nostalgically upon her life with emotional but undemanding Moe.

If anyone sought to "act upon" Libby to "elicit expressions of affection and tenderness," it was Lady Byron herself. She did not want the daughter to have any affection for the mother. All correspondence between Libby and Augusta had first to pass through Annabella's hands. (Not that she asked to read the letters or did so without asking.) Annabella and Libby had many heart-to-heart discussions about life in general and Augusta in particular. Annabella must also have read some of Therese

Villiers' letters to Libby or permitted her to read them.[18]

But Therese, as Augusta's self-appointed advocate, was constantly at cross-purposes with Lady Byron, defending Augusta's actions even though she was not always in sympathy with them.[19] Mrs. Villiers' letters, full as they were of italicized words and the most perfervid emotion, demonstrated to Libby all that her aunt was doing on her behalf.

Mrs. Villiers offered to try to persuade Augusta to give up the Deed and send it to Paris, *providing* that it would remain in Lady Byron's custody. Annabella turned down the offer. She was responsible only for Libby's personal safety, not for her Deed.[20]

Nobody wanted the case to go to court, including Libby's lawyer Stephen. Court action could result in another juicy scandal which Mrs. Leigh could ill afford. Stephen hoped that the affair could be settled out of court after Lady Byron returned to England, but Annabella demurred. It seems clear from the correspondence that she was not at all averse to subjecting Augusta to public disclosures that would destroy Augusta's reputation once and for all—though naturally Annabella claimed only the highest motives.[21]

Therese Villiers was unable to make any headway in her role of peacemaker and was at the point of closing the correspondence since she no longer had any expectation of doing good.[22] Fortunately, she was given a breather because, early in April, 1841, Lord and Lady Lovelace arrived in Paris for a brief visit to see Lady Byron and to meet her intriguing protégé.

To Libby it must have been a welcome change. She had been thrown almost constantly on the society of Lady Byron and friends. On April 14 Libby reached twenty-seven, and in May her aunt would be forty-nine. The age difference was not easy to adjust to, especially when most of Annabella's friends were also older women. Ada was a year and a half younger than Libby, but her husband, thirty-five, was able to bridge the generation gap very nicely between the two young women and Lady Byron. Lovelace was the same age as Henry Trevanion, an ironic coincidence which could not have been lost upon Libby, but the two men could not have been more different in character. Libby and Ada took an immediate liking to each other. Their physical resemblance was striking enough to be noticed by everyone who saw them together, even by those not privy to the relationship. The only difference was in build: Libby was taller and thinner, with "that great, tall childish body of hers" as Ada put it.[23]

The Lovelaces must have gone out of their way to make Libby feel at ease. "I received kindnesses and promises from both," Libby wrote, "and was made to feel that I was to be Ada's sister at all times, which I was really." [24] Whatever Ada did or said was an expression of her true feelings, otherwise she would not have given this impression to Libby. Ada had been brought up to think for herself and speak her mind, a little too bluntly at times. Being the daughter of Byron she had grown used to being fawned upon or ogled at. All this attention could have resulted in arrogance, and Hobhouse, among others, commented on her tendency toward it. But the arrogance was tempered by an innate niceness and kindness. Ada was also under the strong influence of her husband and mother, both of whom held her in line. They did pamper her by taking over the supervision of her three children so that she could give her full time to her vocation, the science of calculation, which had blossomed under the guidance of her great friend Charles Babbage.

The enormous difference between Ada and Libby in every kind of way—background, education, social position, financial security, life experience—might have proved too wide a gulf to bridge if Libby had been a pliant, retiring girl who was self-conscious about her position in the ménage and meekly grateful for any kindnesses. Adversity, however, had taught her that the meek do not inherit the earth, that pride does not always go before a fall, and that money is not necessarily the root of all evil. She believed in herself despite misfortunes which would have crushed someone with lesser pride, and that quality of self-esteem had much to do with the impression she made upon people.

What Libby lacked in worldly goods she made up for in the fascination she seemed to exert on everyone she met. Part of the fascination, of course, stemmed from her life story which was known to most of Lady Byron's close friends who gathered around her in Paris. Libby had always liked to be in the center of things and now she was the object of intense curiosity which was most gratifying to her amour propre. Lady Byron's oft-repeated desire to provide her with the security due someone with her "rank in life" gave her a sense of her own importance which had suffered badly in the Trevanion years. She was undeniably flattered by Ada's friendship and probably offered her any number of "conscientious lumps of sugar" during the sojourn in Paris.

The visit of Ada and her husband came in April, at a time when Paris was at her best. English travelers loved to go there in the spring although it was a beautiful season in their own country. In mid-nineteenth-century England the countryside was still almost the same as it had been in Shakespeare's day. There were great stretches of open unspoiled country, large wooded areas bursting into leaf, streams and freshets swollen by spring thaws. But the heart of London changed little from one season to another except in the parks and pleasure haunts like Vauxhall or Cremorne Gardens. Because of the climate daily life was lived indoors even on fine days.

Not so in Paris. The Parisians, all French people in fact, liked to be in the open air whenever possible. They conducted their business in the street, they ate in crowded sidewalk cafés where the atmosphere was gay and convivial; these customs were noted by many British travelers in their journals and letters. But Sunday in Paris, ah, that was the most festive and delightful day of the week, in contrast to Sunday in London which was quite different, dead almost, the streets all but deserted, and nothing to see or do. In Paris it was a day given over to seeing and doing. It was a family day; the bourgeois head of the house strolled on the boulevards with his wife and children, stopping at the street fairs which sprang up overnight on corners all over the city where the children could watch the Punch and Judy show.[25] All the shops were open, all the cafés. A fortnight in Paris was an endless holiday, especially for those who had money to spend. It was not surprising that Lord and Lady Lovelace enjoyed their visit, but for Libby it was a high point in her life.

Life with Lady Byron did have compensations, and now that Libby had made friends with Ada and Lord Lovelace, the path of the future did not seem quite so tortuous. It was clear that Lady Byron ruled the Lovelace roost as she did all other roosts, but it was possible to adjust to her vagaries and still keep one's identity. To an observer with Libby's sharp eyes and ears the Lady Byron-Lovelace triangle (if such it could be called) must have been a never-ending source of amusement which she would have loved to mimic before the right audience. They were addicted to nicknames of marked ornithological derivation which were used in letters and introduced playfully into conversation. Ada was her mother's "Hopeful Bird" which was shortened to Bird or The Bird with variations such as Brown Thrush, Avis, and the like.[26] Lady Byron was Hen and was addressed thus by her son-in-law in correspondence. His nickname was Crow which does not seem to fit his personality, judging by what we know of him. Actually Hen was an apt name for Annabella; she was tireless in her supervision of Ada's doings, as a mother hen clucks around the barnyard, watching every move of her chicks and flapping defiant wings at any threat to their safety. She was equally henlike toward Libby, writing endless notes in her Journal about the best way to handle this or that crotchet in E. L.'s character. It must have been a relief to Libby when her aunt had Ada and her husband to regiment as well as herself and Marie.

The visit ended all too quickly, but Libby was given many assurances that she and her child were to consider themselves part of the family, so she was sure of seeing Ada in England.

Libby had no desire to return to her native land—she wanted to live in Paris—but she had to do what Lady Byron wished. Although vastly improved in health she was still not strong enough to be on her own, nor would Lady Byron have agreed to it. She had taken Libby and the child under her wing and intended to keep them there.

After the departure of the Lovelaces, Annabella returned to her letter writing with renewed vigor, determined to convince Therese Villiers that *she* was the dupe of Augusta's artful ways as Libby had been. Letters passed back and forth, each more abrupt on Annabella's part than the one before, with neither lady giving an inch. Lady Byron was also making arrangements to leave Paris with her entourage, and now Libby was glad to be able to quit the city. It was discovered that Henry Trevanion was in Paris.[27] Libby was very worried that he might try to take Marie from her, although he had never shown undue interest in the child and had deliberately avoided acknowledging his paternity when he took care of the birth certificate at Morlaix. Since the death of his father, his finances were in better shape, and Georgiana was now receiving the hundred a year due her from the estate. So Henry could, if he wished, continue remaining in Paris and destroying Libby's peace of mind just as he had done at Pontivy and Carhaix. But there was little likelihood of his being able to cause real trouble as long as Libby remained with the redoubtable Lady Noel Byron.

Then, around the last week of May Lady Byron's ménage left Paris and arrived in London. There they would stay for a while settling into the Lovelace town house at 10 St. James's Square.[28] It was only a few hundred yards away from Augusta's lodgings in St. James's Palace.

12

And if we do but watch the hour,
There never yet was human power
Which could evade, if unforgiven,
The patient search and vigil long
Of him who treasures up a wrong.

—MAZEPPA.

IT HAD BEEN TEN YEARS SINCE LIBBY SET FOOT ON ENGLISH soil. There had been big changes in that decade. The railways had begun to supplant the turnpikes and old coach roads, making it easier to travel about the country. People of high rank and wealth were inclined, at first, to eschew this new-fangled means of transportation, feeling that it was rather beneath them, although undoubtedly a boon to the working class who could now get out of the cities on a holiday. Lady Byron was one of the exceptions; she used the railways from the beginning.[1]

She had never, in fact, felt that a gleaming coach and high stepping pair, with liveried coachmen on the box, was a status symbol; it was a means of getting from one place to another. Lord Lovelace always complained that the Hen lacked consideration for horses, ordering her carriage far too often during a day.[2] Ada did not share her mother's indifference to animals; she was more like her father. In addition to an endless succession of favorite dogs, the Lovelace residences were filled with cages of finches, canaries, and rare birds, and parrots were always members of the family.[3] Libby was fond of pets—she was born in a country house, after all—but her life had been too hectic in recent years to take on the responsibility of feeding something other than herself and her child.

Annabella started to look for a country house which would be within easy driving distance to the Lovelace residence, Ockham Park, and also on the railway to the city. After Bifrons and Bath, Libby was not looking forward to life in the country, although St. James's Square *was* a little too close to the palace. She was no longer on such affectionate terms with her Mamma; Augusta was now quite openly antagonistic toward her daughter.[4] This was understandable in view of the suit that had been filed against her in Chancery Court and the fact that her "beloved child" was now living under the protection of an avowed enemy. As for Georgiana, Libby had been estranged from her since eloping to France with Trevanion. It would therefore have been embarrassing in the extreme to run into either Moe or Georgey, something which could very likely happen if one were taking the air on a fine day. It would be especially difficult if she were with Lady Byron. All in all it was probably best to live elsewhere.

House hunting did not prevent Annabella from continuing her correspondence with Mrs. Villiers. Now the subject was a letter which Sir George Stephen wrote to Libby in Paris which had somehow gone astray, and was therefore not answered. He wrote a second letter which also received no reply, and this so galled him that he took his grievance to Mrs. Villiers. She wrote to Lady Byron, accusing Libby of ungracious behavior, for obviously *all* the gentleman's letters could not have gone astray. Therese seemed always ready to take pen in hand for what she deemed a worthy purpose. But Lady Byron was a creature cut of the same, or even of sturdier cloth, and she quickly sprang to her desk to reply, defending Libby against all animadversions.[5] Since Henry Trevenanion had been present in Paris it was logical for Annabella to presume that he could have very easily intercepted the letters. Henry, after all, was quite familiar with Stephen's handwriting. Eventually the letter which Stephen had put into the post on April 29 was returned to him from Paris. It had gone astray, having been improperly addressed. Libby was now exonerated, and despite Lady Byron's testy attitude, Therese Villiers was gracious enough to drop a note July 3 in which she admitted frankly that she had been in error. Lady Byron, alas, was unable to retire from the field without one last salvo. In this letter she vigorously defended Libby again, pointed out how painful the episode had been for her young charge, and implicitly reproached Mrs. Villiers for the part she had played in the latest situation.[6]

On July 9 Mrs. Villiers answered. Her letter was couched in terms which could leave no doubt in anyone's mind that she had given up her thankless role of mediator, and though she regretted disagreeing with Lady Byron, she wanted nothing more to do with the affair.[7] This closed the door on any further communications regarding Libby.

By this time Annabella had settled herself and her household at Esher, Surrey, in a comfortable house, Moore Place, which was built circa 1750–1800. Its park adjoined the grounds of Claremont Palace, then used as a stopping place for guests of the royal family. In 1848, for example, when Louis Philippe lost his throne, he and his family escaped to England where they were given asylum at Claremont. When the young Victoria first ascended the throne she used to encourage her prime minister, Lord Melbourne, to talk about Lord Byron who was one of her girlhood heroes, although a rather naughty gentleman by all reports. Melbourne indulged her curiosity with laundered stories of Byron's escapades, and certainly he knew a number of them inasmuch as the romance of his wife (Lady Caroline Lamb) with the handsome poet had been the scandal of Society. Victoria had always gone out of her way to be gracious to Byron's widow, although Lady Byron rejected all the Queen's efforts to arrange a meeting. Apparently Her Majesty overlooked it, for when she learned that Lady Byron had leased Moore Place she saw to it that Annabella was given a key to the Claremont

Palace grounds so that she could enjoy the magnificent walks and gardens.[8]

So Libby was more than comfortably situated and still on close terms with her aunt. Lady Byron showed her "letters of Lord Byron, relative to the Separation, which, as she often said, might be useful in the Chancery suit." [9] At last Annabella could unburden herself to someone only too eager to listen, someone who could understand the torment of ruined pride which was still painful after twenty-six years.

Besides her preoccupation with "E. L." Annabella undertook the upbringing of seven-year-old Marie. She saw to it that the child would receive an education suitable for a young lady who might enter Society one day under the aegis of her aunt, provided, of course, that she learned to conform. Libby had done her best to bring up her child properly, but there was a difference between France and England in the upbringing of children and their place in a household. Even in French families of great wealth and position, the mother maintained close supervision of her children and kept watchful eyes on nurses and governesses. Children were an integral part of family life and had their meals *en famille* as often as possible. They were taught to observe the strict rules of etiquette which prevailed in France but were allowed to express themselves and take part in conversations among grownups. To the English they often seemed noisy and perhaps unruly.[10] In the households of English society, great and small, the children were supposed to be seen but not heard. Only the poorest class took charge of bringing up the young ones. In households comparable to Lady Byron's, the children were under the entire care of nannies who were in turn supervised by the head nurse who ruled the nursery like a provost marshal. Around teatime, the children's hour, the young were dressed up and paraded into the presence of Mama and Papa and whoever else might be present. An hour was about the limit of endurance the parents were expected to survive with equanimity.

At first, Marie must have been puzzled by such regimentation; she was used to the constant companionship of her mother which she could now no longer enjoy. There is evidence in some of Lady Byron's letters to suggest that Marie responded adversely to her deprivation.[11] It would not have occurred to anyone that it was a traumatic experience for the little girl to adjust herself quickly to life in a foreign country, for to Marie England was a foreign land. Luckily she was pretty and sweet natured, with an awareness of human foibles beyond her years. She had been raised as a Catholic which set her apart from the children of her Church of England relations and neighbors, but in that respect Lady Byron was open-minded and had taught Ada to be the same.

From the standpoint of comfortable living, Libby was in an enviable position, but the village of Esher offered her little in the way of amusement or stimulation. The population was around eight hundred; the center of the social life was the green, the Wheatsheaf Inn, and the White Lion. Most of the villagers lived in cottages but there were a few large residences on the Portsmouth Road, among them Moore Place. It stood back from the road and several footpaths converged on its grounds. (It is now an Inn of the same name.[12]) The Surrey countryside was lovely and Esher was picturesque, but Libby always seemed indifferent to nature, nor is there evidence in Lady Byron's voluminous correspondence and journals to stamp her as a real nature lover. She liked the quiet and simplicity of country life, but if she needed a change of scene she could take the railway to London for a day or so.

To Libby the most agreeable attribute of Moore Place was its comparative nearness to Ockham Park. Ada and William always welcomed visits from Lady Byron and now Libby and Marie were included. It was indeed a lovely place. The manor house was in the most secluded section of the park, surrounded by oaks, chestnut, and fir trees. There was a large sheet of water called Leg-of-Mutton Pond on the property where one could go boating in summer and skating in winter. The house and gardens had been "Italianized" by Lord Lovelace's father and were greatly admired by those who liked the formal Italian style.[13] The family life was one of grace and comfort with a well-trained staff, but the life style was not formal.

Ada's interests and tastes were quite dissimilar to Libby's (she called her Elizabeth), but the two women developed a genuine fondness for each other. Libby loved the luxuries that money could buy, never having had enough of them, and she must have been impressed by the way of living which Ada took for granted. Ada was indifferent to the latest fashions of dress and the baubles that gladden the hearts of women, though she wore the King family jewels on state occasions. Entertaining on a lavish scale was simply not for her. She and William liked certain people a great deal and invited them for frequent visits to Ockham Park and Ashley Combe, but their taste ran to outdoor pursuits which appealed to the country gentry everywhere: riding, walking, drives to various places of local interest. In the winter Ada warned guests arriving from London to be sure to bring warm clothes because there would be skating; a pastime very much in favor at the time and in which she was proficient. Arriving guests were often met at the railway station by an open sleigh in cold weather; it must have been a trial to step out of a heated railway car at the Weybridge station to be met by the Lovelace coachman and driven through the wintry cold to Ockham Park.[14]

One of these frequent guests was Charles Babbage; others were Augustus De Morgan, one of Ada's early tutors in mathematics, and his wife; the Earl of Lovelace was interested in mathematics too but was not in the same class with his brilliant young countess or Professor Babbage. In 1841 Babbage was fifty and a widower with three grown sons, having lost his wife when she was but thirty-five. He was a year older than Lady Byron and had been her friend before he became acquainted with her daughter. In the beginning Ada was the one who kept the friendship going for she admired him extravagantly. By 1841 her grasp of the intricacies of his latest invention—the calculating machine which he called the "analytical engine"—had cemented the friendship. The twenty-six-year-old Countess Lovelace could more than hold her own with him intellectually, but what was more important, she understood his personality and accepted quirks which had earned him a reputation for irascibility among other scientists.[15]

Babbage was inclined to be paranoid about slights, real and imagined, concerning his inventions, and he was always at loggerheads with the Establishment which did not view his machines with the proper reverence. The government was reluctant to grant funds to develop the potential of all those bewildering moving parts unless the damn things would work, and alas, they never quite did in a practical way. Though he had trouble with government officials, socially he was an immense success. He was a tall, handsome man whose father left him well off; he could have dined out every evening if he wished because the ladies adored him. Men who are adored by women usually find women adorable, or at least provocative, but Babbage remained faithful to the memory of his wife. Perhaps his closest emotional tie to any woman was to Lady Lovelace, but it was more in the category of teacher and disciple than anything which could be labeled romantic. It may be that, to Ada, he was a substitute for the father she had never known.[16]

Babbage and the De Morgans were taken with Libby whom they saw frequently at Ockham Park and Moore Place. All who met her at the time remarked on her quiet elegance and the deference she displayed toward Lady Byron.[17] She could never have understood the principles of advanced mathematics which was the bond between Ada and the others, but Libby was sprightly in conversation and attractive to look at. Mrs. De Morgan noticed the resemblance between Libby and Ada; she had known Byron and certain of their mannerisms reminded her of him to an extraordinary degree.

The relationship between the two young women seemed to be taken for granted by most of those who were close to Lady Byron and the Lovelaces. Lady Byron, in fact, encouraged the idea, with Ada in particular, though Ada did not need her mother as a catalyst—she made her own friendships. The "sisters" did not share the same maternal interest in their respective offspring. Libby was a doting mother, partly through circumstances and partly by inclination. Ada was fond of her three children but they were not the center of her life. At this time they were still confined mostly to the nursery: Byron was five, Annabella was three, Ralph was two. Probably Ada would never have been a woman of strong maternal instinct; neither was her mother. As a child Annabella never played with dolls or wanted them.[18] Oddly enough, for a woman who had little empathy for men in her adult years, she preferred playing with boys as a child.[19]

One thing the sisters did have in common was a bent toward music. Byron had once written that he hoped Ada would be musical, "anything save poetical," and she did not let him down. She took up the violin and with the intensity of purpose inherited from her father and characteristic of all her endeavors, she became utterly absorbed in learning to play the instrument. Rather than interrupt her daily practice she walked round and round a billiard table for hours while she played on her fiddle in order to have her quota of exercise.[20] Libby had a pretty talent for singing and accompanying herself on the pianoforte.[21] It conjures up a charming picture, early Victorian School, of the two young women in the drawing room after the evening meal; Libby at the pianoforte and Ada, violin tucked beneath her chin, entertaining those present with an impromptu musicale.

Neither of them was blessed with a robust constitution. Libby's recurrent attacks of pleurisy (judging from descriptions of her symptoms) were not improved by the English climate. As for Ada, her illnesses were harder to define. In one of her letters to "Dear Babbage," she wrote:

I am breathing *well* again today, and am much better in all respects; owing to Dr. L's remedies, he certainly does seem to understand the case, I mean the treatment of it, which is the main thing. As for the *theory* of it, he says truly that *time* and *providence* alone can develope that. It is so *anomalous* an affair altogether.[22]

Indeed it was, as many internal disorders were in that day when a correct diagnosis—and the right treatment—was a matter of luck. Shortness of breath and attacks of indigestion seemed to be the most frequent symptoms, but invariably Ada rallied and continued to drive herself beyond her strength. There is evidence in some of her letters that she had a presentiment—or suspicion—that her trouble *might* be more serious than anyone imagined, much less wished to admit.[23]

Her health did not prevent her from taking constitutionals in the open air whenever possible. Probably she and Libby went for walks in the park surrounding the manor house, just as, twenty-six years before, the young Annabella had walked in the park at Six Mile Bottom with her sister-in-law. They had talked about themselves but mostly about the man who was causing them both such heartache. What did their daughters talk about? About themselves, of course, for no subject can ever be more titillating, but did they also talk about the father whom neither of them had known except through hearsay? There was no reason for skirting the subject inasmuch as they knew what had brought them together in the first place. True, ladies in the Victorian Age did not indulge in overly explicit talk about sex or related aberrations, but they could talk about men, or in this instance, one man. Ada would have welcomed the chance to talk about Byron with someone who shared the same curiosity about him. She had learned to be careful about references to her father when she was with her mother.

In her youthful days there were Byron's poetical works to be found on the bookshelves of her mother's various abodes, but Ada had never displayed undue eagerness to read them, often to the surprise of her mother's friends. Children have an innate diffidence about bringing up matters which they know to be sensitive spots with their parents. After her marriage she had more freedom to express her feelings about her father and to read the works which had made him famous throughout the world. As she grew older she learned more about him from people who had known him for the man he was: a loyal friend, a lover of liberty for the oppressed, an endearing and delightful companion whose scowl quickly turned to laughter, compassionate and wise in most of his dealings, tender with women unless exasperated beyond endurance; this was not the man who had married her mother and deliberately broken her heart. An anecdote reveals that she had not only read his poems but identified herself with some of them. She went to a Queen's Ball dressed in semi-Oriental garb, patterned after one of Byron's exotic, ill-starred heroines, her dark hair in plaits down to her waist woven through with strands of pearls. While she and her husband were chatting with friends, news passed quickly through the assemblage, and all of the guests contrived to stroll past Lady Lovelace to get a good look at her bizarre hairdo.[24]

Libby had to be discreet, of course, but having been assured that she was indeed the "fruit of sin" she was not at all embarrassed about it. On the contrary, it made her feel important, a Somebody worthy to be in the same circle as Lady Byron and Lady Lovelace. It was doubtless good for her ego though it did not augur well for peaceful coexistence with her benefactress. She had been quick to note that everyone, including Ada and Lord Lovelace, walked the chalk line when dealing with her Aunt Annabella. Already Libby had made the discovery that "her strange arrangements were often most painful" although well intended.[25]

In the fall she again had a recurrence of her chronic illness which meant that she was once more dependent upon the ministrations of Lady Byron. There had been some thoughts about her going to a warmer climate that winter to get rid of the chest condition, but now it was not feasible

> without great difficulty and expense, which I was always anxious to avoid. All this rendered me the more desirous to com-

ply with Lady Byron's earnest wish that I should not leave her, which, she used to say, would cost her her life.[26]

It was a strange alliance between these two fundamentally incompatible people, and no more destined to bring lasting happiness than the marriage between Annabella and Byron. As time progressed the same traits in Annabella which had driven her husband frantic affected Libby in the same abrasive way. This does not mean to imply that it was all Annabella's fault. Libby had many of the same qualities which had made Byron difficult to live with if one was emotionally bound to him, as several women besides his wife were to find out. But the situation would some day reach insurmountable proportions.

13

Yet must I think less wildly:—I have thought
Too long and darkly, till my brain became,
In its own eddy boiling and o'erwrought,
A whirling gulf of phantasy and flame:
And thus, untaught in youth my heart to tame,
My springs of life were poison'd.

—CHILDE HAROLD'S PILGRIMAGE

On MAY 31, 1842, A LITTLE MORE THAN A YEAR AFTER the Chancery suit had been instigated, the case was to be heard. It never came to trial. On that same day Augusta's counsel agreed to surrender the Deed without further argument. After two years of pro and con, first between Augusta and Libby in Pontivy, later between Mrs. Villiers and Lady Byron, plus the efforts of Sir George Stephen and the lawyers representing Mrs. Leigh to reach a settlement out of court, it was all over. Whether or not Augusta was frightened by disclosures in public, or induced by sensible advisers to give up the struggle, is unimportant. Much trouble and expense had been incurred by both parties. Stephen had generously refused to take anything for his services, but the other expenses amounted to ninety-seven pounds, not including Augusta's share. Lady Byron paid Libby's part. She could have held Augusta liable for all costs, but she refrained from doing so.[1] At long last the Deed was in Libby's possession.

On April 2 Lady Byron had written to Lady Wilmot-

Horton expressing her aggravation with Augusta about the waste of time and money for such (to Annabella) a niggardly sum. Three thousand pounds *was* insignificant from the point of view of someone who had a substantial yearly income from the more than 60,000 pounds left her by the terms of Byron's will. Annabella's chief complaint was that the "anxious suspense of two years to Elizabeth" had contributed to her illness and destroyed her peace of mind.[2]

Judging by Annabella's arduous efforts on E. L.'s behalf, constantly defending her against all comers, one would assume that all was still well between the occupants of Moore Place. After the severe winter Libby's health was on the mend, and Marie was showing steady improvement at school. Yet on June 9, Lady Byron wrote some "Remarks on E." which she placed in a sealed envelope, not to be opened without her leave. The "Remarks" reveal that, to Annabella at least, all was anything but well.

For some time she had suspected, she wrote, that Libby's "wild and wayward" temper was only an "Instrument for selfish purposes" which, like a cloak, could be put on or taken off as the mood suited her, "for effect." Annabella had reached the conclusions that there were but two holds on "this character":

> Love of approbation and of money.
> The first is comparatively feeble, because it can be never fully gratified but it ought to be cultivated as the best of the two—.
> The latter must be used indirectly, and not in a way *to lower her* in the estimation of others.
> In attempting to hurt those who oppose her she will hurt herself, but this will be, not from recklessness but miscalculation. She expects to make people serve her better by bullying.[3]

What had happened between December, when Ada was so happy for her mother to have E. with her, and the following June? There is no way to pinpoint the exact moment or reason when something goes seriously wrong in a relationship. Judging it solely on the basis of Lady Byron's remarks, Libby does not come off too well. For almost two years she had lived a life of ease and luxury through the generosity of a woman to whom she had turned in desperate need and who had rescued her from almost certain death. Thanks to her benefactress she was now the possessor of a three-thousand-pound Deed of Trust for the future education of her child. She had not been forced to borrow on it or sell it for less than its value. Her daughter, Marie, was being educated in a good school without cost to her. But instead of showing the proper gratitude for these manifold kindnesses by making life agreeable for her benefactress she was, according to Lady Byron, "bullying" those who were trying to help her and indulging in temper outbursts in order to get her own way. In other words, she was biting the helping hand.

There is no doubt that Libby deserved some of the criticism leveled at her by Lady Byron and her circle of intimates. Libby did have a highly nervous disposition and when her temper was aroused she spared nobody's feelings, just as her father had done. Yet before passing judgment one should consider that, for the past year and a half, she had been living a life predicated on the habit patterns and personal preferences of Lady Byron. The two women could not have been less alike in taste or temperament.

By nature and inclination Libby was a man's woman. In spite of all the misery she endured with Trevanion she was passionately attached to him for several years. Later she had turned to M. Carrel in her despair and he had responded as a man responds to a woman with great feminine appeal. She needed men; her sex urge was strong except when weakened by wasting illness. All her life she was attracted to men and attractive to them in varying degrees. Now she was living in an all but manless world. There were men in Lady Byron's circle such as Babbage, Augustus De Morgan, various male relations, and of course, Lord Lovelace, but they were all married or involved elsewhere. Even if one of them had shown interest in Libby she would not have encouraged him. She had no intention of involving herself in another liaison; she wanted marriage. Because she liked masculine society does not mean that she disliked women. She did like the ones with whom she had empathy such as Ada, but unlike her aunt, she did not prefer women to men. Nevertheless there were a few special friends of Annabella's who led interesting, stimulating lives with whom Libby could establish a rapport.

In 1842 the one who occupied first place in the affections of Lady Byron was a woman who, luckily, was able to understand and appreciate Libby because they were alike. She was Mrs. Anna Murphy Jameson, a successful authoress and world traveler, and one of the movers and shakers of the Women's Rights Movement. She was two years younger than Annabella, and she had already established a considerable name for herself in a literary way in America as well as England and Europe. This had all happened before she met Lady Byron in 1834. The introduction was through a cousin of Annabella's, Robert Noel. His relationship to Lady Byron is interesting.

The title and estates of the Barony of Wentworth would have gone to him rather than to Annabella except for a mischance of Fate. His father had been the illegitimate son of Lord Wentworth, and because Wentworth never legalized the union between himself and his mistress, his son got nothing. Lady Noel inherited instead, and after her death, Annabella succeeded to the estates and income. She felt obligated to provide for Robert and his three brothers, as befitted their rank in life; she also supervised their education. Robert became a cultivated, worldly man with friends all over Europe. Through Goethe's daughter-in-law, Ottile, he met Mrs. Jameson and saw to it that this energetic, delightful woman would meet his cousin Annabella. Mrs. Jameson's first impression of Annabella was one word: "implacable." [4] It was a singularly shrewd observation which she should have remembered, but she was a creature of impulse and became instantly charmed by Lady Byron.

In no time Annabella, too, was in the grip of the same infatuation she was later to feel for Elizabeth Medora, but with

Anna Jameson the feeling was returned in full measure. She
had a genuine gift for friendship; many illustrious people admired her, among them Charles Dickens and Fanny Kemble.
Fanny was an enormous success as an actress and social figure,
with great charm and vivacity. She had once met Lady Byron
"many years ago" but through Mrs. Jameson she renewed the
acquaintance.[5] Unfortunately Fanny was not in England during Libby's stay at Esher. In 1834 she had gone on an American
tour and married Pierce Butler, son of a wealthy Southern
planter; the marriage turned out badly, after which she returned to London and took up her career once more. She, too,
was committed to the Women's Rights Movement, as was Lady
Byron.

It was a curious facet of Annabella's character that she
was always attracted to women of ebullient personality, prone
to express themselves in a fervent, emotional manner, yet she
always distrusted too much display of affection. There was
nothing pseudo about Anna Jameson's warm, outgoing personality; she was Irish and redheaded. In common with Lady
Byron her marriage had been a traumatic experience. Unlike
Annabella, she tried to make a go of it for several years and
remained friendly with her husband after separation. Robert
Jameson had pursued her for a long time before she accepted
him, and one can see why. A portrait of her at eighteen, by her
father who was a well-known Dublin artist, shows her to have
been a handsome creature with beautiful red hair and creamy
skin, a somewhat aquiline nose, a firm mouth with the lower
lip slightly protruding, giving the impression of a strong, determined nature. The marriage turned out to be "in name
only."[6] That unsatisfactory phrase could mean anything from
impotence on the husband's part to the wife's refusal to con-
summate the union. One suspects the latter because, in later
years, Jameson had a satisfactory affair with a woman which
only ended with his death.

It is easy to understand the bond which developed between Mrs. Jameson and Lady Byron, both with bitter marital

memories, although the effect on each was quite different. Many years later Annabella's grandson Ralph, who knew her well, commented that

> she renounced the world like the founder of a severe monastic order and would have forced everyone under her power to live a life of Spartan self-denial, and devotion to a somewhat despotic philanthropy. . . . Her horror of the flesh was almost excessive.[7]

Mrs. Jameson never renounced life and was far more tolerant of human foibles. Her chief concern was righting the wrongs of women. She believed in absolute equality between the sexes, feeling that existing laws "let loose the passions of the one sex to prey on the other . . ." creating "a horrid, treacherous warfare even more fatal to the oppressor than to the oppressed." [8]

Her words have a contemporary ring, and in most respects she would have been able to adjust herself to the twentieth century which Lady Byron could never have done. Had circumstances been different, with Mrs. Jameson taking Libby under her wing, it is possible that things would have worked out better for all concerned. She was equipped emotionally and mentally to deal with younger people on their own level, but Lady Byron, though drawn to younger people, was always more of an instructor and dictator than a friend. Mrs. Jameson hit it off with Libby from the start, and with Ada Lovelace, too. Ada confided many things to Anna which she withheld from her mother; this would eventually cause a most vindictive estrangement between Lady Byron and her devoted friend.

Mrs. Jameson stayed often at Moore Place when she was not off on one of her European jaunts, and there she renewed her acquaintance with Libby whom she had met first in Paris. She could not avoid noticing the slow disintegration of the relationship between her beloved Lady Byron and the fascinating but unpredictable "Lanky Doodle." With every passing day the situation was growing more tense. Libby's self-control was slipping, and when she reached a certain point she flew into rages which reminded Annabella of her dreadful honeymoon at Halnaby Hall. Some of these gusts of anger had to do with Lady Byron's arrangements which, to Libby, were "strange and unkind." [9] As an example, Lady Byron gave her sixty pounds a year to provide for her own and Marie's clothes and washing; this was supposed to teach Libby how to economize.[10] Certainly her upbringing left much to be desired in handling money, as Annabella well knew, but it does seem to be typical of her odd insensitivity toward those who were dependent on her. One moment she offered the world, the next she picked at every straw while expecting continuous expressions of gratitude. Libby's lack of proper gratitude and her Byronic temperament became an endless subject of complaint in letters from Annabella to her friends, in marked contrast to her belief in her own generosity and forbearance.

The facts, however, do not bear out the prevailing assumption by Lady Byron's adherents that Libby was an ungrateful virago who made life untenable for the kindly, even-tempered woman who had befriended her. The truth was that Annabella was also a victim of moods which were unexpected and tenebrous, catapulting her suddenly from the height of good humor to the depth of Stygian gloom. No one was safe from them. An old friend of hers, Mr. Howett, who worked closely with her on some of her education projects, had this to say:

> She was subject to a constitutional idiosyncrasy of a most peculiar kind which rendered her, when under its influence, absolutely and persistently unjust. When seized by this peculiar condition of the nerves she was helplessly under its control.
>
> I have seen her of an evening in the most amiable, cordial and sunny humour, full of interest and sympathy, and I have seen her the next morning come down—frozen to the very soul, and no effort on the part of those around her could restore her for the day to a genial warmth. She seemed to take sudden and deep impressions against persons and things, which, though the worst might pass away, left a permanent effect.[11]

He was helping her establish a working school for "education of children of the laboring class," to be built at Kirkby Mallory, but working with her was not easy. Sometimes their meetings would be most fruitful, then for no reason he would arrive to discover "the devil of the North Pole was on her," and he would take his leave after wasting valuable time to no purpose. He was not the only one to suffer from her changeable whims. She had hired a schoolmaster for her school, a man with a wife and five children who had, at her inducement, given up a good position to take the new post. Two years later, without warning, she gave him notice to quit but refused to explain her decision. When he begged Mr. Howett to intercede for him, this was the answer: "If Lady Byron has taken it into her head that you shall go, nothing will turn her." In her dealings with her servants she was equally arbitrary; "anyone who contradicted her must be in the wrong." The result was that it "was no unusual thing for the whole of her domestics to quit the situation in a body." [12]

The unfortunate woman was undoubtedly a prey to menopausal depression, for which there was no help in that day, but it must have been extremely difficult to live with someone so given to glooms and sulks. It is no wonder that Libby wrote: "Lady Byron's temper caused me great misery." [13] Inevitably this simmering hostility would come to a full boil, and one of the parties would seize upon some pretext to call it quits. It was Libby who made the first move: "The suit was concluded in a way, without consultation with me, that showed me that all that had been promised me, unsolicited and unsought, was not sincere, and that I had been in a manner sacrificed in my mother's interest." [14]

Annabella's reasons for this alleged "sacrifice" were: "There have also been in unguarded moments slight allusions to means of working upon her Mother for future advantage—which betrayed to my apprehension, an intended object. In consequence I must, without disclosing my reasons, protect the Mother by my future arrangements." [15]

Annabella must never have recognized how quixotic she appeared to others. The anxiety to "protect" the mother from the machinations of the daughter is all but incomprehensible when one recalls that for close to two years she had systematically denigrated Augusta and defended Libby in her correspondence and doubtless in her conversations.

Libby expressed a wish to leave England as soon as some financial arrangement could be implemented; the doctor had "ordered" her to go to a warmer climate and now was the time to do so.[16] She had a right to expect help from her aunt who had assured her over and over that she would provide for her "as Lord Byron would have done." [17] It would have been the easiest solution for Annabella to give Libby some stated amount per annum, allow her to leave the country with her child, and handle her own affairs. But Annabella did not want the easy way out; she wanted to control the future of Libby and Marie as she had been doing since August, 1840. She had, in fact, consulted with Ada about Libby's future without informing her niece of these consultations.

She and Ada had decided that the South of France was the best location for E. and Marie; the place selected was Hyères. It was, at that time, a small resort town on the French Riviera, popular with the English who wanted to escape the rigors of English weather. Libby could have no objection to Hyères, though it would have been nicer to have taken part in the discussion about her future. But when Lady Byron decided that Libby should be accompanied by a lady who was to live with her on a permanent basis, Libby hit the ceiling: "I knew of no one whose constant society I could wish for and I had never given her in any way to believe that I could submit to such." [18]

Her refusal did not alter her aunt's arrangements in the slightest degree. Lady Byron had promised her protection, and this she would continue to give—but on her terms. Libby would have a companion whether or not she wanted one, and it was decided that her lady's maid would be the ideal choice. A more disastrous decision could not have been imagined, although at the start it seemed a sensible solution.

Mme. Natthalie Beaureppaire had been engaged during the Paris sojourn to serve as Libby's personal servant; her wages had been paid by Lady Byron. Natthalie was a well-educated, well-behaved French woman who "had never lived but in the richest families." [19] As with household servants in that period, she was caste conscious and a bit of a snob. After becoming Libby's maid she mentioned "her desire of being with a lady whose conduct had ever been irreproachable." [20] It was the kind of toplofty remark which Byron always found ridiculous, and Libby had inherited his keen sense of irony. After Natthalie had repeated it once too many times, Libby could not resist commenting that she had better "avail herself of the opportunity of quitting me, as my life and past history were not such as she would wish." [21] Natthalie changed her tune hastily, thanked Mme. Aubin for her frankness, and assured her of her devotion. Nothing would have induced her to quit. Not only was she being offered the opportunity to go back to her own country, but her position was improved. She would function more as a companion than a lady's maid. Her husband Victor, also a servant, was out of a job at the moment and with a little maneuvering he might be given the position of courier. Behind this facade of deference and loyalty was a shrewd, calculating woman who was out to better herself and her husband with little compunction about the means of gaining her objective.

All through June Libby was beside herself with nerves. Every arrangement made by Lady Byron seemed, to Libby, to be "ingeniously painful," as if in an oblique way she was being reminded that she was not really her aunt's "very dear child" but a poor relation.[22] A case in point was the administration of the funds provided by Lady Byron, plus the amount. Lady Byron knew that the medical man, M. Carrel, had suggested the sum of a hundred and twenty pounds per annum as adequate to maintain Libby and Marie in Pontivy. Lady Byron upped it to a hundred and fifty and would also pay Natthalie's wages. Libby felt, and rightly as it turned out, that this sum would not be adequate for a resort on the Riviera and the maintanance of *two* adults and a child. Lady Lovelace privately agreed but had to watch her step with her mother. Libby stated flatly that she would try to find extra money from another source. It would be detrimental to her health and Marie's education to be forever fretting about paying debts. Lady Byron answered, "How can you imagine I will ever let you want either?" [23]

Far more "painful" to Libby's pride was Lady Byron's decision that Natthalie was to have full charge of all financial transactions. The sums would be sent direct to Mme. Beaureppaire who was to render an exact accounting of how the money was spent. It was a humiliating way to handle it and in the end it would backfire most unpleasantly for Annabella.

By the end of June Libby was in a paranoid state but no more so than Annabella. She had asked Mrs. Jameson to help her cope with the rampaging Mme. Aubin; Ada was also enlisted. Everyone who entered the house felt the inimical atmosphere which was blamed entirely on Libby. One friend of Annabella's, Mrs. Louisa Mary Barwell, spent a few days at Moore Place and was so astonished by Libby's rudeness and arrogant bearing, contrasting so markedly with the behavior which Libby had previously displayed, that she concluded the girl was insane.[24] Mrs. Jameson, however, had enough insight to say of Libby, "There is a wish to be and to do right, with an utter blindness to the right." [25]

Whenever things were too rough for Annabella, she behaved more like a migratory bird than a hen: she flew the coop, leaving others to take over. Her excuse was that she was too ill to live under the same roof with her niece. Undoubtedly she was suffering from nervous exhaustion brought on by tension, but once she quit the house and was flitting from one place to another, she continued to dictate her arrangements by letter. Mrs. Jameson was left in charge of the household, surely a

thankless job inasmuch as she had no authority to proceed without first consulting the lady of the manor. But busy as Mrs.
Jameson was with her work and anxiety over her beloved
father's long and terminal illness, she dropped whatever she
was doing to come to the aid of her friend.

The odd part of this domestic crisis was that, in their own
ways, Lady Byron and Libby still cared for one another. Now
that she was separated from her aunt, Libby calmed down
enough to have some perspective. There is a curious parallel in
her reactions and those of Byron after the bird had flown. He
had written tender letters to Kirkby Mallory, full of husbandly
devotion and fatherly pride, as if his wife had merely gone
home for a little visit and to show off the baby. Libby's letters
to Lady Byron concerning plans for her departure were couched
in the most affectionate terms, calling her "dearest Pip" and
showing the greatest anxiety for her aunt's health. As she explained in her autobiography: "I was anxious not to judge
hastily, but trusted that when Lady Byron's health improved
(she was ill) she would be more just and reasonable." [26]

Annabella's response disabused Libby of the idea that all
was forgotten and forgiven. On July 3 Lady Byron was stopping temporarily at Welwyn, where Ada had joined her for
a time to discuss the best way to expedite Libby's journey. In a
letter of that date to Libby, Lady Byron went over the decisions anent finances, making it clear that she might not have
limited herself to a set figure if Libby had been more cooperative. The next day she wrote again, and this letter clearly reveals the split in her personality which caused her so much
emotional pain, and by that same token, was so devastating to
the happiness of almost everyone who had the misfortune to
care deeply for her:

> Do you remember, dear E. that I asked you early in our
> acquaintance not to use affectionate expressions towards me?
> I then felt the possibility of a change in your feelings. You
> did not regard my request, and I suffered myself to believe
> that you had conquered the early impressions to my disad-

vantage which were made upon your mind and were able to love me.

But I ought not to have let me [*sic*] deceive yourself and me (much pain would then have been spared) and should not have accepted your expressions of entire confidence and affection. I will endeavour to forget them. It is enough for me to be your friend—I have never exacted anything in return.[27]

"Able to love me." "I have never exacted anything in return." Poor, bemused, unhappy Annabella.

While Ada was with her at Welwyn she read Libby's letters. Ada felt that E.'s answer to the one quoted above was quite acceptable.[28] Ada told her mother she had reached the conclusion that E. felt it only right for everyone, Lady Byron especially, to compensate her for not having received what was due her as Byron's daughter.[29] Ada could not have known of her mother's many assurances to Libby that she wished to maintain her according to her "rank in life." That phrase appears so often in regard to a number of people that it must have been of prime importance to Annabella.

Ada went on to Cambridge. In a letter to her mother from there, written July 8, she did hint that Hyères might be more expensive than Brittany, although she worded her hint in a way which would not give offense. All her letters to her mother about Libby were masterpieces of tact, but reading between the lines one gathers that she was not unsympathetic to Libby's cause. She was trying to be objective and, wherever possible, to lighten the prevailing gloom.

Libby was a good letter writer, and she did try to convince her aunt that she *was* grateful, that she *did* care deeply and was sorry for the way she had behaved. In all fairness, though, she did have a few grievances. Having fended for herself as best she could while in Brittany, she quite naturally resented having her future—and Marie's—discussed and arranged by Lady Byron and Ada, as if it were a foregone conclusion that she would be in accord with their decision.

Together or apart, Lady Byron and Libby were always at

cross-purposes. Libby could not forget that her aunt had once done all in her power to gain Libby's affection, had said it would cost her her life if they were to separate. Yet this same Annabella now wrote, "From some of your recent letters you have appeared to suppose . . . that I wished for *expressions* of affection. Far from it . . . I shall now dwell only on the many kindnesses I have received from you—or your patient and tender care in illness." [30] Attempting to atone for her past mistakes and to show gratitude for her aunt's protection, she received this response. "As for expenses . . . pray do not pain me by speaking of it . . . Trust my affection, but do not try to fancy that you have corresponding feelings toward me." [31]

Lady Byron went on to Cambridge. Ada returned to Ockham Park so that she and Lord Lovelace would be close enough to Moore Place to help with last-minute details and take some of the heat off Mrs. Jameson. Still, this did not prevent Annabella from issuing daily communiqués and advising Libby. In one letter she warned her not to go to any other source for extra money. [32]

Libby had dared to express a desire to go to France by way of Southampton to Le Havre and up the Seine to Rouen and Paris. She would have an opportunity to go through parts of the country she had not seen. Travelers in France often used the river boats as a welcome and relaxing mode of travel. Coaches and *diligences* were less comfortable and more expensive. Railways were operating in England, but not yet in France. But Lady Byron did not care for this idea; she wanted the entourage to embark from Dover. [33]

Lady Byron seemed to have forgotten that Dover and Calais were dismal memories to Libby, but the fact of the matter is that she did not want the girl to take any route which included Paris. She had been willing to condone her niece's involvement with Trevanion because of her youth and inexperience, but she was never convinced that E. L. had enough moral fiber to withstand temptation. And no city on earth offered more alluring ways to get into mischief. It simply would not do for E. L. to go there, it was up to Natthalie to use a firm hand. One of Natthalie's duties, in fact, was to serve as an espionage agent for Lady Byron and report any wanderings off the strait and narrow path.

Among Annabella's arrangements was one which would prove to be a costly mistake. Libby's drafts and receipts had to be in the same name as the one on her passport, which was Mme. Elizabeth Aubin. But to use a false name in any transaction with a bank was liable to a penalty. Annabella's lawyer Wharton suggested that the drafts be issued directed to Mme. Beaureppaire who would then give them to Libby. M. and Mme. Beaureppaire were, of course, delighted; Libby had no choice.

As the time of departure loomed closer, Libby had a few last things to attend to in London. While she was in town she had a shattering experience which she described with the utmost detail in a letter to Lady Byron. Byron wrote some of the best letters in the English language, many of which, after a century and a half, are as lively in style and timely in thought as to have been written yesterday. Ada inherited this wonderful gift of putting the essence of herself on paper. So did Elizabeth Medora Leigh in this masterpiece of unintended self-portraiture, written in the Lovelace house on St. James's Square before going back to Moore Place:

> If dearest Pip I began my letter with anything else than what occupies me at this moment you might attribute the natural constraint of my letter to other cause and I *know* you will sympathize at what I feel. I have this instant met my Mother. She was crossing the Square coming from York Street as the Carriage drove up to the door. I instantly recognized her—she is unchanged in face—and turned my head as if waiting for William who was ringing at the door. She could not have seen my face—my veil being down—and I saw her before she saw me—her sight and perceptions are not quick—and between the door being opened and my speaking to William, she had reached the Duke of Cleveland's before I got out—which I did quickly. She turned round and looked at the carriage—

for I observed her from the little back window—probabl
from curiosity or thinking it might be you. She was followe
by a dirty-looking rascally kind of servant out of livery who
was playing with his glove and she was dressed (*Augusta*) in
a dark brown kind of muslin gown with white pattern, a black
silk shawl with long fringe and gathered round her as if she
was afraid of losing it and a straw leghorn bonnet trimmed
with white satin ribbons. Her large eyes are ever and indeed
unchanged, her walk is most altered—she shuffles along as if
she tried to carry the ground she walks on with her and looks
WICKED. Oh, were there a thing I had hoped to be spared it
was this. If her curiosity were awakened it is lucky this took
place at Lord L's door—be sure she fears him. I was very
quietly dressed in my old dark silk gown black scarf and white
bonnet—and she did *not* see my *face,* and I well remember
how she never saw or knew anyone and always used to say no
one ever knew people or observed as quickly as me save 'poor
B'—and she used to rely on me for observation.

This has shocked me—pained me, but it is over. I have
drunk quantities of wine since, and now there is nothing left
for me to suffer that I dread. Oh how dearly fondly I loved
her, and had she only stifled the existence her sin gave me—
but God *is* there—and I will do my best to bear as I have ever
done but it is so long, so constant—God forgive her. Oh how
horrible she looked—so wicked—so hyena-like—That I could
have loved her so! Bear in mind one feeling the sight of her
has given me more strongly—If for my good or that of Marie
—intimidate her—she will grovel on the ground, fawn, lick
the dust—all—all that is despicable and bad. You she will not
fear, you personally—but Lord L. Dr. L. or Wharton. Now
we will try and never mention her name—she will live for
years. Oh could I only have loved the memory of my mother,
but had death passed over me the chill—the horror—could
not have been so great. Pity and forgive me if I involuntarily
pain, I do not mean—but I *do* suffer—.

Ada's visit gave me GREAT pleasure yesterday; tomorrow
the children come to me and Thursday she and Lord L. My
will is signed and most satisfactory to me and I hope to everyone hereafter. If climate does not do me good and I never
come back you will find all my letters and papers in order
and I feel that all I have done will satisfy you and not make
me a less dear child to you.

Dearest Pip, I have come up today early on purpose to get you a Daguerotype done of me—I have heard you say it would please you to have one—but the Sun is clouded over but you shall have one and as little ugly as possible. I do not contradict what you say about affection—time will best show you. I no more wish for a "farewell" than you—we have parted—if we meet not again here we shall only meet in happiness hereafter and if we *do* meet again as we *shall* and when I am happy and well—we shall not be the sadder for having had an agony less. My health is as ever bad and tiresome. I have had the little yellow smelling bottle you gave me filled with salts that are now become necessary to me and it never quits me. Oh only think I have a way you can constantly and when you like get parcels to me at Hyères—this will please you—Ada is delighted. I suppose I shall quit London Saturday for I cannot begin a journey Friday. Ada and me will consult about road. God bless you. I will be strong and get over all I cannot help feeling.

ever yr. affect. Child.[34]

Reading this letter one can only feel pity for poor Guss. She had brought much of it on herself, but there is something infinitely tragic about her standing there, her still beautiful myopic eyes squinting at the fine carriage. Did she have any inkling that her "beloved E." was inside peering through the rear window? Her worst enemy could not have wanted Augusta to suffer that final blow to what little remained of her pride. Even Lady Byron was deeply affected. In a letter to E. written July 21, she says: "I could not read of that meeting without great pain and yet I believe it best that you should see what *is*." [35]

Libby was not aware that her aunt was also in London, though not staying at the Lovelace townhouse. Quite often she went to a hotel while in the city. Also, she would not have wanted to run into Libby.[36] A few days earlier she had written to Libby that she dared not encounter the agitation of saying farewell, but that E. was nearer to her heart than ever. One can understand why Mrs. Jameson's sister referred to Lady Byron as "The Sphinx woman." [37] She was an enigma to her husband, to her daughter, her closest friends, even her mother. Libby had a kind of instinctive grasp of her aunt's complex emotional pattern because, in a bizarre way, they reacted in the same compulsive, irrational manner. The difference was that Annabella knew her mistakes but felt compelled to justify them; Libby said she was sorry and thought about something else.

After her hectic day in London, she returned to Esher, somewhat the worse for her unsettling experience and possibly too much wine. Mrs. Jameson was there, loaded with final instructions from Lady Byron who had also sent forty pounds in bank notes for travel expenses. Mrs. Jameson noticed that Libby seemed unusually agitated although glad to see her. After Libby explained what had happened in town, Mrs. Jameson was sympathetic, but time was running short and she had to deliver the messages from Lady Byron, along with the money.

The instructions brought on one of Libby's fits of rage; she berated Anna, her aunt, Natthalie (who had the misfortune to be in the room)—and at first she refused to accept the forty pounds. Bitterly she insisted that it wasn't enough for three adults and a child to travel from Surrey to the French Riviera. She was not going to deny herself all luxuries, no matter what her aunt wished. Finally her anger spent itself and she took the bank notes.

The evening before she was to leave, Ada arrived to bid her "sister" a last good-bye. Although she had been vexed by Libby's recalcitrance, she was sufficiently aware of her mother's ways to recognize that Libby was not solely at fault. She found her in a state of extreme tension, subject to fits of coldness and trembling. Libby was, of course, depressed and upset at the thought of leaving Ada and her husband, and her depression brought on an attack of self-pity which was as human as it was unfortunate. In one of Libby's tirades prior to Lady Byron's departure from Moore Place she had told her aunt that she might go to some other source for extra funds if the 150 pounds proved inadequate. Lady Byron warned her that she would not tolerate this—it was all or nothing from *her*. In one of her letters she had again reiterated that she was to be in full control of Libby's maintenance, and if Libby disobeyed it would annul the agreement.

This had continued to gall Libby and she said as much to Ada. "The last half hour I was there," Ada later wrote, ". . . I was compelled to hear a discourse on the bitterness of dependence and threats of throwing herself down the throat of the first man she could get hold of to marry . . . !'At least I should not depend on charity'—and then came all sorts of vituperations."

It was not the best way for Libby to behave to her "sister" on their last evening together, and probably she regretted the words the moment they were spoken. Fortunately, Ada was half-Byron too and when annoyed she spoke her mind in no uncertain terms. She did that evening, but she was understanding enough to sympathize with some of Libby's tribulations. Distorted they might have been, but occasionally something came out which Ada recognized as true. Had she been in Libby's position *she* would have been angry too.[38]

Inasmuch as Ada wrote this account of the farewell meeting to her mother, she had to word it without implying to her hypersensitive parent that she was on E.'s side in the controversy. Yet one senses that she defended her mother's actions more from filial duty than complete approval. Ada knew there was good in this highstrung, prideful creature just as Mrs. Jameson recognized the "desire to do right."

Libby proved it by her actions. At her aunt's request she had made her will, leaving all her letters and papers to Lady Byron. She always kept them in a strongbox because they were of vital importance to her, perhaps the only things of any value she did possess. They were written proof that Lord Byron was indeed her natural father; she mentioned this several times and so did other people. For that reason the strongbox never left her possession, but to prove that she believed in Lady Byron's assurances of affection and because she thought it would please her aunt, she turned over the box to Lady Byron's housekeeper, to be given to Annabella when she returned to Moore Place.

Natthalie, incidentally, had also urged her to do this, in case of her death, but in view of what was to happen, one wonders if it were part of a well-thought-out conspiracy on the part of the Beaureppaires.[39]

The one paper Libby retained was the Deed. But at six that last evening, when Ada was about to leave, Libby suddenly handed her the precious Deed "to be deposited with Lord Lovelace's papers at Ockham." [40] It was one of her impulsive gestures of trust in the integrity of her benefactors which shows the other side of her nature. It was, alas, this eagerness to show gratitude (which she was always accused of withholding) that would eventually cause her much distress.

Next morning, July 22, she set forth on her journey, accompanied by Marie and the Beaureppaires. In spite of the Byron superstitions which had been instilled in her from childhood, Libby tempted Fate. She began her journey on a Friday.

I 4

'Whom the gods love die young,' was said of yore,
And many deaths do they escape by this:
The death of friends, and that which slays even more—
The death of friendship, love, youth, all that is.

—DON JUAN

ALTHOUGH LADY BYRON HAD NOT WANTED LIBBY AND HER party to take the Southampton-Le Havre-Paris route, they took it anyway. According to a later conversation between Natthalie and Lady Byron, Mme. Aubin had met a French officer whom she wished to marry and arranged to meet him again in Paris. The gentleman was delighted to oblige Madame, but his intentions proved to be entirely dishonorable. That put a quick end to the romance. Lady Byron was surprised to learn that Libby was much more interested in marriage than she was in misbehavior.[1] And this despite what Ada had told her about E.'s determination to find a husband.

Libby makes no mention of this fiasco; probably a woman who has more than her share of success in attracting men does not like to recall the ones who get away. In her autobiography she was more concerned with the pecuniary troubles confronting her. They tried to travel as expeditiously as they could, but by the time they reached Lyons there was not enough money to pay the boat fares which would take them down the Rhône to the Mediterranean. They had a three-day wait while arranging with the bankers to obtain the requisite thirty-seven pounds. When they reached Hyères they were again without funds. Libby had been right in saying that forty pounds would not be adequate for the entire journey, but after writing to Lady Byron, and Natthalie doing the same, more funds were sent which straightened them out temporarily.

Hyères was attractive, typical of a Riviera resort town of the period, with avenues of palatial hotels occupied by tourists and semi-invalids, many of whom were there on a permanent basis. The bath chairs being pushed along the palm-lined promenade were unpleasant reminders of Libby's past, but the summer heat was good for her chest condition. The town was situated on the southern slope of a hill, sheltered from the mistral, though its effects could be seen offshore. The sea inshore could be a brilliant blue while less than a league out one could see the whitecaps and the sails of ships scudding before the wind.

In the valley of the Gapeau, between Hyères and Toulon, were groves of gray-green olive trees and the darker green of cherry trees. The fruit grown there was always the first to appear in the markets of Paris, therefore expensive and not for the poor. Libby had eaten her fill of cherries when she was in Paris with Lady Byron, and bowls of them appeared on the tables of the well-to-do in England. Occasionally she and Marie, accompanied by Natthalie or Victor, would go for an afternoon drive along the coastal road in this charming little valley with the distant range of the Maures on one side and the sea on the other. The luxury of a carriage was only possible when Lady Byron included money earmarked for that purpose. For a few weeks all was peaceful and reasonably serene between benefactress and protégé except that the entourage was always "without money, from all being spent and much owing before any more arrived." [2]

Still, Libby was able to write to her benefactress that she was happy to be back in France. She received an answer from Lady Byron, who said among other things,

"You are happy in the fancied emancipation from fancied chains. Go, and buy experience." Before writing this, Lady Byron had read Ada's account of her last meeting with Elizabeth. By the time Libby had gone to France, Ada had reached a point where she had a better perspective on those last hectic weeks. "I can't help laughing after all." [3]

By now Natthalie had turned over the handling of the finances to her husband, and Victor assured Libby that he was rendering full accounts to Lady Byron of all monies spent. For a while Annabella seemed anxious to make things as agreeable as possible for Libby; she directed her to "get masters for Marie's education" and sent many books to occupy her niece's leisure hours.[4] "She engaged to neglect no expense for my health," Libby wrote, and included money to "hire carriages etc. for my driving out." [5]

Not long after settling in Hyères, Libby was fortunate enough to make a friend who would, in his own way, be as kind in time of need as was M. Carrel. He was Captain Joseph Barrallier, aged fifty-six, of the 71st Regiment of Foot, who had been wounded in the Battle of Waterloo, after which he was awarded the Waterloo Medal. He was placed on half pay until he was able to return to active service with the 37th Regiment of Foot. In 1826 he retired and sold his commission.[6] Since then he had spent much time in the South of France. He met Libby as Mme. Elizabeth Aubin, and until much later he knew nothing of her lurid past. It is possible, however, that he learned she was the daughter of Colonel George Leigh of the 10th Hussars who had once been equerry to the Prince Regent. News got around in that interlocking community composed of career officers in both branches of His Majesty's (now Her Majesty's) armed forces.

The gallant Captain would have found interests in common with the charming English-born Mme. Aubin who had been brought up in the household of a career officer. Captain Barrallier had seen active duty in the Peninsular War; so had Colonel Leigh. The Colonel's father had been a general and his mother was the daughter of an admiral so there was no question of his fitness for being given a commission. Barrallier's father had been assistant surveyor of the Navy at Milford (now Milford Haven).

The Barralliers were eminently respectable people with enough means to live nicely, though the purchase of the coveted commission seemed to have represented a certain sacrifice. Joseph's sponsor asked that "the Appointment should be made to a Regiment going abroad, to save the expense to the parents of a young man in a Regiment at home."[7] He was twenty two when commissioned; prior to that he was educated by his father and served an apprenticeship in the dockyard. Apparently the father had social ambitions for his son which would be greatly enhanced by securing the commission.

In that day the phrase "an officer and a gentleman" meant just that. A young man of good but not noble family who wished to be accepted into Society had a choice of three professions open to him.[8] He could try to become a commissioned officer in one of the armed forces, a clergyman (Church of England), or a lawyer (in that order of preference). It would be a number of years before "medical men" made it up the social ladder. Ridiculous as this seems today, it was a matter of deep concern in the nineteenth century. Captain Barrallier was a kindly, sensitive man of impeccable manners, but without his rank there would have been a problem in bridging the social gap between himself and Mme. Aubin.

Although Libby was more than circumspect in her conversations with Barrallier, she had been indiscreet with Natthalie and Victor, by confiding to them the details of her birth and past. It was an understandable mistake; they were constantly reassuring her that nothing could destroy their devotion and she was more than willing to believe them. For a young woman who was thought in certain quarters to be a ruthless adventuress, she was naive and gullible to an extraordinary degree. The Beaureppaires, alas, were not like M. Carrel or the Captain, but they had succeeded in winning Libby's confidence and she thought of them as friends more than servants.

Letters of affection on both sides continued to pass between Libby and Lady Byron—extra pounds were sent for carriages and schoolmasters—but by the end of summer disturbing signs of growing dissatisfaction were emanating from Esher. The lodgings in Hyères were too expensive; Libby et al. would have to find a cheaper place. It was always unwise to dispute any of Lady Byron's changes of mind, so they looked around for new quarters. They found a country house between Toulon and Hyères which seemed to be in the right price range. Lady Byron appeared to approve, so by November they were settled in the new abode. Toulon was eleven miles from Hyères and not noted for its residential appeal, which accounted for cheaper rent. It was a busy seaport and naval base with a large shipyard, of warlike aspect and bristling with cannon. The city was also known and dreaded as a penal colony; the prisoners were quartered in old rotting hulks, filthy and overcrowded, which had once been galleys.

Libby and the Beaureppaires did try to cooperate, but in less than a month came a letter again complaining about the rent. Libby turned to Victor in this new crisis; he was handling the finances. He enlisted the aid of Captain Barrallier and the mayor of Hyères who both certified that the rent was not unreasonable. This seemed to appease Lady Byron, but in December she reproached Libby for "rendering all the money arrangements as vexacious as possible for her." [9] In addition she

> exacted receipts from me of all the sums that had been paid, saying that I had received them in the name of my maid. I wrote briefly back, regretting only that she could say or think what was so far from being true.[10]

On the advice of the bankers Libby refused to sign the receipt. They informed her "that it was paid by Lady Noel Byron's orders . . . She informed me of the necessity of having that signature to answer the malicious interpretation her conduct, from peculiar circumstances, might be guilty of toward me, and which my signature alone could answer." [11]

What malicious interpretation did she refer to and by whom? She could have been thinking of possible repercussions from Augusta Leigh and her family. Back in October Lady Wilmot-Horton had written to Lady Byron about E. L. who, being her godchild, was always of special interest. In the letter she brought up Mrs. Leigh. Apparently Augusta had been indulging in some breast-beating.[12] Lady Wilmot-Horton asked if she could pass on enough information to Mrs. Leigh so that her mind would be at rest. Annabella answered that Augusta could be told, though not as a message from her, that her daughter was living in circumstances of comfort and peace which might prolong her life. However, Elizabeth feared the inevitable turmmoil that would result if her mother were apprised of her residence and for that reason Augusta could not be told the whereabouts of her "dearest child." [13]

It was a perfectly logical explanation, and doubtless a true one up to a point, for Annabella knew from experience that there was no such thing as logical behavior with the Leighs. No one could be sure that E.'s love for her mother had been irrevocably destroyed by her disillusioning experience in London. If Augusta *were* able to correspond with her daughter, and if her letters were anything like the tender effusions sent to Pontivy, it was possible that the estrangement would be patched up. This was a contingency to be avoided at any cost. As already noted, Annabella wanted no interference from anyone in the arrangements connected with Libby; she guarded that tenuous hold on her niece with jealous zeal. Tragically for her she was still obsessed with that wild and wayward being who first beguiled and then bedeviled her as only one with Byron blood seemed able to do. Yet at the same time she continued to do things and make demands which seemed deliberately calculated to make trouble for herself.

As an example, she accused Libby of not staying within the set figure of a hundred and fifty per anum, although she had insisted on Mme. Beaureppaire being in charge of the finances. She knew, moreover, that Victor had taken over the bookkeeping—they were in frequent correspondence on these matters—and yet, to Libby, she was always writing that Victor "had to go." [14] But she withheld his salary so that, even if he were willing to leave, he had no means of going. At least this was the excuse Victor gave to Mme. Aubin, although he and Natthalie had no intention of leaving. They had latched on to a good thing and hoped to make it better. Reluctantly, Lady Byron did pay Victor the wages due him.

When Libby refused to acknowledge the receipts of all sums sent to her maid, Lady Byron retaliated by not sending the six hundred francs for the rent which was due December 20. Neither did she send the twenty pounds for Marie's education which she had agreed to do. Rather than cause a ruckus with the landlord, and the ménage being without funds, Victor paid the rent out of his salary. Libby had no choice but to send her aunt the requested acknowledgement for all monies received, none of which had passed through her hands.[15]

In answer to that letter Lady Byron wrote to Libby that she would not pay Victor any more money after January first, and Libby was to tell him so. Victor's reaction was to shrug it off with a laugh; if Lady Byron wanted him to go she would have to write to him direct. As a sop to Libby's amour propre, he swore that, rather than leave her and his wife to suffer alone in their precarious condition, he would stay on for nothing.[16]

Lady Byron did not send the money for Marie's education but did send "expressions of affection" [17] which, alas, did not pay the butcher, the baker, and the greengrocer. Clearly it was not going to be possible to stay within the amount of a hundred and fifty per annum, although there is no way of finding out exactly what Victor and Natthalie were doing with the money. Libby stated somewhat ambiguously that "I never saw the letters that passed from her [Lady Byron] to him [Victor], and having no control whatever over the money paid for my maintenance, never having clearly understood its application, cannot explain it." [18]

Judging by later developments it is likely that the Beaureppaires may have padded the expense accounts or juggled them in some way to line their own pockets. And Libby, assuaged by their constant assurances of unswerving loyalty and harassed by her aunt's oft-repeated accusations of extravagance, was fair game for the machinations of this adroit pair. Natthalie was especially clever at playing one side against the other. She was fulfilling her task as Lady Byron's spy, keeping her posted on all Mme. Aubin's activities, while at the same time she was running down her employer to Libby at every opportunity. Lady Byron, of course, had contributed to this by antagonizing Natthalie when she insisted that Victor "had to go."

During January and February, 1843, Libby was pulled in all directions. To her servants she was a valuable pawn and they took care to keep her on their side. She had never liked the country house outside Toulon; neither did the Beaureppaires. It was isolated, unattractive, and dull. All three loved Paris and longed to be there, but the lady who held the purse strings had made her position clear. Go to Paris and risk losing her protection. It is a thorny task to wend one's way through the labyrinth of conflicting statements and justifications stemming from Libby's Autobiography and Lady Byron's letters, in order to reach a conclusion as to who was or was not at fault in the ensuing crisis.

It does appear, however, that the influence of the Beaureppaires was largely responsible for what would prove to be the turning point in Elizabeth Medora's life. But as often happens, the events which precipitate a turning point are seldom recognized for what they are until long afterwards. Suffice it to say that, around the end of February, Victor and Natthalie had convinced Mme. Aubin that she could never reach a satisfactory and equable financial arrangement with Lady Byron; that she was at the mercy of a wily woman who could not be depended upon to abide by *any* agreement. In Paris Libby would be able to find "a more certain and suitable arrangement," [19] and the Beaureppaires would help her. Victor was willing to pay for the journey out of his own pocket and would gladly wait for repayment. By now they both knew how best to deal with Mme. Aubin, how to placate her when angry, soothe her when distressed, flatter her unceasingly, and make her feel that they, alone, were entirely on her side. Still, Libby must have felt an obscure guilt about disobeying her aunt—she was much too virtuous in her self-justification—but it did not prevent her from going ahead. On March 5 she wrote to Lady Byron that she was on the point of leaving for Paris "for reasons of which Lady Noel Byron could not be ignorant." [20]

Lady Noel Byron, meanwhile, had become greatly upset by the recent lack of letters from Toulon, and on March 6 she wrote to this effect:

> Many an anxious hour, and under severe illness, have you of late cost me. . . . When I recollect your birthday last year am I to believe that your tears and your tenderness were feigned? I *cannot* do so. I must first hear from yourself that you were playing on my affection.[21]

In this tragicomedy of errors, the letters crossed in the mail, and to compound misfortune, Libby's explanatory note was lost en route. It would be interesting to know how many thousands of misunderstandings have been due to lost, strayed, or stolen letters. Whether or not Libby's explanation would have healed the breach will never be known. What *is* known is that nine days passed with each side wondering why the other did not answer, a mischance which added more fuel to an already smoldering fire.

Finally Annabella was to learn from her friend Selina Doyle, in Paris, that Elizabeth and her ménage were in that city and had got in touch with Selina and her sister Adelaide. Annabella answered "I am not surprised . . . And as to my pounds, they will only follow many others into the vortex of that family.[22]

Notwithstanding this indirect warning, the Doyle sisters were to play important roles in the next act of this drama.

15

Thus far have I proceeded in a theme
Renew'd with no kind auspices:—to feel
We are not what we have been, and to deem
We are not what we should be, and to steel
The heart against itself.

—CHILDE HAROLD'S PILGRIMAGE

SELINA AND ADELAIDE DOYLE WERE THE UNMARRIED SISTERS of Colonel Francis Hastings Doyle, a longtime friend of Annabella's parents.[1] Following the usual pattern, Selina had first been a friend of Lady Noel before her close relationship with the daughter, Annabella. She had been on the sidelines during Annabella's first season in London and the subsequent romantic involvement with Byron and had commiserated with the distraught bride during her hectic year of marriage. After the separation, while Annabella languished at Kirkby Mallory, Selina was a frequent guest at 13 Piccadilly Terrace and reported what she saw and heard to her unhappy friend.

Byron was too wrapped up in his own troubles to pay much heed to guests or care what he said in their presence, but Augusta suspected Selina's protestations of friendly sympathy. In fact, she had never felt much rapport with a number of her sister-in-law's cronies, and that included the Doyles.[2] The lack of empathy was mutual; none of them wanted Annabella to be reconciled with her husband.

Adelaide, though on cordial enough terms with Annabella,

was never as close to her as Selina. They had both seen Elizabeth Medora in Paris and Esher, when she was on her best behavior and recalled Libby's humility and penitential attitude. She "*had* been better when they first met." [3] These are not traits one would ordinarily think of in connection with Elizabeth Medora Leigh nor would most people consider such characteristics outstandingly attractive or interesting. It is a depressing commentary on the attitude of mind which seemed to prevail in Lady Byron's circle. As long as Libby remained abjectly grateful and self-abasing in the presence of her protectress, she was admirable, but when she had the audacity to assert herself or display pride, she was accused of arrogance or base ingratitude.

The Doyles were away during the explosive period and had not been informed of what happened at Moore Place. Therefore they were kindly disposed toward Mme. Aubin when she wrote them on her arrival in Paris. This was before they received Annabella's warning. Libby and her party settled in a hotel; the "hotel manager" was delighted to welcome them and extend them temporary credit, a connection with the rich Lady Noel Byron being all the security needed.[4] It should be clarified here that Libby would have had nothing to do with arranging hotel accommodations. That was the job of the courier (Victor in this case), who saw to all financial transactions connected with lodgings and traveling. In that day people of wealth or rank were not expected to take any interest in such matters; they had personal servants to handle money, fetch and carry, act as bodyguards, attend to every kind of task which was felt to be menial. Even the impecunious Mrs. Leigh had a rascally flunky trailing at her heels when she ventured to walk outside. It would never have occurred to Libby to keep an eye on Victor and Natthalie; it would have offended their pride, and besides, she believed in their honesty and loyalty.

It was wonderful to be back in her beloved Paris, but with no letter forthcoming from Lady Byron, and funds dwindling at an uncomfortable rate, Libby became alarmed and wrote again to Moore Place. Lady Byron answered immediately. She had received no letter from Toulon about going to Paris and asked what justified this extraordinary step. By then Libby had made contact with Selina and Adelaide. What she had to say about the deterioration of the relationship with her aunt was a great shock to the two ladies. Selina, a loyal friend to Annabella and no friend to Augusta, was not going to accept the word of Augusta's daughter until she heard Lady Byron's side of the story. Adelaide was less insulated to the Byron charm and became Libby's champion.

Selina's letter reached Annabella while she was paying a visit at Ockham Park. Selina reported Libby's conversation in full and asked Annabella to tell what actually had transpired. Selina received two letters in a row, written March 21 and 22. In the first, Lady Byron maintained that she had acted with affection and forbearance throughout, but she also felt she had been "a Cats-Paw to pull the Deed out of the fire—and when I had served the purpose, I was to be turned adrift." [5] The following day she wrote, among other things:

> Adversity is her best friend—and she cannot bear kindness,—at least unless sparingly administered—such is the inevitable result of long servitude. . . . The Slave is not fit for perfect freedom. [6]

That is an extraordinary statement to come from a woman who was involved heart and soul with the abolition of slavery. Her friend Fanny Kemble Butler, back in London and estranged from her American husband, was also an ardent champion of the antislavery cause which was having great exposure in London drawing rooms. Inasmuch as Pierce Butler was a Southern plantation owner who kept several hundred slaves, one can understand why the marriage had fallen apart. So much so in fact, that he succeeded in taking Fanny's children away from her at the time of the divorce, certainly a powerful reason for her passionate involvement with the Married Women's Property Act, which was also one of Anna Jameson's pet causes.

Lady Byron was embroiled in these causes, too, but the more one knows of her magnanimous generosity and manifold charitable activities, the more one has to conclude that she did not possess much generosity of spirit.

When Fanny Kemble first met Annabella, several years earlier, she heard her say that "to treat men as if they were better than they are, is the surest way to *make* them better than they are." [7] It was not an original comment with Annabella, but the youthful Fanny was greatly impressed. After she had been through her own period of travail and heartache, she saw Lady Byron in a more realistic light, as "a woman of profound and fervid enthusiasm, with a mind of rather romantic and visionary order." [8] Annabella may have thought she was treating people as if they were better than they were, but her actions in some cases do not give that impression.

From her standpoint, however, she did have a valid reason for withdrawing her protection from Libby and the Beaureppaires. They, in turn, should have realized the risk they were taking; they knew how implacable she could be when her demands were not met. Lady Byron wrote to the hotel master, explaining that Madame Aubin and the Beaureppaires were using her credit without her permission—"Which I had never done," wrote Libby, "and telling him all she could of the past history of my life that could be unfavorable and painful." [9]

Yet Annabella was outraged on learning from Selina that E. L. was confiding the secret of her birth to one or two people. And worse, far worse, was the fact that Adelaide was listening with a sympathetic ear to the Beaureppaires' tale of woe. Lady Byron was portrayed as a cold-hearted, tight-fisted ogress who had abandoned poor Madame Aubin and her child to the mercy of her servants and had also made trouble for them with the hotel master. That irate gentleman demanded immediate payment of the hotel bill after which they were requested to vacate the premises. [10] Despite Selina's disapproval, Adelaide gave Victor the money for the hotel bill and saw to it that the ménage found other lodgings on the grounds of her destitution. [11]

Again, it must be understood that these financial transactions were the responsibility of Victor, not Libby, though she was the one to be blamed.

While all this was happening in Paris, Annabella was unburdening her soul to her daughter and Lord Lovelace. Although Ada's health was not good she managed to fulfill the social obligations of a peeress and still have time for the project closest to her heart: Charles Babbage's "analytical engine." In the spring of 1843 Ada was hard at work with her "dear Babbage," but being a dutiful daughter she had to give her attention and far too much of her nervous energy to the tribulations of her mother. It was not easy for Ada to harden her heart against Elizabeth merely because of her mother's change of mind. Like her father, she was a steadfast friend. At first Ada had welcomed Libby as a sister because Lady Byron wished it, but as time went on she became genuinely glad to accept her as a member of the family. Notwithstanding the bitterness now existing between Lady Byron and her protégé, Ada still felt that certain of her mother's arrangements had not been quite fair. It was unthinkable to Annabella that her opinions could be questioned, certainly not by her own child.

She blamed Libby for everything that had gone awry, and she was able to back up her assertions in a tangible way which could not be denied. She showed the Lovelaces receipts for sums spent or given to Elizabeth at different times, including gifts and other gestures of kindness, and finally she succeeded in convincing them of her rightness. Annabella may have been desultory in her way of living, but anything that was grist to her mill—letters, documents, receipts for the most trivial items —she saved. The Lovelace papers represent a lifetime of saving on her part, especially of papers pertaining to her first meeting, courtship, marriage and separation from Byron. She claimed that she had saved this huge mass of material in order to have ammunition to fight Byron if he should try to claim custody of his daughter Ada. Before the first Married Women's Property Act in 1882, a man could legally take his children away from their mother, as was the case with Pierce Butler and Fanny Kemble Butler. Annabella had no real grounds for suspecting that Byron intended doing such a thing, but when he wrote to Augusta about returning to England, Annabella was loud in her fear that he might make trouble over Ada, though she knew (since she read his letters to Augusta) that he was returning to see her, the woman who still held first place in his heart. Annabella quashed that plan; she was not going to permit brother and sister to meet again on this earth if she could prevent it. Now years later, she was determined to put an end to Ada's fondness for Elizabeth Medora. Although she had gone to great lengths to bring their friendship about, she had such an inflexible belief in her *rightness* that she found nothing odd in performing a complete about-face.

This does not mean that Ada could have been induced to turn against Elizabeth if she was fully convinced that her "sister" was in the right, and her mother wrong. In her own way, Ada could be as unbending as her mother, and as quick to take umbrage as her father. When she became exasperated enough, she did have a certain amount of the well-known Byron temper. She wrote some very peppery letters to her beloved Babbage when he made a few changes in her notes and papers dealing with his "analytical engine."[12] He made allowances because she was a novice, and because she was a devoted disciple, that was not to be taken lightly when the disciple was Byron's daughter and the Countess of Lovelace.

The truth was that Ada did have certain reservations about Elizabeth, though she would probably have kept them to herself if she had not been prodded by her mother. When she first met Libby in Paris she could not fail to notice how impressed the girl had been by Ada's and her husband's polite assurance, charm, and unassuming ways—hallmarks of the true aristocrat which Libby knew well. It was marvelous for Libby to discover that Ada wanted her to consider herself as a sister. Ada was aware of this homage—so was William—but they were people who gave their friendship with no strings attached.

Then, in Esher, Ada saw the subtle change in Elizabeth.

She was beginning to accept the improvement in her life style as if it were her due; she was no longer content to sit in Lady Byron's shadow; she was not satisfied with occasional donations of money from her aunt; she wanted a definite allowance to spend as she pleased. Ada had not been told that, in the first weeks of infatuation, her mother had promised Elizabeth the moon and the stars, and had later reneged on the promise of a set allowance. Lady Byron had a long memory for facts she wanted to remember, but she tended to forget about things she had not done which she ought to have done. Ada knew that some of her mother's friends had a low opinion of Annabelle's taking Augusta Leigh's daughter under her protection. It was a breach of good taste to permit Lady Lovelace to become friendly with a girl who had lived in sin with her brother-in-law, a girl, moreover, who had been born as the result of incest. Such a creature was unworthy of notice (though a few friends conceded that with such a heritage, Libby's scandalous behavior was only to be expected).

Ada was in no doubt about Elizabeth's paternity. At first she had a doubt or two, "Mrs. L. being married at the time," [13] but there were many aristocratic ladies who became pregnant by a lover and quickly hopped into bed with their husbands so there would be no embarrassing counting of fingers when the child was born. Augusta had had no sexual relations with her husband during her passion for Byron.

Therefore, Ada dashed off a letter to Paris which so perfectly expressed her mother's thoughts and reactions that unconsciously she may have parroted some of Lady Byron's statements. Ada said, in essence, all she thought and felt. It contains, in painful detail, some facets of Ada's character, deeply imbedded in her subconscious, which she would have denied indignantly. The inbred snobbery versus the principle of *noblesse oblige,* the condescension she reveals in treating Elizabeth as her social equal when in reality, she was a nobody—are all there. Yet at the end she betrays the lingering hope that Elizabeth will see the light and redeem herself.[14]

How this letter must have galled Libby's pride. It was

tantamount to saying that Libby should be thankful not to have been treated like a second-class citizen by Lady Byron's coterie, including Lord and Lady Lovelace. Could Libby not have thought: she and I had the same father? Was it *my* fault that I am the result of an incestuous love? Do I not have aristocratic connections on my mother's side, some of them more exalted than Ada's? To be reminded that she was a bastard did nothing to sweeten a temper already soured by her best friend, Adversity.

From then on, through defiance, revenge, or false pride, Libby no longer tried to hide the "secret" of her birth. She let it be known that Lady Byron had told her at Fontainebleau that her real reason for taking her (Libby) under her protection was that Lord Byron had been her father. Selina had not known of this and reported it to Annabella.

Annabella responded with a lengthy explanation as to her reasons for confiding "the secret" to Elizabeth. "The serpent-race will finish my life as they have actually shortened it." [15] Yet she could not cut herself free. Libby's birthday, April 14, was close, and Annabella thought back on the same day a year earlier. Libby had been full of gratitude and sweetness. "I must first hear from yourself that you were playing on my affection," she wrote, "Tell me what I am to think . . ." [16] This from the woman who had reprimanded Libby for expressions of affection.

As can be imagined, all this served to whet Selina's indignation to razor edge. She was amazed that Annabella and her sister Adelaide could have been taken in by Elizabeth's flair for dramatizing herself. [17] She had been told by Natthalie and Victor that Lady Byron had written letters to them, accusing them of having encouraged the move from Toulon and upbraiding Natthalie for not fulfilling her duties as a spy. Lady Byron had also ordered them to leave Mme. Aubin and Marie to their own resources. Adelaide was shocked at the idea of casting Elizabeth and her child adrift in a foreign city. The Beaureppaires also made sure that Libby was acquainted with all that passed between them and Lady Byron, but they assured her not to be alarmed for they would never abandon her.

The one trait in Libby's character which Lady Byron could not quarrel with was her devotion to Marie. Selina had written that Libby was in a great taking about Trevanion, terrified that he might try to take the child from her by some legal maneuver, now that she was not living with Lady Byron. Selina felt it was one more example of E.'s overdramatizing, but Annabella knew that Libby's love for Marie was as fierce and protective as hers had been for *her* only daughter. She knew, too, that Libby did fear that Henry might try to take Marie from her. Irrational perhaps—but so had Annabella been about Byron's taking Ada.[18]

Alas for Libby, the constant prodding from Selina and reproaches from Annabella began to erode Adelaide's stubborn loyalty. Natthalie and Victor were no help either. They were artful enough but a bit too eager to request funds from their new Lady Bountiful. Libby was also to blame for Adelaide's drawing away. Having found a shoulder to weep on, she made the mistake of overdoing it. Eventually Adelaide wondered if she *was* being used after all, and once suspicion enters the door, trust flies out of the window.

With no word from Lady Byron—and no money—the Beaureppaires hit upon an audacious idea. Why not enlist the aid of someone sufficiently important to convince Lady Byron that she was behaving in an unjust manner? They urged Libby to present her case to one of the most renowned and successful advocates in France: M. Antoine Berryer.

Berryer had made a name for himself as a defender of the Bonapartists at a time when the Bourbons had returned to power and any adherents of the former leader were in danger of their lives. From the start he fought for what he believed in regardless of politics.

In 1843, aged forty-seven, this espouser of unpopular causes was at the height of his success socially and professionally, but he always found time to listen to someone in trouble. An interview was arranged between him and Mme. Elizabeth Aubin.

He was impressed by the tall, slender young Englishwoman with her dark eyes and vivacious manner, and her unmistakable air of breeding. By this time Libby knew how to tell her story to create the best impression. M. Berryer, though a busy lawyer, was not impervious to the *douceur* of an attractive female and listened attentively to what she had to say. In fact, he encouraged her to tell him all, good or bad. He was amazed to learn that she was the natural daughter of Lord Byron, the famed English poet and—more important—a loyal supporter of Napoleon. M. Berryer was more than willing to do what he could to induce Byron's widow to pursue a more lenient course with Mme. Aubin, or Mlle. Leigh, which he now called her. He promised to write at once to Lady Noel Byron and was positive that he would succeed where others had failed. Greatly encouraged, Libby returned to her lodgings to await developments. This was in late April.

For some reason, Berryer did not sit down immediately to write to Lady Byron—and after a few days of nail biting, Libby wrote again to her aunt in a last effort to explain the move to Paris. The only response was a visit from Miss Davison, one of the innumerable maiden ladies who seemed to be always in orbit around Lady Byron. Probably through Selina, Miss Davison was delegated to call on the recalcitrant Elizabeth and inform her that she must beg Lady Byron's pardon and give her firm assurances of affection. Until that was done, Libby could expect nothing. Libby complied—she had no choice—but it brought no answer. The Beaureppaires wrote, M. Berryer wrote —silence reigned across the Channel.

They could not know that things had been coming to a head at Moore Place. Following her usual pattern, Annabella had reached the conclusion that her niece was mad, or if not actually insane, guilty of murderous behavior.[19] In a letter anent this to Selina, Annabella wrote that her cousin Robert Noel, a phrenologist by avocation, had once, after subjecting Libby to a phrenological analysis, concluded that her bumps showed a severe destructive tendency. Of course Libby had benevolent bumps too.[20]

For some time phrenology had been the rage in England. From 1832 until 1847 there were twenty-nine phrenological societies flourishing in England alone and as many journals and quarterlies. Everyone was feeling everyone else's head and drawing conclusions; Robert Noel was one of the leading exponents. While Libby was at Moore Place there had been meetings and dinner parties given over to this quasi-parlor entertainment. Annabella was one of that science's most ardent supporters; she liked nothing better than to lecture her young friends on the subject. The Augustus De Morgans were frequent guests and noticed that Lady Byron's philanthropic friends all had one thing in common—their heads were "high in front and at the top." [21] It must have been disconcerting for Libby to sit at the table with these high-domed doers of good—her forehead was on the low side.

Once Annabella had committed herself to the idea that E. might be insane, she thought of Dr. William King. He was formerly Ada's tutor and had become a friend of Lady Byron's with whom he corresponded often. She turned to him for advice on this matter because he was a physician at the Brighton Hospital, also proprietor of a lunatic asylum in Sussex. [22] It was Annabella's notion that Dr. King should go at once to Paris, see Elizabeth, and draw some conclusions about the state of her brain cells. As she explained, Elizabeth was "one whose cradle I had watched with peculiar feelings—(she is a year older than Ada) . . . but the 'law of love' is not for characters in such a state." [23]

She had not yet told him "the secret," but in a letter to him, written May 1, she mentioned that

I have felt that there is a process going on for the disclosure of some truths long hidden, which it may not be in the power of any of us to prevent or retard. You will say why attempt to suppress truth? . . . But there would be affliction to some, and ruin to others in the publication. [24]

She gave him a certificate, in case it was needed, attesting that Mme. Aubin was in reality Miss Elizabeth Leigh, daughter of the Honorable Mrs. Leigh, wife of Colonel Leigh.

Dr. King must have been mystified by these obscure references to "truths long hidden," but armed with Lady Byron's authority to propose certain demands in return for her protection, he set off for Paris. On a Sunday afternoon early in May, Natthalie announced to Mme. Aubin that Dr. King had come to call, at the request of Lady Byron. Libby told her to inform the gentleman that any communication must be made to M. Berryer, acting as her advocate. She assumed that the call was the result of M. Berryer's letter to her aunt.

In regard to letters, Fate was always unkind to Libby. Berryer had written the letter, but somehow it had not been mailed. Full of contrition he met with Dr. King, and after a discussion with him he wrote a second letter to Lady Byron, and one can be sure that he made certain it was posted. In this letter he explained that Mlle. Leigh had told him the full circumstances of her birth and life with Trevanion, and he was fully satisfied that she told the truth. He went on to say, as gracefully as possible, that one hundred and fifty pounds was absolutely insufficient, and not because of any undue extravagance on Mlle. Leigh's part. She wished only for a modest life, the life of a mother whose chief concern was her child. He implored Lady Byron to relax the severity of her conditions which, he felt certain, must have been advised by Dr. King. He hoped that she would allow Mlle. Leigh to live where she chose rather than in some isolated community. In addition he thought that the mother should control the future of her own child.

While the letter was en route, Dr. King made a second effort to see Libby. He was still smarting from the cavalier treatment he received on Sunday and sent in a peremptory message: Libby was to resign all control of herself and Marie to Lady Byron. Only after she agreed to this would there be a discussion of finances. Furthermore he warned her that he was taking no more nonsense and would give her forty-eight hours to make up her mind, after which he would leave Paris for good.

Libby's dander was up; she replied through Natthalie that he might go whenever he wished—she would never agree to such restraint. By this time neither of them was in a mood to discuss anything, but Berryer was a skilled mediator. Ruffled feelings were smoothed down enough so that on the following Wednesday a meeting did take place.

At first Dr. King was in a conciliatory mood, went out of his way to be friendly to the Beaureppaires, made a fuss over Marie, and flattered Libby so that he could win her confidence. According to her, though, he was polite to the Beaureppaires when they were present but when they left the room he ran them down. At no time was Libby won over to him. She knew about his long friendship with Lady Byron and suspected that he was not acting in good faith. After much discussion he offered her three hundred a year (which was the sum agreed upon with Berryer), but the offer was subject to the same rigid conditions she had already refused. Tempers grew ragged. Dr. King became overbearing; Libby became insolent. "I submitted to all the abuse he was pleased to bestow," she wrote, "though it contributed all the more to make me refuse when he said 'Sign—sign—you great fool.' " He was ushered to the door without delay.[25]

Before this stormy session Dr. King had met with Adelaide Doyle. Although she had withdrawn from the field of battle she was not entirely won over to the other side. She told him that, in her opinion, Lady Byron's conduct toward Elizabeth *had* been unnecessarily harsh. By now Annabella had received Berryer's letter which she answered politely but formally declining his offer to help solve the problem. He had made the mistake of defending the cause of the widowed Duchesse de Berry who had fled to England with her husband after the Revolution and who believed that her son had a right to the French throne. Annabella, along with many conservative aristocrats, did not approve of the Duchesse de Berry's personal life and thought Berryer was a bit extreme in his judgments in defending both the Duchess and Libby. She wrote to Selina about it and asked her to inform Dr. King of the true story of Libby's paternity.[26]

But Dr. King had left Paris, thereby depriving himself of some old but well-preserved morsels of scandal. On his return to England, he gave to Lady Byron his considered opinion that E. M. L. was of sound mind. That clinched it. To Lady Wilmot-Horton she wrote that, inasmuch as Dr. King had declared E. to be sane, she had determined to relinquish all communication with her and no longer to pay her the annuity which had been granted her in order to prevent her having to sell the Deed. Nevertheless, Lady Byron would reserve one hundred and fifty pounds per annum to be placed in the hands of trustees—one of which she hoped would be Lady Wilmot-Horton—to be administered by them for E.'s benefit, *provided* the Deed be retained and Libby remain respectable in her behavior.[27] Libby was not to know this, however.

It rankled Annabella that Adelaide Doyle had criticized some of her actions regarding Elizabeth.[28] By withdrawing all support, she had to all purposes left three adults and a child without money to pay for a place to live or food to eat. Annabella's justification was that Elizabeth had disobeyed her three stipulations: not to go to Paris, not to take money from another source, not to withdraw the Deed.[29]

The last is a poser inasmuch as the Deed was among Lord Lovelace's papers at Ockham Park, which surely Annabella must have known. How could E. sell the Deed under these circumstances?

In a letter of May 18 to Lady Wilmot-Horton, Annabella reported that Libby was penniless.[30] Twenty-seven years had passed since Byron wrote his farewell message before going into exile. "Be kind to Augusta—if she is then nothing—to her children." The brief spring of Annabella's youth had been followed by the long winter of her discontent. The happy interval at Fontainebleau when old memories lifted her flagging spirits —all gone, and nothing to take their place.

As for Libby, her wild and wayward temper, her loathing of dependence, and her overweening pride had conspired to do her irreparable harm. Was the control of her own future and that of her child worth the loss of three hundred a year? The future would answer that question. Forced to borrow on the Deed she wrote to Wharton and Ford, Lady Byron's solicitors, asking them to obtain the Deed from Ockham Park and forward it to Paris. Their reply was a devastating blow. They refused to entrust the original copy to the vagaries of the mail; she would have to receive it in person or send someone with her authority to receive it. To Berryer they wrote that Libby "had contracted the Deed on certain conditions, which she had not abided by." [31]

These crushing disappointments were too much of a strain on Libby's overtaxed nervous system. Again she was flat on her back, without funds and far too ill to contemplate a trip to England. Unwittingly she had provided the Beaureppaires with the opportunity to implement their plans. Victor had always maintained that Lady Byron owed him the six hundred francs he paid out of his salary for rent at Toulon. It was decided that Natthalie should go to England and collect this sum, and while she was there she could obtain the Deed from Ockham Park and the strongbox from Moore Place. No longer did Libby entrust this precious possession to her aunt.

Libby was so distracted that she was fair game for any suggestion, but she did hesitate about giving Natthalie the written authority and the key to the strongbox. She may have felt some obscure unease that all was not quite as represented by Natthalie, in her eagerness to act as intermediary. Fearful that the victim would slip out of the net, Natthalie offered to go to see Berryer and ask his advice. Libby agreed to this. Natthalie returned with the assurance that M. Berryer was in complete agreement with all Natthalie's ideas. Finally Libby capitulated:

> I entrusted her with a letter to my mother, whom she much urged me to address. I also gave her the name and direction of my family in case she should be in difficulties in England; and it was agreed that she should go first and consult Lady Mahon, whom she had formerly been recommended to. She obtained five pounds from Miss Davison, and set off.[32]

Miss Davison, like Adelaide, must have entertained a few doubts about Lady Byron's absolute rightness. Not long after Natthalie reached England, Libby began to receive letters from Mme. Beaureppaire—Victor also received some and told his mistress what they contained—and Libby became alarmed: "The letters showed me that she was not acting as had been agreed upon." [33] For once Libby used her head and went directly to M. Berryer with her suspicions and the disturbing letters. Only then did she learn the appalling truth: that Natthalie had lied about meeting the advocate. Berryer had not laid eyes on her for weeks. He sent Libby at once to the British Embassy to consult with Mr. Bulwer. Bulwer was shocked by her story and warned her it was most urgent for her to prevent Natthalie's getting possession of the Deed, or gaining access to the contents of the strongbox. He revealed that the Beaureppaires had a most unsavory reputation and could not be trusted in any way. Bulwer also went to Berryer and reprimanded him for "not having sufficiently considered the case." [34] He and Berryer agreed that Mme. Aubin's only chance was to go immediately to England, countermand the written authority (if it were not already too late), and do all she could to conciliate Lady Byron.

It was excellent advice, but how could she follow it? She was ill, penniless, and alone. Victor had taken himself off for England, but even before leaving he had been insolent. He had lost interest in Mme. Aubin and was after bigger game, i.e., Lady Noel Byron. He and Natthalie wanted to reach her and make their demands before Mme. Aubin had the opportunity to conciliate her aunt, but he did not think such a thing could happen. How could Mme. Aubin go to England and make a personal plea when she was ill and without funds?

But never has Luck or Fate—call it what you will—been more unpredictable than in the case of Elizabeth Medora Leigh. Dickens, the master of coincidence, could have written her story. Whenever she was clinging to the edge of a precipice, someone dragged her to safety. This time it was her friend Captain Joseph Barrallier. He arrived unexpectedly in Paris and paid a call on his former neighbor. He was shocked by the state in which he found her. Gallantly he "refused to listen to the details of my past life or even to look at letters relating to my present." [35] In spite of his refusal, Libby insisted on telling him that she was not at all what he had been led to believe.

The plight of this misguided, helpless young woman appealed to his chivalry, and as befits the honor of an officer and a gentleman he made himself the mentor of Mlle. Leigh (he called her that now) and Marie. He talked the matter over with M. Berryer and was all the more convinced that Libby had right on her side. He was on his way to England to visit his family, and though he did not have a large income it was sufficient to defray traveling expenses for Libby and Marie and to settle them in suitable lodgings in London. Libby wrote afterward:

> He agreed with Berryer that I ought to . . . conciliate Lady Byron. . . . I had a grateful recollection of the kindness I had received from him, listened to the advice he gave me, and acted in accordance with it.[36]

In the early part of June Libby said farewell to Paris a second time and set out for England with Marie, accompanied by Captain Barrallier.

16

I have sustained my share of worldly shocks,
The fault was mine; nor do I seek to screen
My errors with defensive paradox;
I have been cunning in mine overthrow,
The careful pilot of my proper woe.
　　　—"EPISTLE TO AUGUSTA"

LIBBY AND MARIE SETTLED IN LODGINGS AT 8 CHURCH ROW, Old St. Pancras, London, a world away from the palace or St. James's Square. The St. Pancras district was not too far from Regent's Park which Libby had seen through the barred windows of Mrs. Pollen's. Much had happened since that fatal day in July, 1831, when she "put on her bonnet" and walked out of her prison into the arms of Trevanion. Now it was June again and she was back in England, this time through the aegis of Captain Barrallier on whom she "had no claim but pity and kindness." [1] Most women in her predicament would have given up the struggle long since, but Libby was like her mother who, regardless of all her misfortunes, clung to the belief that somehow, some way, things would straighten out.

On the basis of Mr. Bulwer's revelations and her own suspicions, she had reason to distrust all the doings of Natthalie and Victor since they came to England. Yet she was credulous enough to feel that a meeting with her Aunt Annabella would undo all the harm created by the Beaureppaires. Miss Davison, M. Berryer, Mr. Bulwer, Captain Barrallier—all of them had urged her to "conciliate" Lady Byron as if it were a foregone conclusion that it could be done. Nevertheless it would not be easy to show humility and gratitude, that infernal word:

> For what am I to be grateful? Kindness, I feel, but I do not fear having to answer to this charge [ingratitude] from Him who will demand an account of all.[2]

She would discover that it would take much more than repentance to extricate herself from the messy situation in which the Beaureppaires had entangled her, infinitely worse than she could have imagined from Natthalie's letters.

Libby's worst errors had been to have given Natthalie permission to see her mother and other relations and to have given her the written authority to pick up the Deed and the strong-box. With these credentials Natthalie first went to see Lady Byron. Judging by the correspondence between Annabella and various interested parties, Natthalie did a subtle but thorough job of character assassination on Madame Aubin while giving lip service to unquestioning fidelity to her mistress. For the first time Lady Byron learned that the Beaureppaires had been told the "secret" at Hyères, but that Madame Aubin had forbidden them to divulge it to *anyone,* which included Lady Byron. So Natthalie and Victor said nothing, but they resented being lied to by Lady Byron who had represented Mme. Aubin as a "respectable widow." Had they known the truth they would never, but *never,* have accepted the posts of maid and courier. The stigma upon their good name made it impossible for them to find new places. It seemed only proper for Lady Byron and Lady Lovelace to make some sort of financial restitution.

Lovelace wrote to Sir George Stephen for advice on the best course to pursue. Stephen's reply of May 27 did nothing to relieve Lady Byron or Lovelace. Indeed he warned Lovelace and Lady Byron that Libby might be so utterly unprincipled as to decide to utilize the fact of her scandalous origins in order to blackmail her wealthy relatives and extract large sums of money from them at any time.[3]

Until then it was thought that the Beaureppaires were the chief culprits, but Stephen implicated Libby in one of the most noisome of crimes: blackmail. He did not, however, want to be the sole adviser; he suggested that they consult Dr. Lushington (now the Right Honorable Stephen Lushington), inasmuch as he had long been Lady Byron's valued friend and adviser. Sir George Stephen did put forth the idea that it might be sensible for Lady Byron to remit one hundred pounds per annum to Drummond's in Paris, to be paid quarterly to Miss Leigh, which would nullify one of the Beaureppaire's accusations: that Lady Byron had abandoned her niece to destitution. That sum, however, should not be exceeded by Lady Byron in any way.[4] He also urged that a very strong reign be kept on Libby, with Lady Byron retaining strict control through the most effective means possible—money.[5]

Lord Lovelace was understandably upset by the idea of extortion entering into this unsavory crisis, and in order to prevent Lady Byron bearing the full brunt, he decided on another tack. He wrote to Lady Wilmot-Horton, suggesting that Natthalie might be directed to the Chichesters or to some of Libby's other maternal relations in order that they might stop Natthalie's tongue wagging about the secret which would surely result in disaster for Mrs. Leigh.[6] In other words, it would be up to the Chichesters to assume responsibility for Libby and the Beaureppaires. Actually Lovelace was in a dilemma. He knew that his mother-in-law objected to any further contact with Augusta, who invariably brought trouble in her train.[7] However, he was a kind man and did not relish the thought of Elizabeth being in Paris without a sou, regardless of her behavior. He felt it would be unfair to prevent Elizabeth's "agent" Natthalie from going to the mother for possible aid.

After posting his letter to Lady Wilmot-Horton he informed Lady Byron of what he had done, with the wry comment that the situation might humble the Chichesters whose pious, yet aristocratic bearing consistently reflected a holier-than-thou attitude.[8]

He hoped this would smooth the Hen's ruffled feathers; she had a long standing grudge against Augusta's relations.[9] Unfortunately for Lovelace, Annabella had been writing letters on her own before receiving this one. She expressed herself firmly on the subject to Lady Wilmot-Horton about Natthalie's threatened visit to St. James's Palace to see Augusta.[10] Extraordinarily enough she gave as her reason for trying to keep Natthalie away from Augusta that Augusta *could* not give any financial assistance to her daughter and should thus be spared a meeting with her daughter's emissary. She had thus told Natthalie to go first to Lady Wilmot-Horton. For a wonder she had considered adopting Stephen's suggestion about the one hundred pounds per annum to be administered by trustees.

On the receipt of Lord Lovelace's letter, Annabella wrote hastily to Lady Wilmot-Horton countermanding his suggestions. With one of her abrupt mind changes she was now unequivocally against Natthalie's meeting any member of Augusta's family. Even when confronted by threats of extortion and further vexations, Annabella could not bear the thought of Augusta having anything to do with her wayward daughter. Neither was she happy about Lord Lovelace taking it upon himself to offer suggestions on her behalf. But in spite of her efforts to keep the Chichesters and Augusta in the dark, she was frustrated. She received a disturbing letter from Dr. King, written June 2 at Brighton.[11]

It seemed that he met Lord Chichester on the street; Chichester took him aside to ask a few questions. He apologized for bringing up the subject but he had heard that Dr. King had been to Paris and he was anxious to know how matters stood. He was curious to know what King thought about Elizabeth assuring the doctor that he was a relation and knew quite a bit already about the situation.

Chichester seemed to be in possession of much of the information which Annabella had wanted to withhold. Therefore it was almost certain that Augusta would know too. Annabella should have known that such gossip could not be kept secret. There were many English people living or making extended visits to Paris, and a large proportion of them were friends. Annabella herself had friends there. Before the Beaureppaires left Paris, they had probably regaled *their* friends with their troubles. Certainly Libby had done her share of talking out of turn, and one can be sure that people would listen to such a wild tale, embellished as only a Byron could embellish it.

Chichester knew about the Berryer incident. (Inasmuch as Mr. Bulwer of the British Consulate had discussed the matter with both Libby *and* Berryer, it is not surprising that news about it would find its way back to England.) Lord Chichester, however, was chiefly concerned with Libby's behaviour in France after leaving Lady Byron. Augusta maintained in her letter to Annabella that Libby had behaved herself after parting from Trevanion, but she had also written that certain people were not so willing to believe Libby's letters. It was an excellent opportunity for Chichester to get the facts from Dr. King who was not only trustworthy but had been in Paris at Lady Byron's request to call on Elizabeth Medora. Dr. King must have possessed a remarkably objective mind, considering the rough treatment he received from Libby. He expressed the opinion that the girl's deportment as regards sexual morality was above reproach. But she had a willful nature and resented any attempt by anyone to control her life or that of her child.

Apparently the Chichesters had already decided on their own that they might contribute something to Libby's support, but they did not wish to interfere with any of Lady Byron's arrangements. This was not discussed openly, only by indirection, but Dr. King thought it worth while passing the information on to Lady Byron. She did not take kindly to the suggestion. Had she been more flexible she might have saved herself and the Lovelaces embarrassment by acting on the idea, but it was not in her to take the easy way out of any predicament.

Such was the state of affairs when Libby arrived in London with the notion that a few tears and apologies would solve things. She got in touch with Sir George Stephen whom she considered to be acting for her, not realizing that he had, to some extent, gone over to the other side. He called on her at her lodgings and seemed to have lectured her on the virtues of obedience and gratitude to Lady Byron in return for her generosity and kindness. By this time such an idea was a very sore subject indeed, and Libby's impulsive reaction was to go on the defensive. She retorted that her aunt's kindness was due to fear that she would disclose family secrets. It was an uncalled-for remark, but apparently Stephen decided not to remonstrate with her, although he gave Lady Byron a full report of the meeting which did Libby's cause no good.

Lady Byron was already upset by the fact that Elizabeth had come to London, and what was even more reprehensible, had already allowed someone—a man—to defray the costs of the trip. Captain Barrallier had been Libby's neighbor and adviser at Hyères, had called on her in Paris, and had then agreed to acompany her and Marie to England. In Annabella's lexicon Libby had therefore entered "a life of Vice."

Captain Barrallier had gone to the office of Lady Byron's solicitors Wharton and Ford where he had an unsatisfactory interview with Gerald Blisson Wharton. He was given no hope of a reconciliation between Miss Leigh and Lady Byron. He went to see his family outside London, then to the city where he called on the firm of Banon and Smith in Westminster. They were army agents with whom he had done business in the past. He wanted some money to help defray the additional expense of maintaining Miss Leigh and her child. In the course of the conversation with Smith, who was also a solicitor, he mentioned that Miss Leigh was the daughter of Lord Byron by the wife of Colonel George Leigh—which "created great interest." [12]

It is a mild way of describing the amazement which must have greeted him after this bombshell. For in one of those incredible twists of Fate which were an integral part of Elizabeth Medora's life, Captain Barrallier happened to be talking to a man who revered Lord Byron almost to the point of idolatry.

17

I have not loved the world, nor the world me,—
But, let us part fair foes; I do believe,
Though I have found them not, that there may be
Words which are things,—hope which will not deceive,
And Virtues which are merciful.

   —CHILDE HAROLD'S PILGRIMAGE

THOMAS SMITH HAD SPENT SOME YEARS IN GREECE AS AN
army agent and at one time was secretary to the chief justice
of Corfu.[1] In August, 1823, a week after Byron's arrival in
Greece on what would be his last journey, he met Smith on
the Island of Ithaca at the home of the resident governor.
Byron and his party, along with some English officers and local
bigwigs, had finished dinner and gone to the drawing room.
Smith was awestruck at finding himself standing close to "the
great object of my curiosity and engaged in conversation with
him without presentation or introductions of any kind." He
had heard that Byron was inaccessible, haughty, and rude to
"the visiting English," but it proved to be untrue.

Byron seemed to have taken a liking to Smith and talked
at length on all kinds of subjects including Lady Byron and
Ada. "He spoke of 'Ada' exactly as any parent might have done
of a beloved absent child," Smith wrote, "and betrayed not the
slightest confusion, or consciousness of a sore subject [the sep-
aration], throughout the whole conversation." The next day
the whole party rode into the surrounding country on a

lengthy sightseeing tour where "Lord Byron ceased to be more than one of the party, and stood some sharp jokes, practical and verbal, with more good-nature than many of the ciphers whom one is doomed to tolerate in society."

The journey took them along the coast, also a side trip to the Island of Cephalonia. They were entertained by the local dignitaries as befitted the hero who had come to liberate the country from the Turks. That he was also financing the expedition played no small part in their eagerness to make him welcome. Byron singled out Smith. "His conversation was not merely free—it was familiar and intimate, as if we were schoolboys meeting after a long separation." The Byron charm was working overtime, but Smith was to get a dose of the Byron temper, too.

After an outing in which Byron swam too long in the heat of the day he was grumpy and feverish. The explosion took place in a convent, or rather a hospice, where the party were guests for the night. The abbott launched into a dull and meandering address of welcome, interrupted suddenly by Byron who snatched a lamp and ran out of the room yelling, "Will no one relieve me of this pestilential madman?" The next day his lordship was "all dejection and penitence," but in a short time he "revived; and, lively on horseback, sang, at the pitch of his voice, many of Moore's melodies and stray snatches of popular songs of the time in the common style of the streets." [2] Like father, like daughter!

The impact of that powerful personality on Thomas Smith was still strong after twenty years. It is no wonder that he was interested in Captain Barrallier's comments about Miss Leigh. He was, in fact, on fire to meet the woman who claimed to be the daughter of his hero. A meeting was arranged and Libby brought Marie with her. Smith found her "a very lively and agreeable person" and was delighted with her "pretty little daughter." [3] He could not have failed to notice the Byronic traces in Libby's features: the same curve of the jaw, the rounded chin, the full lower lip with its hint of sensuality belied by the ladylike grace of her manners.

The writing of Thomas Smith reveals an idealistic, generous nature coupled with the overweening adulation for the nobility so prevalent in that period. If Miss Leigh had the right to claim the benefits due her noble blood but was deprived of them by the cruel circumstances of her birth, he was going to see that justice was done. It never entered his mind that he would have to scale an impregnable fortress occupied by the redoubtable Lady Byron and her cohorts. He was bemused by the memory of a hero and beguiled by a young woman who also claimed to be the daughter of that hero. This is not to suggest that he fell in love with Libby; such an assumption would be intriguing but still sheer fiction. He was prepared to do battle, but he was clearheaded about it and did not intend to plunge into the fray without preparation. He suggested that Miss Leigh write a full account of her life as it pertained to the present situation so that he could examine the facts and work out a suitable plan of action.

Thus it came about that Libby wrote her Autobiography. It was written under stress; she leaves out words here and there; some passages are almost illegible and are further hard to read because she wrote on both sides of thin notepaper. Yet her vocabulary is good and shows the result of a well-rounded education. The last half which was dictated to some unknown person is not as well phrased. After reading it Smith was more than ever determined to work out an arrangement with Lady Byron agreeable to both parties. He knew better than to risk a personal confrontation after reading the Autobiography, but it was possible to reach Annabella through an intermediary. He discovered that his best avenue of approach was the Right Honorable Stephen Lushington, and through a mutual acquaintance he requested a meeting.

Smith's object was to make peace for his client with Lady Byron. He made it clear that he was acting for Libby [4] and that he was not a party to any extortion attempts, nor was extortion ever Libby's intention. He assured Lushington that her mistakes in Paris were due to the machinations of the Beaureppaires who had then left her to fend for herself and her child while *they* came to England for the express purpose of obtaining money for themselves—*not* for Miss Leigh, as they were saying.[5] Because of them, Miss Leigh was now in severe financial straits and was dependent upon the generosity of Captain Barrallier, who was strictly a friend and nothing more. The Captain and Smith had finally persuaded Miss Leigh to humble her pride and beg Lady Byron's forgiveness. Lushington was impressed by Smith's bearing and by his statements.[6]

A week later, July 21, Smith met again with Lushington who had meanwhile received two letters from Lady Byron. The gist of them was that she was not to be moved by arguments on behalf of Miss Leigh. Mr. Smith was not properly informed of Lady Byron's conduct in the matter, nor did she intend to make it more known. She regretted Miss Leigh's trouble but would not consent to renew any communication with her.

Smith was shocked by the implacable tone of Lady Byron's letters and could not understand what had changed her so radically. Nothing could have been more affectionate or maternal than her letters up to the time Miss Leigh left Toulon for Paris. Why had this move given such deep offense? Smith felt it had been justified. Lushington knew Lady Byron's moods very well indeed. He had dealt with her for more than twenty-seven years and knew that she could change her mind without warning, but that nobody on earth could force her to change it. Smith argued that it was a case of starvation for Miss Leigh and her child, that Captain Barrallier had to return to France and could not go on helping her with his limited means. When this plea failed he tried to persuade Lushington that it was important to Lady Byron's and her daughter's peace of mind, not through fear of extortion but for simple human kindness. "What was the girl to do for bread?"[7]

Lushington had only a cursory knowledge of the conflict.

He had been brought into it at a late date, and he did not wish to be involved any further. He thought Smith should go to Sir George Stephen who had formerly acted as Miss Leigh's lawyer. He suggested, too, that it would be wise for Miss Leigh to see him and to deport herself with decorum. Smith did not feel that Sir George would be useful when Lushington had failed.

Lushington replied, "There may be others of the family to whom he has access. I believe that is the only chance for Miss Leigh. I am not at liberty to say more—do you understand me?" [8]

Smith agreed to discuss it with Miss Leigh, though he doubted she would take his advice. He asked if Lushington knew that Victor Beaureppaire was in London and threatening to insult Lord Lovelace in a public place so that he would be arrested and taken to Bow Street. There he intended to give a full account of Miss Leigh's history which would go down on the police docket and become a matter of public record. Lushington replied that he did indeed know the scoundrel was in London, because Victor Beaureppaire had brought a court action against Lady Byron to extort money. This was a dismaying piece of news for Smith, but he absolved Miss Leigh of any complicity. He assured Lushington that Victor and his wife were operating independently of his client.

Smith had been so sanguine about his success that he was unable to hide his disappointment. The two men parted, not on hostile terms, though both of them recognized that only a miracle could effect a reconciliation.

While Smith was going all out to help his client and relieve Barrallier's financial problems, Libby was having her own difficulties with her "loyal" maid, Mme. Beaureppaire. Barrallier had urged Libby to keep on good terms with Natthalie, no easy task for a girl with a short fuse, but she had tried. The trouble was that everything Natthalie was doing served to widen rather than close the breach between Libby and her benefactress. Libby had discovered through Smith, via Lushington, that Natthalie had gone to Moore Place and demanded that Lady Byron hand over the strongbox, which Annabella sensibly refused to do. She would only release it to its rightful owner. This was before Libby's arrival in London. When Libby requested the return of the box, it had vanished. Everyone at Moore Place had looked high and low for it, but to no avail. Suspicion pointed to Natthalie's having stolen it because it had been in its usual place before she arrived to claim it. Lady Byron wanted to advertise its loss, but Lushington advised against any unnecessary publicity.

When Libby met with Natthalie and demanded the truth, Natthalie denied all guilt, but her protestations of innocence had a hollow ring. The two women quarreled acrimoniously until Libby could no longer endure Natthalie's insolence. She asked for the key to the box. Natthalie refused and berated Libby for everything she could think of including base ingratitude. That was all it took to infuriate Libby, especially from a woman who was now revealed in all her malicious duplicity. After a screaming row Natthalie flung the key at her former mistress and stormed out of the door. It was the last time Libby would have any direct contact with either of the Beaureppaires, but it was not the last of the turmoil they would cause.

The court action against Lady Byron and Lady Lovelace which was instituted by Victor (and Natthalie as a willing accomplice although she tried to weasel out of it) was not for withholding back wages but for fraud, a criminal action. Lady Byron was accused of misrepresenting facts when hiring them with a resultant loss of their characters. This prevented them from getting the kind of employment to which they were accustomed. If found guilty, Lady Byron would then be liable for damages. Victor had found a smart lawyer, a Mr. Dod, and if all progressed as hoped the amount of damages awarded could be sizable.

Libby had no connection with this action, nor would Smith or Barrallier have countenanced such a move. When

Smith met with Sir George Stephen on July 26 he formally dissociated both himself and Libby from the legal action which had been instituted against Lady Byron by the Beaureppaires.[9] Stephen seemed to have agreed that Libby was not involved in a conspiracy with the Beaureppaires, but they were using her as the fulcrum of their lawsuit, and she was thus guilty by association—in the minds of the defendants.

Stephen was willing to disentangle her from the web in which she was caught, but it would take time and patience. He must sometimes have pondered on the vagaries of human nature and the caprices of fate which dragged him into this maelstrom of deceit. A year and a half ago he was moving heaven and earth to restore the Deed of Appointment to Elizabeth Medora, at the request of Lady Byron. Mrs. Leigh was the arch villainess; Elizabeth was the innocent victim. Lord and Lady Lovelace were on terms of familial affection with Elizabeth. Natthalie was the ideal lady's maid—capable, attentive, and respectful.

Now all of them were likely to be involved in a distasteful trial which would delight the gossip columnists, the pamphleteers who specialized in smut, whisperers in the court circles frequented by Mrs. Leigh. With Victoria on the throne and the straitlaced Prince Consort dictating the morals of Society, it might go hard for the unfortunate Mrs. Leigh. Lord Lovelace expressed himself feelingly on the subject of the Beaureppaires. At Hyères they had remained in the service of Elizabeth although she had told them the details of her past. Not a word of complaint about wages or loss of characters until their stay in Paris dashed their expectations of making a further killing.[10] Only when they found the game was up did they become alarmed about their reputations. In Lovelace's opinion it was so clearly a case of blackmail that a trial would be sure to bring out the facts and they would then be shown up for the perfidious wretches they were. In fact, if Victor continued to write libelous letters villifying Lady Byron, which he was doing, it would be smart for Lady Byron to take the initiative and bring an action for libel and slander against Beaureppaire. It would prove to the world that Lady Byron had nothing but contempt for the charges, but more importantly, it would force Mrs. Leigh and the Chichesters to protect *their* reputations by buying off the damned scoundrel.

What Victor lacked in talent he made up for in gall. In very bad French he wrote to various people, including the present Lord Byron, informing them of Elizabeth Medora Leigh's scandalous romance with her brother-in-law. This was scarcely earth-shaking news to either his lordship or his wife. Victor also attacked Lady Byron and her daughter for having misled Natthalie when she had been hired as a maid for "Madame Aubin." Not only had Annabella and Ada lied to Natthalie, they were now refusing to give her or Victor good references to enable them to get another job. Victor intended to make the whole thing public; indeed, like a madman, he threatened to appeal for help to Queen Victoria and to the government and to both houses of Parliament.[11]

It was a large order for one man, but it was just possible that he might make good his threat. It did, however, provide Lushington and Wharton with some idea of what to expect from the prosecution if the case came to trial. Lushington was not as hopeful about the outcome as Lord Lovelace. After he had gone over Lady Byron's statement of her case, there was no doubt in his mind that Natthalie *was* hired by Lady Byron (not Miss Leigh) with Lady Lovelace playing some part in the transaction; that Miss Leigh's real name was not used but a false one; and that Lady Byron used that name in addressing all her letters to Miss Leigh. He had to inform Lady Byron that he did not think Victor's action could be defended with much success.[12]

Libby was beside herself with apprehension. Sir George Stephen had informed Thomas Smith that so far he had been unable to obtain the strongbox. Everyone blamed everyone else for its disappearance. The loss of the box alone would have been enough to upset Libby, for it contained all she owned of any real value, with the exception of the Deed, still at Ockham Park. How bitterly she must have regretted her gullibility in giving Natthalie the key; the wretched woman might have stolen the precious documents to sell at some future date. Oddly enough, on August 9 Sir George Stephen had written to Smith that he would "feel truly rejoiced to be the means of extricating her from her present false and painful position." [13] But he could not undertake it unless Miss Leigh agreed to Lady Byron's terms: surrender of the Deed to trustees, a written expression of contrition, and a return to seclusion in France. If the terms were accepted he was convinced of his success: "My only object is to effect an arrangement that may conduce to the peace and comfort of all parties, in the most distressing case that ever fell to my knowledge." [14]

Smith could not quite see how Miss Leigh could "surrender" something she did not possess. Stephen wrote to Lushington about it. If mediations fell through he felt it only fair to return the Deed to its rightful owner. Stephen must have been an understanding gentleman with more than his share of kindness, for he did make a tremendous effort to help Libby while knowing that it might redound to his disadvantage where Lady Byron and the Lovelaces were concerned.

The Deed and the strongbox were not all that concerned Libby. Her position as regards Captain Barrallier was growing untenable. He wanted to return to France but hesitated to do so until he was satisfied that her affairs were straightened out. As with M. Carrel, Barrallier was helping her from simple goodness of heart. She had not succeeded in making any headway with her maternal relations or attempted to meet with her mother. Lord Chichester had twice written to her, urging that she make it up with Lady Byron, but that was all. In her desperation to relieve Barrallier of the financial burden she wrote to a number of her relations. As was customary she made copies of most of these letters which she turned over to Smith for safekeeping. One of them, to the Honorable D'Arcy Osborne, serves as an example:

> When I was a happy child, you used to be kind and good natured to me. Now that I am in suffering and misery, will you refuse me what I am compelled to ask all who will give it me—aid and protection? I am sure you will not, if you will let me tell you why I am so.
>
> Your cousin,
Elizabeth Medora Leigh.[15]

Beside her relations she seems to have written to certain people whom she knew to have been close to Byron. John Hobhouse was one of them, and he reacted as follows: "Elizabeth Medora Leigh stating herself to be *child* of Lord Byron and starving—some imposter I *hope*." [16]

He made this comment in one of his journals. Although he had known Libby as Augusta's daughter and Byron's favorite niece—and had been told about the girl's elopement with Trevanion—he no longer had much contact with the Leighs, and he was *persona non grata* with Lady Byron. Ada he did know, but she did not make a habit of discussing family secrets, so there was no way that Hobhouse could have had any knowledge of Libby's plight. It would be interesting to speculate on what his reaction might have been if he *had* known; it might have augured better for Libby's future. Hobhouse was a bit stuffy and straitlaced on certain subjects, but he was very well off now that he had succeeded to the title of Lord Broughton, and he had been utterly devoted to Byron.

Out of all the painful, begging letters Libby wrote, the only one to be answered was one to the Duke of Leeds. He sent her ten pounds. Her brother Frederick (called Fred) seems to have had some dealings either with her or with others involved in the situation. Assuredly she could have done without him. He had never been anything but a trial to his mother, in danger of losing his commission in the Navy by dishonorable discharge because of his rash behavior and reckless gambling. And now, suddenly, he was making it his business to meddle in the Beaureppaire-Byron-Lovelace imbroglio.[17] How he would interfere is not spelled out—but whatever he did would be certain to make trouble for the Leighs and the Chichesters, unless they put a stop to his foolishness. Lord Lovelace feared he might try to contact Lady Byron, and he urged his mother-in-law to have no dealings whatsoever with Frederick, to avoid him as she had avoided his mother.[18] It was unlikely that Libby had anything to do with her impetuous brother's plan. She did not need him to add to her difficulties; she had quite enough without him.

Inasmuch as Libby had failed to get any response from her relations other than the Duke of Leeds, and with nothing forthcoming from Thomas Smith's efforts, she decided to make one last, desperate move. On August 12 she went to St. James's Palace and sent in her card to Mrs. George Leigh.[19] It was in the evening, at a time when she knew that her mother would be likely to be "at home." Society in that day abided strictly by the rules of etiquette and nowhere was it more formal than at Court. A caller, no matter who it was, was accompanied by a servant who was sent in with the card while the caller remained outside.

As Libby waited she must have been on tenterhooks. What to say? How to behave? She had not seen her mother since that painful afternoon outside the Lovelace town house, nor had they corresponded. Although the Chichesters and her mother knew she was in London, and not living with Lady Byron, none of them had tried to see her. But "dearest Mamma" had never been known to hold grudges. A good cry would resolve everything. The servant returned. "Not at home." To others Mamma was at home but not to her daughter. If Augusta had cut Libby dead in public she could not have inflicted a worse blow to her daughter's pride. There was nothing for Libby to do but accept this stinging rebuke and go with head held high.

There is no way of knowing what went on in Augusta's mind. For twenty-nine years she had managed to keep her position at Court in spite of huge expenses, unruly sons, abandoned and ruined daughters. She had lived down the lurid scandal of the separation, at least enough to avoid further trouble with Lady Byron. She was fifty-nine, afflicted with a dropsical condition, dowdy and chronically broke. Most people who knew her felt she had suffered enough and were willing to forgive—with certain reservations.

The Honorable Mrs. George Lamb, a friend of Mrs. Villiers and Lady Byron, wrote to Annabella that Augusta was contrite, but not contrite enough.[20] As with Therese and Annabella, she seemed to have wanted Augusta to wear a hair shirt until it was replaced by a shroud.

Natthalie had tried to see Augusta and had been in contact with Lady Wilmot-Horton and the Chichesters, so Augusta could not have been ignorant of what was going on or the disaster which could befall her if all the details of Libby's birth and fall from grace became generally known. All because of that wretched daughter, the loving, vivacious Libby who had once been the light of her life. Augusta was on bad enough terms with Georgey these days without a possible confrontation between Georgiana and the sister who had stolen her husband. At that moment the distracted woman probably wished her daughter dead. Nevertheless it was unwise of her to risk alienating Libby when it was important to win her loyalty.

For Libby did not take her humiliation lightly. In her anger she did the first thing which came to mind: she wrote a vituperative letter to her mother. The original and a copy she gave to Barrallier to turn over to Smith. In a note to Smith, Barrallier said, "If you do *not* approve of the letter to Mrs. Leigh, retain it." He was worried about its effect on the mother who he hoped would rally to her daughter's aid or at least persuade her well off relations to come forward. Smith thought the letter was: "very proper and natural under the circumstances but is it not somewhat premature? A day or two may make an important change—." [21]

He decided to retain it for a while until all other avenues of communication were explored.

This letter was not published along with Libby's Autobiography when that document was published in 1869; it was considered too "harsh and unfilial." [22] Perhaps it was to Victorian eyes, but fortunately the copy, in Libby's hand, is included with the manuscript for her Autobiography.

> August 13th, 1843
> 8 Church Row
> St. Pancras.

My Mother,

The motive that led me last night to ask what I have long since hoped to be spared, to meet once more, you, I so tenderly loved, was not as you have given me the right to do, to accuse and reproach you, nor yet to seek to awaken your pity for the misery I owe alone to you—.

Since I was made to understand you could never have loved me, the child of your guilt, in whom you have been but a means to satisfy your ambition, a sacrifice to be made to those you feared, then to throw me on the world, destitute, homeless and friendless. I have expected and sought nothing from you—but now compelled to seek aid and protection from all who will give it. I once more remind you I am your child. The world and strangers will tell you in harsher terms all you owed me—do owe me—could I have felt I was writing to a *Mother,* I would have said much, now I can only beg you, by the memory of my father, the brother to whom you, and the children you love and which by my destitution owe all— no longer to forget and neglect what you still owe

> your child
> Elizabeth Medora Leigh.

It was one of those angry letters which should have been kept a few days and reread in a calmer mood, but Libby was too desperate to think clearly. Life was closing in, each day more frustrating than the one before. She had certainly courted disaster, because she was, after all, a Byron, and the Byrons were disaster-prone. Their history is a dark legend of emotional instability and actual insanity, but in spite of this terrible heritage, Elizabeth Medora, like Byron, had some inner strength which kept her from slipping into the abyss. And there was Marie to sustain her when all else failed. To keep Marie at her side, to control the child's future was an obsession. As long as there was any possible alternative she would never bow to the dictates of Lady Byron and turn over Marie's upbringing to anyone else.

In her desperation she clutched at any straw and the response from the Duke of Leeds seemed to prove an alternative.

On August 23 she wrote him again. She gratefully acknowledged the receipt of the ten pounds, quickly summarized her life giving special attention to Lady Byron who had first been very kind and later very cruel, and from whom she learned "of the infamy of my mother, once so dearly loved, that I owed my birth to incest and adultery." [23] She mentioned that her only resource was the Deed which was not payable until the death of Lady Byron and her mother. All efforts of her adherents to arrange a meeting with her former protectress had met with distrust and disdain. Three times she had "humbly asked pardon," but it had not been granted. Inasmuch as she was almost a stranger to the Duke she could only beg him to consider her position and its causes.

She gave it and a copy to Barrallier who enclosed it in a letter to Thomas Smith, and wrote the following comment: "It is entirely her own composition. I do not like it." [24] The Duke must not have liked it either, for nothing came of it. That branch of Augusta's family kept themselves as aloof as they could from the endless crises which beset the Leighs. By this time they must have realized that helping Augusta's family was a little like trying to clean the Augean stables.

It was inevitable that the Right Honorable Stephen Lushington would run into heavy weather with Lady Byron when he advised her to make an out of court settlement with the

Beaureppaires. People seldom had courage enough to tell Annabella in so many words that she had been wrong. She denied that she had represented Libby as a widow to Natthalie and Victor, then went on to explain in her inimitable manner that in Paris someone had asked if Mme. Aubin were a widow, and that she had told them the truth.[25] However, it was quite evident to everyone concerned that Annabella had used the name Mme. Aubin in her correspondence with Libby and the Beaureppaires.

Lushington was not one to be dissuaded by equivocation. He pointed out that, if it came to a trial, neither the Beaureppaires nor Lady Byron would be witnesses. Lady Lovelace and Miss Leigh, possibly Lord Lovelace also, would be examined on the stand, and some letters might be included as exhibits for the prosecution. He was letting her know, in a polite way, that her unwillingness to settle would only embarrass Ada and her husband.

While Annabella was digesting this bitter pill, Smith decided to send Libby's letter to her mother. On September 4 Augusta wrote to Gerald Blisson Wharton that her daughter had called upon her and she wished to find out if Lady Byron had withdrawn her protection. Wharton sent the letter to Lady Byron and enclosed her reply with a covering letter to Lushington.

As a result of the urging of Sir George Stephen, backed up by Lushington, the Deed was finally returned to Libby. Smith and Barrallier advised her not to borrow on it. It was more sensible to accept Lady Byron's conditions. Libby capitulated on two of them: she would humbly apologize to Lady Byron and she would retire to seclusion in France, but she would not surrender the Deed. Smith sided with her on this, for the Deed was now her sole asset, unless the strongbox turned up and had not been rifled. The decision was given to Sir George who passed it on to Lushington, who passed it on to Lady Byron, in the customary routine.

It should come as no surprise that Annabella had changed

her mind about one of her demands. Originally there had been the three stipulations; now suddenly another stipulation was added by the insatiable Lady Byron. "She must sign a statement of the sums received by her during the period when she represented that she was 'abandoned' to the charity of servants." Annabella went on sternly to say that whether or not Elizabeth agreed, or no matter what she tried to do, nothing would "ever induce her to resume the character of protectress, or give her (Medora) the slightest reason for saying that she was restored to favor." [26] Libby was guilty of what Lady Byron called "parricidal" conduct. A strange word to use since "parricidal" means killing one's parents and Lady Byron was by no means Libby's mother.

It is odd that she demanded Libby's statement about monies received when she had the signed receipts in her possession, sent from Hyères.

Again stalemate. There was nothing for Stephen and Lushington to do but wait until Libby was in such financial hardship that she would *have* to surrender the Deed. Possibly Annabella might have been more willing to compromise a little if Victor had not, at that inopportune moment, made himself more obnoxious than usual.

He and Natthalie had returned to France, leaving final details of the court settlement to be handled by Mr. Dod. Reluctantly Lady Byron had agreed on a sum less than asked, but Dod was prepared to send the proposal to Victor for acceptance. Before he could do it, Victor sent an "anonymous" letter to Lady Byron (hardly anonymous; it was in his handwriting) which he addressed as follows: "The Lady Noel Byron, *femme de mauvois foi,* Moore Place, Esher, Surrey."

It was obviously the work of a madman. It stated that "a reward was offered for any information concerning 'the unfortunate Elizabeth Aubin, natural daughter of Lord Byron,' aged twenty-nine years, and of her daughter, aged nine years, who had been 'abandoned' by her adoptive mother, 'the very wicked Lady Noel Byron' and by the 'virtuous princess,' her half sister Lady Lovelace, and by her 'rascal of a brother-in-law the Seigneur Harpagnon de Lovelace.' Anyone with information of these unfortunate creatures . . . should get in touch with 'Mrs. Leigh, her mother, at St. James's Palace, where he would receive the promised reward of a hundred lashes of the knout' . . ." [27]

Victor injected the only laughable touch in the proceedings, but nobody was in a mood for laughter. Annabella was positive that Libby was involved with the "infamous scoundrel" Victor and his perfidious wife, and alas for Libby she was never freed completely from the accusation of collusion. As for her association with Captain Barrallier, Annabella wrote to Lady Wilmot-Horton that she would never provide any money so long as Libby retained her immoral connection with the captain.[28]

Nevertheless there were a few intrepid souls who dared to feel that it was unchristian to leave the woman absolutely penniless, and one of these was Lady Wilmot-Horton. Annabella always took umbrage at criticism, but to ease her uneasy conscience and to keep her promise to Byron she decided to provide a set amount per annum, but with a strange stipulation: it must be allowed to accumulate without Libby's knowledge *until* she was not under someone else's protection and in dire need. Neither did she inform Smith or Barrallier of this decision.

Without this vital information and with increasing desperation, Libby thought of asking the aid of a police magistrate to force the return of the strongbox. She now believed that its whereabouts were known to Lady Byron and the Lovelaces, but she was dissuaded or perhaps decided on her own not to carry out that idea. In October she moved to cheaper lodgings and wrote to Barrallier (still in England) to address her as Mme. Aubin, Aldenham Terrace, Old St. Pancras Road.[29] She asked if he would be kind enough to accompany her to Smith's office so that she could terminate her business affairs with him.

Smith was greatly chagrined that he had failed to reconcile

Miss Leigh with Lady Byron. After five months of patient ne-
gotiation all he had accomplished was the return of the Deed.
(At some later period the strongbox seems to have been returned to Libby, though she does not state how or when it
happened.) Smith also regretted that he had failed in his efforts
to defray some of Barrallier's expenses, but the gallant Captain
seems to have taken his losses with good grace. There is no
record of what took place when Libby parted from her loyal
friend and protector so that he could return to France. Probably there was a certain amount of relief on both sides, for a
well-intended plan which goes awry is bound to put a strain on
any association.

Libby made no further effort to see or communicate with
her mother, but according to some local gossip in Esher she
did try on one occasion to see Lady Byron at Moore Place.
The story was that Medora Leigh (she was always called that
in local journals and histories) paid a surprise visit at Moore
Place. When Lady Byron learned that the girl was at the front
door, her ladyship "left hurriedly by the drawing-room window,
jumped into a carriage and did not stop until she reached
Brighton." [30] This curious incident is not mentioned in any
of Lady Byron's correspondence or by Libby. Anecdotes of all
kinds proliferated through the years about one of Esher's best-
known residents, Lady Noel Byron, but they were always so
biased in her favor and often so inaccurate factually that they
cannot be accepted without question.

On December 7 of that same year, 1843, Sir George Stephen
wrote to Lady Byron and informed her that for some time he
had heard nothing either directly or indirectly about Miss
Leigh.[31] From the lengthy and unaccustomed period of silence,
Sir George inferred that she might have sold the Deed or found
other sources of financial help unknown to him or Lady Byron.
She had not as yet sold or borrowed on the Deed. Sometime between October and December she transferred her legal affairs
to Sir John Hughes, a solicitor.[32]

He seems to have been of entirely different caliber from

her other legal advisers. There was no touch of the sentimental about him; he was down to earth, inclined to quibble over details, a no-nonsense man. Libby was no longer full of belief in her star, the Byron star. Now she knew it for what it was, not radiant with light but dark with evil omen. Nothing withers so quickly as charm in the arid climate of failure. To Hughes she must have been a half-sick, desperate woman with an illegitimate child and no visible means of support. The sensible thing was to contact Henry Trevanion. As father of the child it was his obvious duty as a gentleman to contribute to Marie's support.

Such a proposition was anathema to Libby. She told Hughes that it would be a long day before *she* would write to Henry Trevanion. It was not one long day, but an endless succession of long days. Christmas was approaching, the worst time of year to be friendless and poor in a huge city. It must have recalled the days when she was "a happy child" at Six Mile Bottom, the holiday visits, the jingle of sleighbells, the arrival and departure of those same uncles, aunts, and cousins who turned their backs on her now. Such memories must have been hard to bear when she looked at Marie.

On Christmas Day she wrote to Hughes authorizing him to contact Henry. She doubted that anything would come of it, "but it is worth more to be fooled in this manner than to fool yourself, if only once, in believing unjustly in someone's guilt." [33]

Actually Hughes had not waited for her to give him permission. He had already written to Henry in an effort to feel him out about Marie. There had been no reply. Now he wrote again, enclosing Libby's note. In January, 1844, Trevanion answered:

> I am sending you back the letter of Miss Leigh's. I am extremely sorry that it is entirely out of my power at the moment to contribute to the education of the young girl who was the object of your letter. . . . At the moment I find it difficult to maintain myself.[34]

Henry was far from destitute, now that he had his income from his father's estate. He had bought some property in Brittany at Botives in the commune of Malguenac, Morbihan, where he now lived. How cleverly he avoided responsibility. "The young girl who was the object of your letter" was not an acknowledgement of paternity and without it there was no hold on him. A natural child had no legal claims upon the father without this recognition.

Sir John Hughes was a realist. Trevanion had turned her down—there was no way of coercing him—she would have to do what she was told and that was that. He made contact with the trustees and ascertained what had to be done before his client would be able to draw on the annuity. Libby was allowed to retain the Deed but she would have to leave the strongbox with its contents in Hughes' charge. She must leave England for good and live "in seclusion in France." She was ordered by Hughes to make a new will leaving all she possessed to Marie. Libby obeyed and gave the document to the lawyer. She had no alternative but to turn over the strongbox to him.

On May 27, 1844, Libby borrowed five hundred pounds on the security of the Deed from a Captain Hugh Cossart Baker so that she could pay her debts.[35] It is the last known fact about her activities in England. As far as her maternal relations and Lady Byron were concerned, she had gone with her child to France, and everyone breathed easier. If any of them ever felt a qualm about the treatment she received, they could always say with some truth that she brought it on herself. Everyone expected that she would come to a bad end. The sentimental novels of the day abounded in virtuous heroines who resisted temptation, but for those who did not, the wages of sin were paid in full. The road ahead for Elizabeth Medora Leigh could only lead downhill to the workhouse or the streets.

But unpredictable and wayward as ever, she refused to provide a proper ending to her life story.

Book Three

REDEMPTION

18

MADAME ELIZABETH AUBIN HAD NOT ENTERED A LIFE OF vice nor was she in a house of correction. True to her agreement to live a secluded life, she and Marie had found lodgings in a *pension* at St. Germain-en-Laye, a charming little town about thirteen miles outside of Paris. At the time it was a favorite summer residence for Parisians, on a hill above the Seine which commanded a magnificent view of the surrounding countryside as far away as Paris. Its terrace, about a mile and a half long and over a hundred feet wide, was one of the finest promenades in Europe. France was home to Libby. She loved the life, the people, and she was close to the city she adored. Best of all, she was free.

The annuity provided enough for her immediate needs, and if she was prudent about money she could enjoy the life of many a single woman with restricted income. It did not allow for many luxuries, but she could afford to mark time, to plan for her future. She was careful to pay the interest on the loan secured by the Deed; she wanted no trouble on that score. In the main, life showed promise. She was only thirty, not considered too old in France for a "widow"; she was still willowy and attractive. About her there was a provocative aura of mystery, and she was delicate enough to fit the style of the period.

Exotic fragility was all the rage in Paris; it was chic to look consumptive. Libby's dark coloring was also in her favor; it was the fashion for women to look like the dark-eyed beauties who peered through the lattice windows of a sultan's harem.

In this eminently respectable *pension* she had an ideal opportunity, if she took advantage of it. She could not hope to make a brilliant match, but she might find some older man, perhaps a widower, who could offer the security of marriage. She had no illusion that she might capture the heart of some young man of wealthy and important family. He might make her his mistress—and his family would not object to *that*—but marriage was a deadly serious business involving contracts, dowries, fully attested social backgrounds. Selecting the suitable wife was the family's prerogative in most countries, but it was especially true of France. Libby had not changed her thinking about marriage and would not agree to a liaison, regardless of the inducements.

All this, however, was in the realm of wishful thinking; the realities were another matter. Although she tried to live within her income she was incapable of prudence about money. Byron's mother had managed to keep herself and her son on a hundred and fifty per annum, but Libby did not—could not—follow in the same footsteps. There was also Marie's education to consider: a knowledge of languages, social deportment, all the airs and graces of well brought up young ladies in Europe as well as England. It was important for Marie to have as many advantages as possible to counteract her background. If it were in Libby's power, she wanted her child to go to the proper school where she would meet the proper friends who would in turn open the proper doors which would lead to a proper marriage.

It was equally essential for Libby, as Marie's mother, to present the best facade she could afford. The annuity was simply not elastic enough. She was able to borrow ahead on the annuity for a time until the trustees called a halt. Before they would advance any more money the funds would have to accumulate again. By the end of 1845 Libby was again in dire straits. She had been so sure that she could manage her life once she cast off the "fancied chains," but the will-o'-the-wisp of freedom had led her into a treacherous bog. She could not turn back nor could she move forward unless she borrowed on the Deed or sold it outright. It was a crucial moment, and this time she had to make her own decision, a decision which would dictate the future course of her life.

Was a life of leisure worth the endless begging, the loss of pride and self-respect? It could go on for years, each year more degrading than the one before until there came a time when she would be like her mother whose charm had faded with the decline of her fortunes. There have been women like Augusta Leigh in every period and country who cling to the periphery of fashionable Society without the means to do it correctly; an embarrassment to their friends and objects of contempt to their enemies. It is true that in Augusta's day there was little choice in the matter unless a woman had intelligence enough to make her own mark in the world. But for every Anna Jameson or Fanny Kemble there were a hundred Augusta Leighs.

Libby made her bitter choice. She placed Marie in the Convent of the Nativity situated in St. Germain. There the child would receive a decent education, kind treatment, and meet girls of good families. Libby had never forgotten her weeks in the convent outside Carhaix; it had not worked out for her but perhaps it would for Marie. After attending to Marie's immediate needs, Libby went to work as a servant in the same *pension* where she had been a paying guest. It would have been a difficult transition for any woman to make. For a woman of her background it was astonishing.

The kind of work required of her is not stated, but it is probable that her duties were not too onerous and somewhat in keeping with her education. It speaks well for her previous behavior that the proprietor would agree to the arrangement. Yet it must still have been a difficult period of adjustment, especially for Libby, for only in fiction or drama does reformation take place overnight. To control her unstable temper, to accept her position with a smile, to work long hours whether or not she felt up to it physically, to live on equal terms with those who had formerly waited on her; it was not easy. There must have been times when she looked back on the days of plenty at Moore Place and wondered what could have possessed her to throw it all away.

Perhaps the very drama of it gave her a certain wry satisfaction. According to the mores of the time she was close to the bottom rung of the ladder, and she once had been close to the top. If this spectacular fall were to become known in England, there would surely be a great shaking of heads and "I told you so's." What a pity that a woman with so much to offer should come to such an ignoble end. In this connection, however, the French were more hardheaded about going into service. To be sure, there were snobs in France, especially among the parvenus and certain members of the new-rich bourgeois, but the average Frenchman placed a higher value on earning one's bread and keeping out of debt than living a life of impecunious gentility for the sake of appearances. Moreover, servants in all but the wealthiest or noblest of households were on terms of equality with their employers which would not have been permitted in England.

One day a new guest came to board at the pension. He was Colonel Jacques-Philippe Delmas de Grammont, Commandant of the 8th Hussars. He brought his orderly with him, a young soldier named Jean-Louis Taillefer. Taillefer was thirty-four, a good-looking, stockily built fellow of sturdy peasant stock. He still had two and a half years to serve in his term of military duty and was considered an excellent soldier. Colonel de Grammont was a fine man, interested in many things besides soldiering. He was later to be known as the author of the "Grammont Law" which deals with the humane treatment of animals in France. It is told that on one occasion Napoleon III presented him to Prince Albert as "the author of the only good law we

have given to the Republic." The Grammont name was a respected one of the *ancien régime;* later Colonel de Grammont
became a senator and a general. That such a man chose Jean-
Louis Taillefer as his orderly proves that the young soldier was
no boorish peasant. And indeed, everything known of Taillefer
shows that he was a man of integrity and sensitivity.

In the course of their daily duties Taillefer and Madame
Aubin saw a lot of each other, helped one another with their
routine tasks. A friendship developed. Soon Jean-Louis was
head over heels in love with her, but a soldier was not allowed
to marry during his term of duty. Under those conditions
courtship was a tricky business for Taillefer. Madame Aubin
was not interested in a love affair, nor was it likely that she
was greatly interested in Jean-Louis—at the beginning.

She was, after all, reared in the household of a career officer who had once been equerry to the Prince Regent. In the
rigid caste system of the British armed services, the foot soldier
was so far down the line that he would never have had the
least contact with a colonel's daughter. There was a caste system in the French military also. If Libby had been staying at
the *pension* with Lady Byron, for example, she would doubtless
have met Colonel de Grammont, as would Lady Byron, but the
Colonel's orderly would have been treated in the same way
that the Leighs treated the Colonel's manservant; with civility
but not equality. That Taillefer was of peasant stock was not
against him—many peasants with patched clothes had money
salted away in Paris real estate—but it was not in his favor
either, socially speaking.

Still, it was pleasant for Libby to be admired so ardently
and treated with such respect. It could not have taken long for
Jean-Louis to learn that Madame Aubin was no ordinary
woman but a lady who had been forced by reverses to become
a servant. Her appearance and demeanor would have told him
that. She must have been a tantalizing enigma as well as a
handsome woman, and with the stubbornness and pride of a
peasant he set his heart on making her his own. He was no

selfish neurotic like Trevanion; he was a straightforward, virile man without a wife and children cluttering up his background. His intentions were honorable although he could not marry until he was through with his term of duty, and in terms of romance that was a long time.

For close to a decade Libby had lived a sterile life entirely contrary to her nature. She had managed to bank the fires but the embers still retained a spark which could be fanned into flame. In April she would be thirty-one, an age when unmarried ladies without a fortune had to face the fact that their chances of marrying were almost nil. But the Byrons were a lusty breed and did not take well to abstinence. At thirty-one Augusta had just put an end to her passionate affair with Byron and would continue bearing children by her husband for a number of years. At thirty-one Byron was just beginning his fervent romance with the youthful Contessa Guiccioli after a period of debauchery in Venice which would have exhausted the vigor of most men. It is surprising that Libby resisted temptation as long as she did before she succumbed to the kisses and embraces of the enamored Jean-Louis Taillefer.

In May she found herself pregnant, but this time there was no question about her future. Taillefer accepted his full responsibility. Not only would he marry her when it was possible but he would adopt Marie, too. There was a risk, of course; he was a soldier and Colonel de Grammont could be called up suddenly for active campaigning. Jean-Louis could be wounded, even killed, but when was any path trod by Elizabeth Medora Leigh not attended by risk?

Toward the end of November Madame Aubin did not feel equal to continue working at the *pension,* which she had been doing up to then, with the full approval of her employer. Taillefer had already arranged for her to go to St. Affrique, a market town in southern France, in the department of Aveyrons. The town was a few miles from his native village of Lapaeyre. Libby left with Marie for St. Affrique and took lodgings in the house of M. Lamothe, the local apothecary, and let it be known that she was there for her health. Later she moved to the house of "the Widow Girbal," an inn. Lamothe and Mme. Girbal knew Jean-Louis for he was popular in their town. Libby settled down to await her confinement.

Aveyrons was not picturesque like Brittany or Normandy, nor did it have the beauty and climate of the Cote d'Azur. Neither did it glow with a sense of history, that mystical identification with the past to be found in so many parts of France such as the neighboring region of Provence or the Loire Valley. In other words, neither in Libby's day nor the present day has it been a section which the average foreign tourist would select to visit above all other places. It does, however, possess an industry which sets it apart and most of the countryside is given over to it. The caves of Roquefort honeycomb the cliffs overhanging the little market town of Laguiole about fourteen miles from St. Affrique and not too far from Lapaeyre. The famed cheese is made from the milk of ewes, and the fields in the area are sown with wheat, rye, and oats to feed these valuable creatures. Other than providing fodder for sheep, the soil is poor, but the peasants who own the land, like peasants throughout the country, would not dream of living elsewhere. This was the land of Jean-Louis's birth, these were his people; and now Elizabeth Medora would be part of it one day. If there were times when she felt like "Ruth . . . amid the alien corn" she never let anyone know it.

Although she could never hope to become a husky peasant woman, her health seemed to have taken a turn for the better. This time she seemed likely to carry the child to full term without incident which would indicate that some of her past difficulties were due partially to a depleted nervous system brought on by her hectic life with Trevanion. On January 27, 1847, she gave birth to a healthy boy. On that same day Taillefer arrived in St. Affrique. The purpose of his brief visit was to recognize the child. On the birth certificate Libby called herself Elizabeth Aubin, age thirty (*sic*), not married. The baby was christened Jean-Louis Elie (always called Elie) and eleven-year-old Marie was godmother. When mother and child were able to travel, Taillefer bundled them off to Lapaeyre. There was barely time to arrange for their care and lodging before he had to report to Colonel de Grammont. He would not be able to rejoin Libby for eighteen months. Until then she would have to go it alone.

A foreign bride coming to a strange community and meeting her husband's family and friends for the first time faces an ordeal which has been described so often that it has almost become cliché. But a bride, at least, has the security of her husband's name and a wedding ring to carry her over the rough spots, and indeed most families try to present a united front to the world regardless of their private opinions of the new addition to the family.

Libby had nothing in her favor except the knowledge that Jean-Louis's intention to marry her was well known. But she was English, she was a mature woman, she had a daughter going on twelve by some previous and mysterious alliance, and she had a baby by Jean-Louis which was conceived out of wedlock. Fortunately she had proved that she was able to bear children and had produced a husky son. Moreover, it was not a black mark against her to have borne a child before marriage; a peasant farmer in most countries liked to know he was not going to be saddled with a barren wife. That the woman bore a son was a plus mark; it meant another helping hand in the barnyard and the fields.

What could cause trouble was that this particular relationship did not conform to the accepted pattern, and neither did Madame Aubin. She was different in appearance, with that "great, tall, childish body," a marked contrast to the short, broad-hipped, big-breasted peasant women. She was also a lady, which could have been a detriment, for the peasants of Aveyrons were no different from the Bretons and Normans. To them all outsiders were unwelcome and anything strange was suspect. How did a lady become involved with a humble soldier, even if he was one of their own? No matter what Jean-Louis may have told his family and neighbors in explanation, everything about the affair was odd.

The majority of these people led severely circumscribed lives; most could neither read nor write except with great difficulty. The women grew up, were courted, married, had children, grew old, and died without knowing anything of the outside world. The young men did leave long enough to fulfill their military service, but most of them came back to their native villages, married local girls, and stayed there for the rest of their lives. A few may have had dreams of a different life, but it was a rare man who could realize even a part of his dream. In comparison to the bourgeois class all of them were poor, at least they appeared to be, though appearances in some cases were deceiving. One thing Libby shared in common with them. She was poor, too. Having left St. Germain-en-Laye, she was no longer abiding by the terms of the trustees and thus was not receiving the annuity. Until this year, however, she had managed to pay the interest on the loan from Captain Baker, but from then on she could not do it.[1]

It would have come as a surprise to her maternal relatives and to Lady Byron's intimates to learn that Elizabeth Medora Leigh could adjust herself to this kind of existence. Probably they would have refused to take such an idea seriously; they were all convinced that she was a willful, ungrateful creature who could never become a truly responsible member of society. The most interesting part of it is that she did manage it—by being herself. If she had tried to curry favor by descending to the peasant level of culture and education, they would have recognized the insincerity and resented it. They would also have been quick to take offense if she had gone to the other extreme and put on airs. And the traits of character which had caused the most trouble in her former life were the ones most likely to be understood by the people who surrounded her now.

She was proud; so were they. She had endured much; so had they. Too much or too little rain, crops ruined, an epidemic of anthrax or some other disease among the livestock; such disasters could strike any one of them. All they could do was salvage what they could and start over. So, obviously, had Madame Aubin. They could respect her for that. Her emotions were close to the surface; so were theirs. Impulsive acts of kindness, outward expressions of affection or dislike were taken for what they were, not analyzed for hidden motives. Stubbornness was not a fault; it proved one had a mind of one's own. Bursts of temper were not frowned upon; no peasant ever spared the rod and spoiled the child. And Libby also had another attribute in her favor; she was thought to be a woman of great beauty.

All reports of her stemming from this period of her life mention her appearance. Her beauty was quite often remarked on and her appearance frequently noted. She was never considered an outstanding beauty in England, but then beauty is not only in the eye of the beholder but a question of time and place. London Society of the Georgian and Victorian eras boasted some of the most ravishing women on earth, and the same was true of Paris. In the company of such nonpareils Libby could not hope to compete on an equal basis, but in the village of Lapaeyre she was a *rara avis*. She also was one of those fortunate women who grow better looking as they grow older.

As time went on the people of the village began to feel a growing respect for this stranger, but they were not quite ready to welcome her into the fold all the way. She did, however, conform to what was expected of a woman. She took care of her house, was a good mother, went to mass and church regularly, accepted the meagerness of her lot without complaint. Hard work tired her, and there was much she had to learn which the neighbor women knew almost by instinct. Many of her ways were new to them also. And there was something about her which made her an object of endless curiosity and speculation.

Libby had never minded being noticed and she knew how to make the most of it. There is no need to speculate about her ability to charm people when she wanted them to like her, and one can be sure that she wanted these people to accept her. It was a relief that she was not expected to show constant gratitude, and nobody patronized her. She did have to prove herself, of course, but she could reassure herself that she was better born, better educated, better able to conduct herself properly in any social situation. She had been brought up to value these attributes, which was one of the main reasons why it had galled her to be made to feel inferior to those around her. This did not happen in Lapaeyre. It was important for her to feel superior; it gave her the inner security to carry her through the difficult months still ahead.

In this connection it is likely that Jean-Louis indulged in some plain speaking before he had to return to duty. She had borne his child; he had assumed responsibility for her and her daughter; he had the right to make certain demands. Thrift is ingrained in the makeup of a French peasant farmer; a wife would have to learn to live within her means and not embarrass him by running up debts. Jean-Louis was well aware that *he* was on trial in the village, too. He had taken a calculated risk in bringing his mistress to Lapaeyre; he knew he could be criticized for intending to marry a woman of different nationality and background. And there were other personal questions which could nag at a man in his position. He was not, after all, a romantic youth in love with love. He was thirty-four when he met Madame Aubin. At some time or other he might have wondered if she gave herself to him through genuine passion or took him for a lover because she had given up hope of doing better. His doubts were outweighed by his love.

Was Libby a woman in love? One can only judge by her subsequent behavior and draw one's own conclusions. The idea put forth in one case: that she married out of her class as a kind of oblique revenge against her mother's aristocratic family connections, as well as Lady Byron and the Lovelaces, seems very wide of the mark. Nevertheless a year and a half on trial in Lapaeyre must have seemed an eternity to her. Probably there were times when she regretted her choice, other times when she was frightened that Jean-Louis might regret, too. It is a normal emotional reaction.

Spring, summer, fall, winter; 1847 came to an end. January 27, 1848, was Elie's first birthday. He was at the crawling stage, a fine, healthy boy. On April 14 Libby was thirty-four. May 19 was Marie's thirteenth birthday. She seems to have inherited her mother's good looks, but the ups and downs of her life had a sobering effect upon a nature which might have been far different.

At thirteen Marie was not as precocious as her mother had been at the same age, but she was more mature in her thinking. She loved her mother and knew that she was loved in return, but she was not blind to Libby's faults. She knew the facts of her mother's birth as she did her own. She had seen how all this affected her mother's behavior and attitude toward life, but instead of becoming defiant as Libby had done, Marie became introspective. As a young child she had seen that a life of ease with Lady Byron had not made her mother happy, although there had been compensations for Marie.

She had gone to a proper school, arranged and paid for by her Great-Aunt Annabella; she had been on familial terms with her second cousins, the young Lovelace children. Unfortunately she had never been able to put down roots long enough to establish youthful friendships. She had to depend largely upon herself. Being a normal little girl she must have liked wearing pretty dresses and owning the trinkets dear to the hearts of little girls everywhere. It was fun to have things to play with, a doll, perhaps, to dress and undress. Good things to eat, comfortable beds to sleep in, and no worry about the means to pay for them; all these and more Lady Byron had provided for her. But creature comforts did not insure happiness, not if the grownups could not get along with each other. Especially not when one of them was the mother she loved so well; the only constant in a world of change.

But during her weeks in the convent at St. Germain she had seen that the nuns seemed happy without worldly goods.

She was too young to fully comprehend that this happiness was the result of rigid self-abnegation; all she knew was that she felt an attraction for the life inside a convent. After going to Lapaeyre she still felt the call toward the religious life, and the longing to return grew stronger as time passed. She did not say too much about it, however, because her mother needed her. Among the peasant farmers she was known and remembered as a quiet girl with a firm but gentle way of conducting herself. She was a source of great comfort to her mother, and it is likely that her presence contributed much to Libby's growth as an individual. If Marie did talk about her hopes and aspirations to become a nun, Libby would have understood, though she might inwardly have flinched at the thought of losing her daughter. She could remember back fourteen years, when she found a measure of peace cut all too short by the birth of this child who now was dreaming of a cloistered life.

On June 4 Libby and Marie and Elie celebrated Jean-Louis's birthday in absentia. In a month, God willing, he would be through with his term of duty. As the time approached Libby must have been beset by the usual feminine doubts and worries. Would she live up to the image carried in his memory for eighteen months? Toward the end of July he was back, and her worries were groundless. He wanted to marry her immediately, but as usual with Elizabeth Medora Leigh there was a hitch in the proceedings.

She thought she had given the civil authorities the necessary proof of her identity, but it was not enough. She had to write to the English Consulate in Paris, and there followed an uneasy waiting period. She had used the name Elizabeth Aubin on Elie's birth certificate and woman-like had knocked two years off her age. Her dealings with the British Embassy in the disastrous Paris interlude had been difficult, and there was the worry about what Lady Byron might have written to Mr. Bulwer during the dispute over finances. Her aunt had done a thorough job of queering Libby with the hotel manager, so she could have done the same elsewhere. As a matter of fact, the Embassy did have some dubious information in their files about E. M. Leigh that had been supplied by Lady Byron, but apparently it was decided to let well enough alone. The "proper papers" were furnished, and she was known officially as Mlle. Elizabeth Medora Leigh. The annuity from Lady Byron via the trustees, though not being paid to Libby at the time, helped to establish proof of her identity. The path was clear at last.

In France, especially with villagers and inhabitants of small towns, the most important celebration in a woman's life was her marriage. It was, in fact, an occasion celebrated by everyone in the area. Families might be at loggerheads and neighbors might be feuding bitterly, but on a wedding day grievances were put aside. Such was the case with Libby's wedding.

On August 23, 1848, the civil ceremony took place; the religious ceremony was performed on the following day. In her bridal veil with a wreath of imitation orange blossoms, the traditional thing to wear, Elizabeth Medora must have been lovely to see, with her dark eyes and hair and her tall, slim body. One can be sure that she followed the custom of the country and pressed the wreath under glass which was then displayed in some prominent spot in the living quarters she would share with her husband.

The women of the village had been making preparations for days. After the ceremony there were the usual dancing, drinking of toasts, eating—more toasts, more eating—until the bride and groom were able to sneak away at midnight. It was a strange contrast between this wedding and the dreary ceremony in the chapel of St. James's, when Henry Trevanion took Georgiana Leigh as his bride, and Libby had been maid of honor. Libby had traveled far in the ensuing twenty-two years, from the country house at Six Mile Bottom to a little village in southern France where, as Madame Jean-Louis Taillefer, she would live out the rest of her life. Now she had rights to demand instead of favors to accept. The last chapter of her life was about to begin.

19

LIBBY'S YEAR AND A HALF HAD NOT BEEN WASTED. SHE had proven herself, and now that she was an integral part of the community, her prestige continued to grow. Oddly enough she was still addressed as Madame Aubin in her business dealings rather than by "the common name of Taillefer." According to custom it was part of her wifely duty to be the family cashier and handle business transactions. It would have been amusing to watch the reactions of those who had known her in England, had they been told of Elizabeth Medora's success as a businesswoman.

This was not the only change in her life style. One would have reason to think that she might walk all over a man once she had "rights to demand," particularly a man who loved her as devotedly as did Jean-Louis. The fact of the matter is that Libby was equally in love with him. Nothing else can explain her metamorphosis. For she did undergo a profound change, which was reflected in the attitude of everyone who knew her in that period. Her neighbors grew to love her for her goodness and piety, and years after her death they still spoke of her with deep affection. The devotion of this simple, good man called forth all that was best in her because it was love freely given.

For the first time she knew what it was to share her life with someone who accepted his part of the bargain wholeheartedly.

This is not to say that her life was idyllic; it was as hard as the lives of most peasant women. The farmhouse was cold in winter, hot in summer, hard to clean, ridden with insect pests, buzzing with flies in the summer. The washing was done in the *lavoir,* a public shed over a stream in the village where the women took their places and beat the dirt from clothes and bed linen with big flat paddles. Men and women alike smelled of sweat and the barnyard. If one wanted a hot bath one went to a bath house in the nearest market town—on market day. Even in Paris most places had no running hot water. A hot bath was a luxury seldom afforded except after an illness like scarlet fever, measles, smallpox, and the like. Then the hot water arrived by cart inside a large receptacle which could be used as a bath tub. It was very difficult to keep oneself clean in a farmhouse where the water was either taken from the well or lugged from the nearest stream.

Libby's only labor-saving devices were Marie or possibly the daughter of a neighbor who was paid a few sous for helping with the chores if Libby was too worn out. It would be a mistake, however, to think that her living conditions as regards cleanliness were a giant step down the ladder from her former way of living. In that period some of the larger country houses and city mansions had big tanks for storing water, but it had to be brought in by hand and heated on a stove. With all the hue and cry of the present day about air and water pollution—and adulterated foods—one forgets that these are not new problems.

In the nineteenth century water was almost always polluted to such an extent that water itself acquired a dangerous reputation. Nobody drank it except when nothing else was available. Country people fared better provided they lived on the upstream side of other farms. As late as 1814, while Libby was living in the Old St. Pancras section of London, the Fleet River ran through the district and became known as the Fleet

Ditch as it meandered through the streets, a noisome stream lined with houses on both sides whose drains emptied into the turgid water which was open to the skies. The stately homes of England had no inside plumbing except cesspits which were either abandoned when full or cleaned out by polemen (a well paid profession, not without reason), who carried their stinking buckets through the house at night if there was no other means of egress. There were sewers in London but there was one house in Wimpole Street where none of the waste matter reached the sewer in thirty years because the drains were improperly constructed.

Thus, anyone living in a large city, or even a town, was used to unpleasant smells, and indeed the personal habits of the most exalted members of the nobility would not pass muster today. One was supposed to wash one's hands before and after meals, but that sinister liquid, water, was too risky for faces. Much better to wipe one's face each morning with clean linen. It is not hard to see why a naturally fine skin was a prized rarity along with good teeth, sweet breath, and reasonably clean hair. The general health of city dwellers was never good; all suffered from assorted bronchial troubles, peckish appetites, and general malaise. When one considers that milk, the most easily contaminated of foods, was carried by a milk girl through the streets and fetid alleys in open pails, it is not surprising that so many were tubercular. The rich, at least, could escape to the country in the hot weather or go to the seashore and various spas. Life in the country, even with the humblest peasants, was more healthful than life in the city. So, despite the rigors of her lot, Libby was doubtless in better physical condition than she had been for many years.

Along with the hardships she had compensations. Through some means, perhaps eked out of Jean-Louis's pay while serving in the army, Libby had acquired a piano. No one in the area had ever seen one and it was the talk of the village. Her neighbors could hear her accompanying herself as she sang the songs of the day. One wistful ballad seemed to be her favorite; the gist of it was that "the only good thing that is left to me is to have cried sometimes."

The piano was not the only thing which intrigued Libby's neighbors. An individual never changes completely; he or she repeats the same pattern in varying degrees until death. Libby had the Byron trait of saying and doing things which would titillate the curiosity, even to shock. Augusta once said to Hobhouse, "Byron is never so happy as when he can make you believe some atrocity against himself." [1] The French call such a person a *mauvais farceur*. Libby would not have made shocking comments about herself, but she had her little attention-getting devices.

She let it be known, for instance, that she was "the daughter of a great lord from across the Channel." This would have been enough in itself to create a lasting impression. It is doubtful that any of the villagers had ever heard of Byron or was familiar with his poetry; a book was seldom found in a peasant farmhouse. But their awe and respect for the nobility was deeply ingrained in spite of the Revolution. All in all one can safely assume that Madame Taillefer's or (Mme. Aubin's) presence in the community brightened all their lives.

This would not have happened, though, if she had set herself too far apart from others. There was in her a "desire to do right," and she had impulses of kindness and tenderness which endeared her to people. They were not, as Lady Byron described them, "conscientious lumps of sugar," offered as bait, but sincere efforts to be useful. Because of her good education she often helped her neighbors with reading and writing. They got into the habit of coming to her with documents and papers which needed explaining; sometimes she wrote letters for them. She was also a devout Catholic, which endeared her to the village curé.

When August, 1849, rolled around, Libby and Jean-Louis had been married close to a year. Marie was fifteen, Elie was three and a half. He was now a good-looking youngster with reddish brown hair and a firm chin and was the pride of his parents. Libby's health seemed good, her husband adored her, she had two fine children and the good will of her husband's people and neighbors. At thirty-five Elizabeth Medora had come to terms with life.

One day she woke up not feeling well. Probably she performed her daily tasks the same as always, for summer was a busy time. Later she felt headachy; still later she had chills and fever. At the onset these symptoms were not too alarming — people often had fevers of various sorts—but the fever worsened, the headaches were more severe, she suffered from intense thirst and nausea and severe pain in the back. Then, on the third day, came the dreaded eruption which extended rapidly over her entire body. Smallpox! Now all that could be done was to pray that by some miracle she would pull through, and if she did survive, that she would not be disfigured with pockmarks. There is no need to dwell on the clinical progress of this horrid disease; then as now there was little to be done to make the patient comfortable.

The pox was no stranger to anyone. It was known to be contagious, but it was not yet known what caused it or what precautions should be taken to prevent it from spreading to everyone in the family. Incredibly, many in a family did *not* come down with it, unless it became epidemic. Most farmhouses had but one large room, though there may have been an extra one in the Taillefer house. Marie would have tended her mother, and Jean-Louis and Elie would have been in and out of the dwelling, yet none of them seems to have contracted the disease. How Libby came to catch it will never be known.

She must have known the despair which afflicts anyone, especially an attractive woman, who has the pox. The disease is unpredictable, sometimes leaving its victim unscarred, sometimes miserably disfigured. It soon became apparent, alas, that Libby was not going to recover. When she knew she was going to die, she accepted her fate with quiet dignity and was in full possession of her faculties until almost the end. On August 19 she was able to write a letter to Sir John Hughes, which was not posted, however, until September 3. She wrote her own will in English:

> I declare that all my previous wills are null and void. I also swear that any other document is null and void. I bequeath all my worldly goods to my husband Jean-Louis Taillefer including the Deed of Appointment under the will of the late Lord Byron, to my husband and children. I also declare here that I forgive my mother and all those who have so cruelly persecuted me, as I hope myself to be forgiven. I ask my solicitor, Sir John Hughes, to send to the above Jean-Louis Taillefer, the box which has all my papers in it which he still holds. I sign this August 23, 1849.
>
> E. M. Leigh.

Two witnesses also signed it, neighbors who were barely able to scratch out their names. Ironically, August 23 should have been a day of rejoicing. It was her first wedding anniversary.

The will was written under extreme duress, without time to ask legal advice, otherwise some errors could have been corrected which later transformed it into a legacy of woe. Jean-Louis was too dazed by grief to be of help. Life was reluctant to release Elizabeth Medora. She lingered for six days, growing steadily weaker as she passed into a coma. Before she lost consciousness she begged Marie not to forsake Jean-Louis and to take care of Elie. On August 29, 1849, at four in the afternoon, she died.

The entire village followed her coffin to the cemetery. She was laid to rest, as her father had been, in a simple country churchyard.

Fourteen years later M. Bonal, the parish priest of Lapaeyre at the time, had occasion to write to a certain M. de Waroquier. Bonal's brief note proves, as nothing else could, the indelible mark Elizabeth Medora left upon the memory of those who had known her:

M., the Abbé Singla, has seen with his own eyes, the respect
I have for the tomb of the pious, charitable Englishwoman,
whom I did not have the honour of knowing myself, but of
whom everyone speaks to me with the highest praise. I, myself, take care of the flowers on the tomb, I have also planted
there a beautiful cypress and a fine tombstone with an iron
cross on top.

The homage of Lapaeyre had been no passing thing.

20

Byron ALWAYS BELIEVED THAT THE CURSE OF THE BYRONS brought misfortune not only to themselves but to those closely involved with them. Like most superstitions its truth depended largely on coincidence, but if Byron could have known what problems lay ahead for Elizabeth Medora's heirs he might have said, "There, you see, it *is* true."

Jean-Louis was completely crushed by the loss of his wife, and had it not been for Marie he would have suffered a real breakdown. She was his comfort in those first despairing weeks. She tended the house, took care of her little brother, did what she could to pick up the pieces of their shattered lives. She it was who arranged for the probate of her mother's will by writing to Sir John Hughes. On September 3, 1849, she informed him of her mother's death and enclosed Libby's letter to him. He received them on September 8. Until then all who had once known Libby had lost track of her, and it was a number of years later before all facts were put straight.

Sir John Hughes had sent Marie's letter (in which Libby's letter to him was enclosed) on to Lord Chichester. Apparently the two had been in communication with each other on some matter. Through Lord Chichester, Augusta heard the news about poor, unfortunate Libby's death, although no particulars about it seem to have been mentioned to her, such as the date and cause of Libby's death, or even the fact that she had been married to Taillefer. The news was relayed by Lady Wilmot-Horton to Lady Byron.[1] Annabella's reaction is not given in any available record, but one can assume that she had her feelings, as she did when she heard the news of Byron's death. The only expression of regret that came from Lady Wilmot-Horton was her worry about Marie, who now had to get along on her own in a foreign land.

It is significant that Marie made no attempt to communicate directly with her maternal grandmother or the Chichesters. Of course, she had not known them personally, but neither did she write to Lady Byron whom she had known well. Libby had forgiven them all on her deathbed, with a special forgiveness for the "dearest Mamma" she had tried to hate but never ceased to love. Marie forgave everyone because there was no bitterness in her, but they had all belonged to another life. Her only tie to them was her mother, and now that tie was severed. Although she was only fifteen, necessity forced her to think and behave like an adult and she handled matters amazingly well.

If she could have read Lady Wilmot-Horton's letter she would have been taken aback to see herself referred to as an "unfortunate child." Unhappy yes, having lost her mother, but she had health, a family, a home, compassionate neighbors, the comfort of her religion, and the bright promise of her vocation to dream about. She was fortunate in the things which are important.

At this juncture Sir John Hughes entered the scene, and there he would remain for fourteen years. In view of his maneuvering during that time, one cannot avoid the suspicion that he did not act on behalf of Libby's interests; that he was playing a double game. The situation was ideally suited for pettifoggery. He was dealing with a young girl and a French peasant without the means to fight a long, costly court action in

England, which operated with a different code of laws in another language.

One of Hughes's first actions was to file an affidavit that there was no legal representative of the late Elizabeth Medora Leigh. This, despite the fact that he had acted as her solicitor, had induced her to leave her private papers in his care, and *as her solicitor* had been in touch with Lord Chichester. In a letter to Marie he quibbled over Libby's holographic will which he found hard to read, though he knew she had written it on her deathbed. He could not read the names of the witnesses. Who were they and were they present at Elizabeth Medora's death? In the year 1844 she had made Marie the sole heir. Now someone named Taillefer and another child were included. Although Libby had called Jean-Louis her husband, he asked Marie if her mother was married to this Jean-Louis Taillefer. If so, why did she sign her name Elizabeth Medora Leigh? And why did the death certificate refer to her as Madame Elizabeth Aubin? Until Marie could answer these questions to his satisfaction, he could do nothing.

Certainly he had a right to question the confusion of names, but as will be seen, the answers did not satisfy him. Explanations and documents which seemed in order in St. Affrique were sloughed off by a prominent London solicitor. It could be that he was trying to protect Marie's interests, feeling that she was too young to understand that by the terms of the new will she was no longer sole heir. But at no time did she contest the will; she had, in fact, been instrumental in admitting it to probate, through Hughes.

According to English law of that day a holographic will was valid even without a signature. In France the law required that it be dated and signed by the testator, Libby had fulfilled these requirements. As regards probating the will, prior to 1857 in England probate might, if uncontested, be made in common form, i.e., by the executor's own oath.[2] It is true that Libby had not appointed an executor, but obviously Marie and Taillefer expected Hughes to act as their representative in England.

Their mistakes were made through ignorance rather than intent to defraud, but Hughes seems to have made little effort to advise or protect them. Instead he obstructed them. During these two years of haggling certain events occurred in England which further confused the issue.

On May 3, 1850, Colonel Leigh died, leaving his widow loaded with debts.[3] Augusta was sixty-six and seriously ill with heart disease and dropsy, barely able to keep herself and her numerous dependents. She was so hard up that she was forced to sell a number of Byron's letters which should have been kept secret. Her only comfort in those unhappy months was her daughter Emily, Lady Byron's godchild. Emily's position with her mother was very like Marie's in regard to hers. Emily was the only Leigh willing to take on responsibility for her mother's various problems. Had Augusta been less harassed and in better health she might have used her influence to force Hughes to take a more lenient view in the probating of the will. Although their relationship had ended in bitterness, death has a softening effect upon the hardest of hearts. If Lady Wilmot-Horton wondered what would become of "the unfortunate child," Augusta would surely have wondered about Marie, too. She had, after all, arranged for the Deed of Appointment to safeguard Marie's education, the one trouble being that it was only payable on the death of Lady Byron and Augusta.

Nevertheless, if the will were probated so that the heirs had a legal right to the Deed, there would have been nothing to prevent them from borrowing against it if it was necessary. They did need money desperately, for legal fees and proper advice, but they were stalemated. It was impossible for Jean-Louis or the local advocates to fathom the intricacies of all that was going on in England. Always some new complication would arise. Meanwhile the strongbox remained in Hughes's possession and the will was not admitted to probate. Until that was done the Deed was of no more value than a scrap of paper. They had given up hope when a savior appeared.

In 1852 G. de Waroquier of Toulouse, formerly Colonel

in the 8th Hussars which was de Grammont's regiment, went on a holiday with his children to St. Affrique. He was a native of that town and was following the French custom of returning to his birthplace for a brief summer sojourn. His well-to-do relatives still lived in St. Affrique and took an interest in what was happening in the community. They had heard about the beautiful English lady, daughter of a British lord, who had married one of the Taillefers of Lapaeyre. They knew about her sad death after but one year of marriage and of the trouble her grieving widower was having with her will. The sad, romantic story was told to de Waroquier with indignant embellishments. Jean-Louis Taillefer was a God-fearing, hard-working farmer, but he was poor. How could he hope to win out against a prominent advocate in faraway London, who had powerful connections? M. de Waroquier agreed that it was unfair and decided to investigate the matter.[4]

After talking it over with Jean-Louis, he looked up Colonel de Grammont who was a personal friend as well as his former superior officer. De Grammont told him about the romance between his orderly and the charming Madame Aubin in St. Germain; he spoke highly of her and praised Taillefer's career as a soldier. His opinion carried weight and convinced de Waroquier that the cause was worthy. He got to work but soon discovered that Hughes was no more impressed by *his* efforts than he had been by anyone else's in that part of France.

De Waroquier refused to give up. He questioned Marie at some length. Did her mother have any influential friends who might impress the authorities? Marie recalled a few, among them Lord Brougham, from the old days at Hyères.[5] After a turbulent political career, in 1838 Brougham had bought land in Cannes, then a small fishing village. Such was his renown that he put the place on the map. He seems to have met Libby at Hyères and was disposed in her favor, particularly since he had known Byron and some of his friends. When he received a letter from de Waroquier, asking for assistance, he agreed to do what he could. He got in touch with a former grand chancellor of the French Embassy in London who promised to expedite things. De Waroquier also corresponded with M. Roux, a friend of his who was a secretary of the French Embassy, and he also wrote to Lord Melbourne in his attempt to bring about a "prudent settlement of Elizabeth Medora Leigh's claims." [6]

As late as 1857 he still had not given up. He was now more concerned with Elie, eleven and a half years old, who was now in his charge. Apparently De Waroquier thought that Lady Byron might take an interest in the boy's future, inasmuch as he was the son of Elizabeth Medora Leigh and more important—the grandson of Lord Byron, and he wrote an emotional plea to Lady Byron on Elie's behalf.[7]

De Waroquier was doomed to disappointment in his hope to enlist any interest in Elie from Lady Byron. She was undergoing her own ordeals which had preoccupied her from 1850 on. The diligent efforts of de Waroquier always met with further reasons for delay from Hughes. In one letter Hughes stated that five hundred pounds had already been borrowed against the Deed and no interest paid since 1847. It would also take from seven hundred to eight hundred pounds to clear the will and admit it to probate. Until all these financial matters were attended to, nothing could be done, including the release of the strongbox.

De Waroquier was a stubborn adversary. While he was absorbed in the litigation he was also concerning himself with the immediate problems of the Taillefer family. Jean-Louis had suffered an accident which lamed his right foot, making it difficult to farm his property. Marie was still in charge of the house and Elie, though her longing for the life of a religious was as strong as ever. De Waroquier was thoughtful and also practical. In 1855 he arranged for Jean-Louis to go to Toulouse where he became a coachman for de Waroquier's son Arthur. The elder de Waroquier took over the upbringing and education of Elie, then nine, which left Marie free to pursue her vocation.[8]

In 1856, aged twenty-two, she returned to the Convent of the Nativity in St. Germain, where in due course she took her final vows and became Sister Saint-Hilaire. She let it be known that she felt bound to expiate the sin of her birth as well as that of her mother, and she was more strict with herself than was necessary. In her Book of Hours she remembered her mother, drawing a memorial tombstone on which she inscribed "Elizabeth Medora Byron," also some lines of Lamartine (changing *he* to *she*):

> Stretch over her thy pardoning hand.
> She sinned—but Heaven is a gift;
> She suffered—'tis but innocence;
> She loved—'tis the seal of forgiveness.

As for the man she never knew, whose love produced her mother and whose blood ran in her veins, she had only tender thoughts. "Poor Byron," she used to say, "I am very fond of him." [9]

De Waroquier did not feel that his responsibility was finished now that he had taken care of the personal needs of the family. He gave up the Deed as a hopeless cause, but he was determined to extract the papers from Elizabeth Medora's strongbox so that they could be turned over to her heirs. M. Roux in the French Embassy presented Hughes with a letter from de Waroquier. He requested that the strongbox be forced open in the presence of Roux. Hughes, and one other legal adviser. Roux was to look over all the papers, keep what he felt were germane to the cause, and burn the rest. If he found *any written evidence* of Elizabeth Medora Leigh's true paternity, it was to be included in the papers saved. [10]

On May 19, 1863, the box was opened in Hughes's office. Present were Roux, the chancellor of the French Embassy, a lawyer selected by Hughes, and Hughes himself. The box contained letters, drafts of letters, and scattered notes, more than enough to prove that Elizabeth Medora was indeed the "child of sin." To Roux's dismay, he was told that it was the custom in England to burn all papers which tended to show immorality, and such was the case with these. Roux objected strenuously—who among them was qualified to be the arbiter?—but he was overruled by the highhanded Hughes and his cohort. Everything was burnt except two letters: the one from Libby to Hughes giving him permission to seek aid from Trevanion, and Trevanion's letter of refusal. They were sent to Sister Saint-Hilaire. Not only did none of Libby's heirs receive a farthing from the Deed but her precious papers, which would have proven to the world that she had the right to call herself a Byron, were destroyed. The destruction of personal papers by fire was no stranger to those with the name of Byron.

Monsieur de Waroquier's eleven-year struggle had come to nothing, but he never lost interest in the Taillefers. Jean-Louis remained in the service of the family until he was accidentally killed when he fell to his death from a collapsing tower. Sister Saint-Hilaire died in 1873, greatly beloved. Elie, a good-looking, agreeable fellow, was a disappointment. He seems to have been a rolling stone, first a clerk, then a wine broker, then a commercial traveler. He was frequently in some kind of scrape and came to no good end on January 22, 1900, aged forty-four.[11] Byron would have made much of the date. It was the anniversary of his birth.

While Libby was struggling to take care of herself and Marie at St. Germain, two people once close to her were also trying to salvage their lives. Henry Trevanion had continued to live on his property in Brittany while Georgiana and the three girls remained in England. Georgiana was now intensely bitter toward her mother whom she blamed for all her troubles. Agnes, the second Trevanion daughter died in 1844, at sixteen.[12] About that time Georgiana decided to try it again with Henry; she and her two surviving daughters went to join him at Botives.

Henry had never shown interest in the welfare of his family, but he was getting on and life was lonely. Perhaps he and

Georgiana could make a go of it. But the reconciliation was doomed from the start. If Henry had taken a liking to his two daughters, it might have been better, but there was no real communication with them *or* Georgey. Bertha, the eldest girl, was in her late twenties and destined for spinsterhood. She died in 1858, at thirty-two.[13] The youngest, Ada, would fare better. She lived until 1882, and oddly enough, by the terms of Byron's will (leaving his estate to Augusta and her heirs on the death of Lady Byron), Ada would eventually receive twenty-eight thousand pounds, a goodly sum in that day.[14] She, in turn, left it jointly to one of her Trevanion cousins and to Geraldine Leigh, the daughter of Augusta's youngest son, Henry Francis Leigh.[15] So, by a long and very roundabout way, some of poor Guss's heirs profited by her brother's generosity, although she herself never received a pound.

As for Henry and Georgiana, they parted for good. Georgiana returned to England and Henry died alone on Christmas Day, 1854,[16] aged fifty. There is no indication that he was remembered with love and respect by his neighbors. By his death, however, Georgiana inherited his share of the Trevanion estate and was henceforth independent.

And now, to Lady Byron and her daughter. Much had happened between May, 1844, when Libby left England, and her death in late August, 1849. Annabella used Moore Place as home base but was still traveling about, sometimes accompanied by Mrs. Jameson. Ada had her husband and children to occupy her and was also working closely with Charles Babbage. In November, 1844, Hobhouse sent her a pamphlet he had written about Byron, in which he showed great insight and appreciation of his friend's character. It was written to persuade certain important people, among them the Dean of Westminster Abbey, that Byron should have a place in Poets' Corner. The famed sculptor Thorwaldsen had created a marble bust of Byron before he left for Greece, but it had been refused by the Dean and was still in a crate in a custom house. The pamphlet did not change the Dean's mind, but the bust was accepted with pleasure by the Library of Trinity College, Cambridge, Byron's alma mater. Lady Byron and Mrs. Jameson viewed it before it left London and Anna wrote later that Annabella had tears in her eyes.[17]

Hobhouse had a copy in his London house and saw to it that Lady Lovelace could view it alone after a dinner party to which she and Lord Lovelace were invited. Ada looked at it for a long time in silence, then thanked Hobhouse quietly for giving her the opportunity.[18] This gracious gesture plus the pamphlet made her all the more eager to find out whatever she could about her father. This did not, however, prevent her from working with Babbage on a project which would plunge her, her husband, and her mother into utter disaster.

On the surface nothing was amiss except that Ada was totally absorbed—too much so. Her friend and teacher Augustus De Morgan felt that such dedication was dangerous, that her desire to reach beyond the "present bounds of knowledge" might impair her health.[19] The truth is that she and Babbage were trying to develop an infallible system for betting at the race track. The Lovelaces, along with most of the aristocracy, loved the races and indulged in betting, though Babbage was more interested in the system than in placing bets. For a time Lovelace was involved with them in perfecting the system, though he was no match for Ada or Babbage. Little is known about the mechanics of this brainchild except that it was based on intricate calculations which were indeed foolproof when dealing only with consistent mathematical figures and signs. Man and horse, unfortunately, are equally notorious for inconsistency. This system was therefore no more infallible than any other and the Lovelace losses were becoming formidable. Lord Lovelace decided to quit before he was ruined and extracted a promise from Ada to do the same. Lady Byron knew nothing about all this.

In 1846 the Lovelaces leased Ockham Park and moved to Horsley Towers estate at East Horsley. The new tenant of Ockham Park was none other than the Right Honorable

Stephen Lushington, then Judge of the Admiralty Court.[20] The Lovelace finances were a bit troubled but they could have straightened things out if both had stayed away from horses and jockeys. Lovelace did, Ada did not. She had already shown that single-minded tenacity which drove her relentlessly toward the mastery of anything she set out to accomplish. The system *could* not fail; she would prove it was workable. Babbage encouraged her. His stubborn refusal to admit there could be imperfections in any of his analytical inventions was a flaw in his character which would augur ill for the woman he revered so much.

From 1847 on Ada became hopelessly involved with book-makers. It was unthinkable that one in her position would deal with them directly, so Babbage transferred one of his servants to the Lovelace ménage, a young woman named Mary Wilson who served as Ada's lady's maid. Her main function, however, was to act as go-between for Ada with the bookmakers. Ada was now living two lives. To the world she was the charming Countess of Lovelace with her three children and devoted husband; in private she was in the power of unscrupulous men who had no compunction about threatening to expose her if she did not pay up her debts. She dared not confess to her husband that she had broken her promise; she feared his wrath and the risk of losing his love. So she pawned the Lovelace family jewels.

Lady Byron still knew nothing of her daughter's double life; she was occupied elsewhere. In 1848 her cousin Robert Noel introduced her to the Reverend Frederick Robertson of Brighton. He was an immensely popular preacher and a genuinely fine human being. He was also remarkably handsome. When Anna Jameson saw Lady Byron with Robertson she recognized the "great mutual attraction" although Annabella was fifty-six and Robertson was in his thirties.[21] Not that there was ever any hanky-panky; Robertson was married and faithful, and Lady Byron was—Lady Byron. This friendship was the one happy experience in the last years of her long and lonely life.

Ada had made the tragic blunder of becoming friendly with a man named Crosse, one of the betting crowd and thoroughly reprehensible.[22] Nothing indicates that the association ever reached serious proportions but she had written him some indiscreet letters which could, if released, blemish her hitherto spotless reputation, especially in the Age of Victoria.[23] The time came when she had to redeem the family jewels or risk losing them, so she was forced to turn to the one person who had enough means to help her and would protect her secret— her mother. Shocked as Annabella was that her daughter could be guilty of such sordid doings, she redeemed the jewels and agreed to say nothing to Lord Lovelace. Twice, in fact, did she have to redeem them as well as pay off certain debts.[24] Ada had not learned her lesson the first time. This did not make for harmony between mother and daughter and there would be less as time went on.

The emotional tension brought on by this double existence contributed to the slow but steady breakdown of Ada's health. She was assured that there was nothing to worry about, which used to be the stock answer given to an anxious patient when the doctor suspected but could not be positive (before X rays and exploratory surgery) that there might be everything to worry about.[25] Lord Lovelace did what he could to make things pleasant for his ailing wife and encouraged her desire to know more about her father. In 1850 they visited Newstead Abbey, owned since 1818 by an old college friend of Byron's, Colonel Wildman. Wildman had the means to restore it to its ancient beauty and through the years had collected many Byron artifacts and memorabilia. Almost everyone who had known Byron made a pilgrimage to Newstead and Wildman was more than delighted to welcome the Lovelaces.[26]

It was a moving experience for Ada to walk through the apartments once occupied by her father and kept as they had been in his day. To stand at his bedroom window and look out on the swans in the lake, to see the Byron coat of arms and Byron family portraits, to walk in the park and see the elm where Byron had carved his initials along with Augusta's caused her to undergo a profound change of heart about her mother's marriage. While there she wrote Lady Byron some letters in which she expressed her feelings clearly. Annabella's reaction can be best explained by some excerpts from a letter she wrote to her daughter about the visit to Newstead:

> If the Mythic idea generally entertained of your father affords you satisfaction, do not forget, dearest Ada, how much of it is owing to my own line of conduct. . . . I was his best friend, not only in feeling but in fact. . . .
> It often occurs to me that my attempts to influence your Children favorably . . . will be frustrated and turned to mischief so that it would be better for them not to have known me . . . if they are allowed to adopt the unfounded popular notion of my having abandoned my husband from want of devotedness and entire sympathy . . . whilst he wrote to me privately (as will hereafter appear) 'I did—do —and ever shall—love you'. But from the whole tenor of my conduct and more particularly from the circumstances a few years ago which necessitated a disclosure till then withheld from you & Lovelace, you must be convinced of my repugnance of anything like self-justification. Only the strongest conviction of its being a duty toward others would force me to enter into it.[27]

An estrangement which had festered between Ada and Lady Byron for a long time now surfaced after the visit and continued until the summer of 1852.

Annabella had the Reverend Robertson to commiserate with her, and soon she had confided everything to him about "the secret." In the past two or three years she had refused to write or see Augusta despite importuning letters with desperate appeals for financial help, which if not met *"must end in the ruin of us all."* [28] After Colonel Leigh's death in May, 1850, Emily Leigh wrote her godmother, Lady Byron, of her mother's wretched financial condition and broken health.[29] Annabella liked Emily and finally decided, early in 1851, to meet Augusta once more before they both died. She made it clear, however, that this meeting was not going to lead to any offer of financial assistance. She arranged that they meet at Reigate, at the White Hart Hotel; Augusta could take the railroad there. Augusta was frightened of railroads, but she agreed to make the trip.[30]

The meeting was on April 8, and Augusta had thought it would be between her and Lady Byron. To her surprise there was a third party present, Robertson. Augusta did not know the real purpose of the meeting until confronted with it. Annabella wanted to extract another confession of guilt from Augusta before a witness, and some show of true repentance, before a witness. The meeting was unsatisfactory; when they parted Annabella felt that nothing had been resolved. They would never meet again, but Annabella could not let go.

In October when she heard that Augusta was dying, she wrote briefly to Emily: "I have a request to make . . . whisper to her [Augusta] *from me* the words 'dearest Augusta'—I can't think they would hurt her." On October 12 Augusta breathed her last.[31]

On December 10, 1851, Ada became thirty-six. The Lovelaces had left their London town house on St. James's Square and were now living at 6 Great Cumberland Place. Ada's health had continued to deteriorate and early in 1852 her illness was recognized for what it had been for some time, "internal cancer." [32] There is no need to dwell on the despair she must have suffered long before the disease exacted its own brand of suffering. Prior to this Annabella had taken the youngest child, Ralph, now thirteen, under her wing and was supervising the boy as closely as she had her own daughter. He had almost no playmates his own age and spent most of his time with tutors.[33] Byron, the oldest (seventeen) was turned over to Lord Lovelace's sister and a governess because his father was too distracted by Ada's illness.[34] Fifteen-year-old Annabella King spent much of her time with her grandmother.

By summer Ada's sufferings were acute. Mattresses were affixed to the walls and on the floor of the sickroom to prevent her from bruising herself when she tossed about.[35] The only position in which she was even remotely comfortable was on her hands and knees.[36] She reconciled with her mother; Annabella was always at her best in a sickroom. Finally Ada was compelled by fear and pain to make a full confession to her husband about her double life and the part her mother had played in redeeming the jewels and paying debts. Although Lovelace was horrified that his beloved Avis, his sweet Bird, was in the toils of unscrupulous scoundrels, he was even more appalled that Lady Byron had kept it a secret from him. Faced with the almost impossible task of straightening out his wife's entanglements, the distraught man was so beside himself that he could not forgive his mother-in-law or thank her for coming forward.[37]

Then Annabella made the discovery that Lovelace had also been guilty of betting and going into debt, while she had thought he was keeping Ada in line. She jumped to the conclusion that he was partly responsible for the estrangement between herself and her daughter, though this was entirely wrong. She grew so hostile to him, in fact, that they were not on speaking terms although she was now living under his roof to be near Ada.

Mary Wilson had kept Babbage informed of Lady Lovelace's illness, accusing Lady Byron of using harsh measures in dealing with the patient, putting her under restraint and the like.[38] Apparently, Lady Byron must have felt that Mary did know too much for she dismissed her in the presence of Lovelace and his tormented wife.[39] Ada managed to write to Babbage that she had to see him. Although unwelcome now, because of Lady Byron, he came at Ada's bidding. She gave him a paper purporting to be a will and asked him to be her executor. On August 12 she sent him a note stating he was to have six hundred pounds of her insurance money to buy back the letters from Crosse.[40] Babbage turned violently away from his former friendship with Lady Byron and planned to publish an account of Ada's misery at the hands of her mother, but he was dissuaded by John Murray, Byron's publisher. Mrs. Jameson offered to hear his side of the story and, if possible, to patch things up with Lady Byron, but nothing much came of her efforts.[41]

On November 27, Lady Byron was alone in her room in the Lovelace town house; Lovelace was in his room struggling with making some order out of chaos. Ada was on her deathbed. Lady Byron wrote in her Journal that she sat—

> in the hearing of her groans, and of the little bullfinch singing carelessly his wonted airs. In the next room one whose feelings are far from being in harmony with mine—.[42]

The objectivity of her thinking at such a time is almost frightening. A few hours later Ada died, released at last from months of martyrdom. She had already stated that she wished to be buried beside her father in a vault at Hucknall Torkard. It must have been the most bitter blow to Annabella, this request of Ada's to lie beside Byron for eternity. Even the funeral arrangements were not her choice. Robert Noel stated that Lady Lovelace's funeral was too ostentatious—"escutcheons and silver coronals everywhere." [43]

After the ordeal was all over, Lovelace wished to make it up with Lady Byron. The grief-stricken man wanted to turn back the clock to the days when he and Lady Byron were affectionate friends. Annabella, alas, had to have the last word, and was determined that he admit he was wrong and that she was right in the long dispute between them. After endless bickering she put an end to the correspondence. And this was not to be the final *coup de grâce* she would inflict on someone.

After Ada was dead and gone, Annabella found out that her daughter had confided in Mrs. Jameson, that Anna knew things which had been withheld from her. It caused a breach in the friendship which was not mended. In addition to receiving Ada's confidences, Anna had made a point of championing Ada's reputation when it was whispered that she had been in the hands of bookmakers.[44] In a letter written in 1854, Annabella took exception to something Anna had said when they were still on speaking terms. "You tell me you have 'shielded the memory of Lady Lovelace from the cruel world.' If the world is cruel, let it alone." [45]

In vain did Anna try to straighten out the estrangement. Finally the heartbroken woman, in an ecstasy of anger and grief, destroyed all but two of Lady Byron's letters written through the seven years of their association.[46] She was so upset, in fact, that she could not bear to see Robert Noel again, and he had been one of her staunchest friends. Anna's numerous other friends knew how prostrated she was by the cessation of her attachment to Lady Byron. Fanny Kemble, more clear-headed perhaps than most of them, stated her feelings on the subject with singular astuteness:

> I never thought theirs a real attachment, but a connection made up of all sorts of motives, which was sure not to hold water long, and never to hold it after it once began to leak. It was an instance of one of those relationships which are made to *wear out,* and as it always appeared so to me. . . . I pity Mrs. Jameson more because she is mortified than because she is grieved, and I pity Lady Byron because she is more afraid of mortifying than of giving her pain. It is all very *uncomfortable* but real sorrow has as little to do with it now as real love ever had.[47]

Early in 1853 Lady Byron decided to renew her correspondence with Lord Lovelace. She had recently lost her close friend Robertson through death, and it may have been that this untimely tragedy gave her more understanding of Lovelace's bereavement: "To you, Lovelace, I have been the most faithful of friends, and at no time, more actively and self sacrificingly than in the last year and a half." [48]

Even then she was driven by the need to justify herself and

to remind him that he owed her gratitude. Two days later he answered the letter:

> And yet with all your severity and coldness, which drives me into these indignant remonstrances with you, the last page of your letter is too true for me not to re-echo and confirm it. You have been too noble and generous (in some things), self denying in all, for me not to bear ready testimony to it. In most fine qualities you have not your equal on earth, and my love for you is as ardent as ever, however you may repell it. I hold you in respect and admiration more than ever—but your want of sympathy (in spite of your gentleness) with those who do not feel exactly as you do, has cruelly destroyed what certainty, and hope, and comfort remained to me.[49]

Even had she tried to profit by this stern rebuke, it was too late for her to change her ways, if indeed she ever could. At sixty-one she was lonely, restless as always, but she had a full life. Strangers meeting her for the first time could not believe that this gentle, fragile little woman with her widow's cap atop her silvery hair could be as heartless as some of her husband's verses made her out to be.

Also in 1853 she was invited to a luncheon party. Among the guests was a woman she was anxious to meet for several reasons, one of them being that the lady was the author of a best seller. Only a year before *Uncle Tom's Cabin* had been published in America, and now everyone in England was reading it. Harriet Beecher Stowe was equally eager to meet Byron's widow. Though twenty years younger, she hit it off with Lady Byron from the start. They had interests in common; Lady Byron had sponsored two runaway slaves who had made their way to England. Mrs. Stowe might have taken Mrs. Jameson's place with Lady Byron, but she had to return to America.

Three years later she returned to England. She received a note from Lady Byron, now living in Ham Common near Richmond. Annabella wished her to come to see her; she wanted a confidential talk. By then she was seriously ill with a "gradual ossification of the lungs," one of those odd Victorian maladies not listed in a modern medical dictionary.[50] In point of fact, she had progressive heart disease. The two women met in Lady Byron's sickroom and the purpose of the visit was revealed.

Lady Byron did not think she had long to live and wanted to explain certain matters in strictest confidence to someone from another country who would take an objective view "out of the sphere of personal and local feelings."[51] After this preamble Lady Byron launched into the whole story of her marriage, separation, and relationship with Augusta. Mrs. Stowe described the next bit of conversation thus:

She asked if Mrs. Leigh was beautiful.

"No, my dear, she was plain."

"Was she, then, distinguished for genius or talent of any kind?"

"Oh no. Poor woman; she was weak, relatively, to him and wholly under his control."

"And what became of her?"

"She repented and became a truly good woman."

"Was there a child?"

Lady Byron said there was one, a daughter, who made her friends much trouble, being of a very difficult nature to manage. Despite a passage of more than forty years, Mrs. Stowe described Lady Byron as speaking "with intense, repressed, emotion" as if it had all happened yesterday.[52]

One can imagine the effect of this Greek drama of incest, betrayal, and revenge upon the sensibilities of a Congregational clergyman's daughter with a deep sense of right and wrong. Mrs. Stowe was an arch feminist, in many ways ahead of her time, but she was living in an era of sentimental prudery and must have been shocked beyond belief. She was convinced that Lady Byron's "policy of silence" was a fact, and that she was the first to hear the monstrous "secret" in full detail. She was too forthright a woman to understand the duality of Lady Byron's nature, and indeed, it is difficult for anyone to comprehend the compulsion which forced Annabella to tell all to a comparative stranger. *Unless* it was because Mrs. Stowe was an author. Byron had a myriad of champions. Could she not have one?

Mrs. Stowe returned to America and they never met again. Seven years later, on May 16, 1860, Lady Byron died. She was not buried beside her husband and daughter nor even among her own people. By her wish she found her final resting place in a London cemetery, Kensal Green, surrounded by strangers.[53]

In 1868 there appeared *My Recollections of Lord Byron*, written by the former Contessa Guiccioli, now married to the Marquis de Boissy, a wealthy Frenchman who took pride in introducing his wife as "the former mistress of Lord Byron." [54] The Marquise was understandably prejudiced against Lady Byron and did not mince words. On the other hand, when visiting England in 1832, she had met Mrs. Leigh [55] and extolled her as the only person who stood by Byron at the time of the separation. A separation, moreover, which had been forced on him by his heartless, prudish wife. This was too much for Mrs. Stowe. Only too well did she recall Lady Byron's description of a bitter quarrel with Byron in which he said, "The world had made up its mind that By is a glorious boy, and the world will go for By—right or wrong." [56] It was time that someone set the record straight about that glorious boy.

In 1869 *MacMillan's Magazine* published some articles which told the "true story of Lady Byron's married life," written by Harriet Beecher Stowe. In 1870 her book *Lady Byron Vindicated* appeared in the bookstalls. But with the best intentions she did her friend the worst kind of disservice. The book was too sentimental and biased, even for *that* day. In America as well as England the Victorians took a dim view of her scandalous allegations. Indignant letters appeared in *The Times* of London, denunciatory articles were written, books were published. Many thought Mrs. Stowe was little better than a muckraker for shedding light on events which should have remained in darkness, if indeed any of them were true.

There were those, however, who knew that the story *was* true. One of them was Thomas Smith, though his views on

Lady Byron did not coincide with Mrs. Stowe's. For twenty-six years he had kept Elizabeth Medora Leigh's Autobiography among his papers along with numerous letters. He never intended publishing them, but in the interests of truth and justice he agreed to turn over the material to Charles Mackay who did publish it in 1869: *Medora Leigh, A History and Autobiography*. And in so doing he did Libby a great service.

Until this publication, her story, though scarcely a secret, was not known to the world. For the first time the public at large learned of the existence of this "child of sin" and read the saga of her life. Lady Byron did not emerge in the book as an angel of forbearance or generosity. Her defenders and detractors locked horns. The skeleton in the Leigh closet could no longer be concealed, much less ignored.

When Lady Byron talked to Mrs. Stowe on that summer afternoon, she never suspected that her confidences would turn into boomerangs. Unwittingly she performed one more service for the wild and wayward daughter of the two people who spoiled her life and whom she loved to the day of her death. The glorious boy had the last laugh, after all.

Notes

CHAPTER 1

1. Malcolm Elwin, *Lord Byron's Wife* (London, 1962), 311. Quote from Byron's letter to Augusta Leigh, September 17, 1816.
2. *Ibid.*, 53.
3. Quote from a letter by Francis Wormald, Newmarket, to Lady Delamere re my request for information about E.M.L.'s birthplace. From *A History of the Wilbrahan Parishes* by Canon H. P. Stokes (London, 1926).

> At the Lodge (now Swynford Paddocks, residence of Capt. Malcolm Bullock, M.P. and Lady Victoria Bullock) formerly lived Colonel Leigh, whose wife the Hon. Augusta Leigh was the sister of Lord Byron. The poet often visited here—here he wrote "Corsair," etc. The sad story of Medora Leigh is connected with this house.

Mrs. Wormald further writes: "I myself seem to recollect hearing of a tree in Swynford Paddocks grounds called 'Byron's tree' under which it is said Byron wrote some of his poems."

Note: The photograph of the house at Six Mile Bottom, birthplace of Elizabeth Medora (included in the illustrations) may be the house mentioned above. It was either burned or torn down and remodeled later.

4. Elwin, *op. cit.*, 193.

CHAPTER 2

1. Lord Broughton (John Cam Hobhouse), *Recollections of a Long Life* (London, 1910), Vol. II, 191–2.

2. Leslie A. Marchand, *Byron: A Biography* (New York, 1957), Vol. I, 473–5.
3. Elwin, *op. cit.* 243. Extract from letter of Augusta Leigh to Byron. Also footnote 1, 243. Lady Byron refers to the fact that E.M.L. was called Medora until about three when the name was dropped in favor of Elizabeth or Libby.
4. *Byron, A Self-Portrait. Letters and Diaries, 1798–1824,* ed. Peter Quennell (London, 1950), Vol. II, 529. Letter dated Ravenna, 1820, from Byron to Hon. Augusta Leigh.
5. Broughton, *op. cit.,* Vol. I, 191–7.
6. *His Very Self and Voice, Collected Conversations of Lord Byron,* ed. Ernest J. Lovell (New York, 1954), 101. Quote from Byron's Memoirs, later destroyed but recalled by his friend Samuel Rogers.
7. *Ibid.,* 87–8. A statement by Caroline Lamb. Also Elwin, *op. cit.*
8. Harriet Beecher Stowe, *Lady Byron Vindicated, A History of the Byron Controversy* (London, 1870), 243.
9. *Ibid.,* 439.
10. Broughton, *op. cit.,* Vol. II, 215.
11. Elwin, *op. cit.,* 375.
12. Broughton, *op. cit.,* Vol. II, 268–9.
13. *Ibid.,* 270.
14. Earl of Lovelace (Ralph Milbanke), *Astarte: A Fragment of Truth Concerning George Gordon Byron, Sixth Lord Byron,* recorded by his grandson, new edition by Mary Countess of Lovelace (New York, 1921).

CHAPTER 3

1. Doris Langley Moore, *The Late Lord Byron* (London, 1961), 15. Also, Broughton, *op. cit.,* Vol. III, 39.
2. Moore, *op. cit.,* 148.
3. Broughton, *op. cit.,* Vol. III, 40.
4. Medora Leigh, *History and Autobiography,* ed., Charles Mackay (New York, 1870), 30.
5. *Ibid.*
6. Moore, *op. cit.,* 16–7.
7. Elwin, *op. cit.,* 310. Also Earl of Lovelace, *Lady N. Byron and the Leighs* (England, privately printed, 1877), Preface 25.
8. *Ibid.,* 425.
9. Ethel C. Mayne, *Life of Lady N. Byron* (New York, 1930), 235–7.
10. *Astarte,* 238. Letter dated July 18, 1816, from T. Villiers to Lady N. Byron.
11. *Ibid.,* 238, same letter.
12. Quennell, *op. cit.,* Vol. II, 451.
13. *Lord Byron's Correspondence,* ed. John Murray (New York, 1922), 186–7.
14. Mayne, *op. cit.,* 289.

15. Marchand, *op. cit.*, Vol. III, 1044. Letter dated Genoa, November 7, 1822, from Byron to Augusta Leigh.
16. Quennell, *op. cit.*, Vol. II, 750. Letter dated August 12, 1823, from Byron to Augusta Leigh.
17. Add. Ms. 31037 British Museum, Leigh Family Papers.
18. Quennell, *op. cit.*, Vol. II, 377. Letter dated December 18, 1816 from Byron to Augusta Leigh.
19. Moore, Thomas, ed. *Letters and Journals of Lord Byron with Notices of His Life* (London, 1830), Vol. IV, Letter No. 307 dated February 2, 1818 from Byron to Moore.

CHAPTER 4

1. Material relative to Trevanion family, courtesy Christine Hawkridge North. Also, J. Berlase, Jr., *The Parochial History of Cornwall* (London, 1838). Also, J. L. Vivian, *Visitations of Cornwall* (Exeter, 1887). Material relative to Caerhays Castle from Christine Hawkridge North.
2. Moore, D., *op. cit.*, 159. Quote from Augusta's letter to Lady Byron.
3. Leigh, *op. cit.*, 30.
4. Moore, D., *op. cit.*, 452.
5. Leigh, *op. cit.*, 30.
6. *Ibid.*
7. Mayne, *op. cit.*, 310.
8. Leigh, *op. cit.*, 31.
9. *Ibid.*, 30.
10. *Ibid.*, 31.
11. *Ibid.* This sentence was deleted in the published version, but is in the original manuscript. "She [Georgie] said she alone was to blame as she had been activated by jealousy . . ."
12. Mayne, *op. cit.*, 340.
13. Quennell, *op. cit.*, Vol. II, 410. Letter dated June 3, 1817, from Byron to Augusta Leigh.

CHAPTER 5

1. Mary Browne, *Diary of a Girl in France in 1821* (New York, 1918). Material relative to Calais in that period is scattered through the pages.
2. Leigh, *op. cit.*, 31.
3. *Ibid.*

CHAPTER 6

1. *Leaves from the Diary of Henry Greville* (New York, 1929), 49 (June 29, 1828).

2. Encyclopedia Brittanica, 11th Edition: "Thorobred," gives an interesting sidelight on the Godolphin family. All thorobred racing stock throughout the world traces its lineage back to three stallions: The Byerly Turk, the Darley Arabian, and the *Godolphin* Barb (or Arabian). The last-named stallion was brought into England from France about 1730 and was eventually sold to the Earl of Godolphin on whose estate the animal died in 1753.

3. Add. Ms. 31037 British Museum. Leigh family papers. Letter from Augusta to Lady Byron.

4. *Ibid.*

5. *Ibid.*

6. *Ibid.*

7. Leigh, *op. cit.*, 31.

8. *Ibid.*, 37. Quote from E. M. Leigh's letter to her cousin The Hon. D'Arcy Osborne.

9. *Ibid.*, 31.

10. *Ibid.*, 31.

11. Greville, *op. cit.*, 101.

12. Leigh, *op. cit.* The material having to do with Lady Byron was deleted entirely by Mackay in the published version. This was summarized from the original manuscript.

13. Mayne, *op. cit.*, 341.

14. *Ibid.*, 342.

15. *Ibid.*, 342–4.

16. *Ibid.*, 344–5.

17. Leigh, *op. cit.*, 31.

18. *Ibid.*, "When she found it was [illegible] to endeavour to make me employ means to destroy my child she agreed with Georgie that I should again accompany them . . ."

19. Earl of Lovelace, *Lady N. Byron and the Leighs* (England, privately printed, 1877) 135.

CHAPTER 7

1. Leigh, *op. cit.*, 37. E. M. Leigh's letter to the Duke of Leeds.

2. *Ibid.*, 31. The published version differs here and there from the original manuscript. The original wording is: "We were all taught to dislike and deceive him. But I pitied him, strange to say—and would have done anything to hide his faults or expose him."

3. *Ibid.*, 32.

4. Broughton, *op. cit.*, July 1, 1831.

5. Leigh, *op. cit.*, 31.

6. *Ibid.*, 31. The published version differs from the original. In second paragraph the original reads: "I found Georgiana in my room, apparently in great distress of mind. . . . She begged forgiveness of me and entreated me never to abandon Henry. . . ."

7. *Ibid.*, 31.
8. *Ibid.*, 31.
9. Lovelace, *op. cit.*, 111.
10. Leigh, *op. cit.*, 31.

CHAPTER 8

1. Leigh, *op. cit.*, 32.
2. Leigh, *op. cit.*, 32.
3. Gunn, Peter, *Dearest Augusta* (New York, 1968), 243.
4. Roger de Vivie de Regie, *Le Secret de Byron* (Paris, 1927), 78.
5. Philip Carr, *The French at Home* (London, 1930). All descriptions of French village life and customs are culled from this book.
6. Anna Bowman, *In and Out of Three Normandy Inns* (New York, 1892).
7. Leigh, *op. cit.*, 32. This quote is from the original manuscript. The published version differs slightly, with minor deletions.
8. Mayne, *op. cit.*, 347.
9. Sedgwick, Anne Douglas, *A Childhood in Brittany 80 Years Ago* (New York, 1919). Description of life and customs in Brittany culled from this book.
10. History of The Order from *Biographical Sketch of Rev. Mother M. Hyacinth,* Foundress of The Daughters of the Cross in America by one of her novices. Sent to me by courtesy of Mother Mary Clarissa, D.X. St. Vincent's Academy, Shreveport, La.
11. *Ibid.*
12. Leigh, *op. cit.*, 32.
13. *Ibid.*
14. *Ibid.*
15. Gunn, *op. cit.*, 243.
16. de Regie, *op. cit.*, 78.
17. *Ibid.*, 74–5.
18. Gunn, *op. cit.*, 243.
19. *Ibid.*, 243.
20. *Ibid.*, 243.
21. *Ibid.*, 244.
22. *Ibid.*, 243–4.
23. Leigh, *op. cit.*, 37. Letter from E.M.L. to her cousin Hon. D'Arcy Osborne.

CHAPTER 9

1. Leigh, *op. cit.*, 32.
2. Sedgwick, *op. cit.* Details of life in customs of Finistère from this book.
3. *Ibid.*

4. *Ibid.*
5. Add. Ms. 31037. Leigh family papers. Letter dated January 23, 1826, from John Hanson (Byron family financial adviser) to Augusta Leigh regarding H. Trevanion's financial prospects.
6. Ms. 31037. Leigh family papers. Letter dated May 10, 1835, from Augusta Leigh to John Trevanion (Henry's father).
7. *Ibid.* Undated letter from Augusta to John Tevanion.
8. *Ibid.* See Note 7.
9. *Ibid.* Letter written in July, 1835, by Augusta Leigh.
10. Leigh, *op. cit.,* 32.
11. Browne, *op. cit.* See also *Childhood in Brittany.*
12. Moore, *op. cit.,* 431.
13. Leigh, *op. cit.,* 32.
14. Mayne, *op. cit.,* 347.
15. Leigh, *op. cit.,* 32.
16. Sedgwick, *op. cit.* Descriptions of peasant house.
17. Leigh, *op. cit.,* 32.
18. *Ibid.*
19. *Ibid.*
20. Lovelace, *op. cit.,* 138. Letter dated March 16, 1841, from Lady N. Byron to Mrs. Villiers. Also letter dated January 20, 1841, from Lady N. Byron to Augusta Leigh.
21. *Ibid.,* 164. Letter dated July 3, 1842, from Lady N. Byron to E. M. Leigh.
22. Mayne, 352.
23. Lovelace, *op. cit.,* Extract from "Narrative by Lady N. Byron," 1841.
24. *Ibid.,* 124. Mrs. Leigh's Statement #2.
25. *Ibid.*
26. Elwin, *op. cit.,* 426.
27. Leigh, *op. cit.,* 33.
28. Lovelace, *op. cit.,* 140. Letter dated March 18, 1841, from Mrs. Villiers to Lady N. Byron.
29. *Ibid.,* 130. Letter dated February 27, 1841, from Mrs. Villiers to Lady N. Byron.
30. *Ibid.,* 147. Letter dated August 6, 1841, from Lady N. Byron to Mrs. Villiers.
31. Carr, *op. cit.*
32. Lovelace, *op. cit.,* 140.
33. Gunn, *op. cit.,* 245.
34. Mayne, 347.
35. Leigh, *op. cit.,* 32.
36. Trevanion Family Genealogy, from *Visitations of Cornwall.*
37. Lovelace, *op. cit.,* 134. Letter dated March 9, 1841, from Mrs. Villiers to Lady N. Byron.
38. Leigh, *op. cit.,* 32.

CHAPTER 10

1. Lovelace, *op. cit.*, 119.
2. Broughton, *op. cit.* Diary, February 24, 1834.
3. Moseley, Maboth, *Irascible Genius: A Life of Charles Babbage, Inventor* (London, 1964), 160.
4. Lovelace, *op. cit.*, 139. Letter dated March 15, 1841, from Lady N. Byron to Mrs. Villiers
5. *Ibid.*, 119.
6. *Ibid.*
7. *Ibid.*
8. Mayne, *op. cit.*, 348.
9. *Ibid.*, 348.
10. Mayne, *op. cit.*, 348.
11. Elwin, *op. cit.*, 316. See Note 2.
12. *Ibid.*, 294.
13. Lovelace, *op. cit.*, 120. From Narrative of Lady N. Byron, 1841.
14. Mayne, *op. cit.*, 394.
15. Leigh, *op. cit.*, 33.
16. Mayne, *op. cit.*, 353.
17. Leigh, *op. cit.*, 35.
18. Mayne, *op. cit.*, 349.
19. Leigh, *op. cit.*, 33.

CHAPTER 11

1. Browne, *op. cit.* The author describes the approach to Paris in a traveling carriage.
2. "Astarte," *op. cit.*, 186.
3. Lovelace, *op. cit.*, 137. Letter dated March 10, 1841, from Lady N. Byron to Lady Wilmot-Horton.
4. Leigh, *op. cit.*, 33.
5. Mayne, *op. cit.*, 353–4.
6. Mayne, *op. cit.*, 349.
7. Mayne, *op. cit.*, 350.
8. Gunn, *op. cit.*, 247.
9. *Ibid.*
10. Lovelace, *op. cit.*, 125.
11. *Ibid.*, 128. Letter dated February 26, 1841, from Earl of Lovelace to Lady N. Byron.
12. Mayne, *op. cit.*, 354.
13. *Ibid.*, 355.
14. *Ibid.*, 356.

15. *Ibid.*
16. Lovelace, *op. cit.,* 144. Letter dated March 26, 1841, from Lady N. Byron to Sir George Stephen.
17. Mayne, *op. cit.,* 358.
18. Leigh, *op. cit.*
19. Lovelace, *op. cit.,* 136. Letter dated March 9, 1841, from Mrs. Villiers to Lady N. Byron.
20. *Ibid.,* 140. Letter dated March 15, 1841, from Lady N. Byron to Mrs. Villiers.
21. *Ibid.,* 145. Letter dated March 27, 1841, from Lady N. Byron to Mrs. Villiers.
22. *Ibid.,* 148. Letter dated April 8, 1841, from Mrs. Villiers to Lady N. Byron.
23. Mayne, *op. cit.,* 356.
24. Leigh, *op. cit.,* 33.
25. Browne, *op. cit.* A description of the author's first Sunday in Paris.
26. Mayne, *op. cit.,* 355.
27. Lovelace, *op. cit.,* 157. Letter dated June 11, 1841, from Lady N. Byron to Mrs. Villiers.
28. *Ibid.,* 154. Letter dated as follows: 10 St. James Square, June 8, 1841, from Lady N. Byron to Mrs. Villiers.

CHAPTER 12

1. Mayne, *op. cit.,* 408.
2. *Ibid.,* 395.
3. Moseley, *op. cit.,* 197–203. In letters from the Countess of Lovelace to C. Babbage there are many references to "the mutual and endearing interest in birds and dogs," also in letters to Lady Lovelace from Babbage.
4. Lovelace, *op. cit.,* 151. Letter dated April 13, 1841, from Lady N. Byron to Mrs. Villiers.
5. *Ibid.,* 157. Letter dated June 11, 1841, from Lady N. Byron to Mrs. Villiers.
6. *Ibid.,* 159. Letter dated July 8, 1841, from Lady N. Byron to Mrs. Villiers.
7. *Ibid.,* 159. Letter dated July 9, 1841, from Mrs. Villiers to Lady N. Byron.
8. C. K. O'Mahoney, *Literary Associations of Esher and Thames Ditton* (London, 1943).
9. Leigh, *op. cit.,* 33.
10. Carr, *op. cit.*
11. Lovelace, *op. cit.,* 161. Letter dated December 6, 1841, from Countess of Lovelace to Lady N. Byron.
12. O'Mahoney, *op. cit.*

13. Brayley, E. W., *The History of Surrey* (London, 1878).
14. Moseley, *op. cit.,* 164.
15. *Ibid.,* 104. Chapter 11 deals with Babbage's "unhappy art of making enemies."
16. *Ibid.* There are many references throughout the book about Babbage's devotion to Lady Lovelace and her touching concern and respect for him.
17. Lovelace, *op. cit.,* 181. Letter dated April 10, 1843, from Louise M. Barwell to Lady N. Byron.
18. Mayne, *op. cit.,* 6.
19. Elwin, *op. cit.,* 84.
20. Mayne, *op. cit.,* 434.
21. de Regie, *op. cit.,* 43.
22. Moseley, *op. cit.,* 174. Letter from Lady Lovelace to Babbage.
23. *Ibid.,* 174. Letter from Lady Lovelace to Babbage. ". . . if only my breathing and some of the other etceteras do not make too rapid a progress *toward* instead of *from* mortality."
24. Mayne, *op. cit.,* 434.
25. Leigh, *op. cit.,* 33.
26. *Ibid.*

CHAPTER 13

1. Mayne, *op. cit.,* 357. Byron to Lady Wilmot-Horton.
2. *Ibid.*
3. *Ibid.*
4. *Ibid.,* 376.
5. Frances Ann Kemble, *Records of Later Life* (New York, 1882). Letter to Mrs. Jameson dated Philadelphia, October 26, 1834.
6. *Ann Brownell Murphy Jameson, Letters and Friendships 1812–1816,* ed. Mrs. Stewart Erskine (London, 1915), 12.
7. *Astarte, op. cit.,* 186.
8. Erskine, ed., *op. cit.,* 333. From her "manifesto—a . . . statement of certain principles regarding the social and relative position of women." Preserved in Weimar among the correspondence of Ottile von Goethe.
9. Leigh, *op. cit.,* 33.
10. Lovelace, *op. cit.,* 181. Letter dated April 8, 1843, from Lady N. Byron to Selina Doyle.
11. Mackay, *op. cit.* Part III, 50.
12. Mayne, *op. cit.,* 452. Extract from *Robertson of Brighton* by Frederick Arnold.
13. Leigh, *op. cit.,* 33.
14. *Ibid.,* 37–8.
15. Mayne, *op. cit.,* 357.
16. Leigh, *op. cit.,* 33.
17. *Ibid.*

18. *Ibid.*
19. *Ibid.*
20. *Ibid.*
21. *Ibid.*
22. *Ibid.*
23. *Ibid.*
24. Lovelace, *op. cit.*, 181. Letter dated April 10, 1843, from Louise M. Barwell to Lady N. Byron.
25. Mayne, *op. cit.*, 359.
26. Leigh, *op. cit.*, 34.
27. Mayne, *op. cit.*, 358.
28. Lovelace, *op. cit.*, 165. Letter dated July 8, 1842, from Countess of Lovelace to Lady N. Byron.
29. *Ibid.*
30. Mayne, *op. cit.*, 358.
31. *Ibid.*
32. Lovelace, *op. cit.*, 166. Letter dated July 13, 1842, from Lady N. Byron to E. M. Leigh.
33. *Ibid.*, 167. Letter dated July 17, 1842, from Lady N. Byron to E. M. Leigh.
34. Mayne, *op. cit.*, 360–2.
35. Mayne, *op. cit.*, 362.
36. Lovelace, *op. cit.*, 169. Letter dated July 21, 1842, from Lady N. Byron to Countess of Lovelace.
37. Erskine, ed. *op. cit.*, 360.
38. Mayne, *op. cit.*, 363.
39. Leigh, *op. cit.*, 34.
40. *Ibid.*

CHAPTER 14

1. Lovelace, *op. cit.*, 188, May 27, 1843. Extract from Lady N. Byron's Memorandum of N. Beaureppaire's Statements.
2. Leigh, *op. cit.*, 34.
3. Mayne, *op. cit.*, 326–3.
4. Leigh, *op. cit.*, 34.
5. *Ibid.*
6. The War Office Records Centre, Middlesex, England.
7. Commander-in-Chief's Memoranda, W.O. 31/207 Public Records.
8. R. J. White, *Life in Regency England* (New York, 1963), 59–60.
9. Leigh, *op. cit.*, 34.
10. *Ibid.*
11. *Ibid.*
12. *Ibid.*, 172. Letter dated October 1, 1842, from Lady Wilmot-Horton to Lady N. Byron.

13. *Ibid.*, 172. Letter dated October 4, 1842, from Lady N. Byron to Lady Wilmot-Horton.
14. Leigh, *op. cit.*, 34.
15. *Ibid.*
16. *Ibid.*
17. *Ibid.*
18. *Ibid.*, 35.
19. *Ibid.*
20. *Ibid.*
21. Mayne, *op. cit.*, 363.
22. *Ibid.*, 174. Letter dated March 14, 1843, from Lady N. Byron to Selina Doyle.

CHAPTER 15

1. Elwin, *op. cit.*, 85.
2. Broughton, *op. cit.*, Vol. II, 325–6.
3. Mayne, *op. cit.*, 363.
4. Leigh, *op. cit.*, 35.
5. Mayne, *op. cit.*, 363.
6. *Ibid.*, 363.
7. Kemble, *op. cit.* Letter to Mrs. Jameson dated Philadelphia, October 26, 1834.
8. Elizabeth Armstrong, *Passionate Victorian* (Macmillan, 1938), 271.
9. Leigh, *op. cit.*, 35.
10. *Ibid.*
11. Mayne, *op. cit.*, 364.
12. Moseley, *op. cit.*, 170. Letter from Lady Lovelace to Babbage.
13. Mayne, *op. cit.*, 356.
14. Lovelace, *op. cit.*, 176. Letter dated March 24, 1843, from Countess of Lovelace to E. M. Leigh.
15. Mayne, *op. cit.*, 363.
16. *Ibid.*
17. Lovelace, *op. cit.*, 180. Letter dated April 4, 1843, from Lady N. Byron to Selina Doyle.
18. *Ibid.*, 181. Letter dated April 8, 1843, from Lady N. Byron to Selina Doyle.
19. *Ibid.*, 204. Letter dated September 26, 1843, from Lady N. Byron to Lady Wilmot-Horton.
20. *Ibid.*, 180. Letter dated April 7, 1843, from Lady N. Byron to Selina Doyle.
21. Mayne, *op. cit.*, 394.
22. Lovelace, *op. cit.*, 185. Letter dated May 13, 1843, from Lady N. Byron to Lady Wilmot-Horton.

23. Mayne, *op. cit.*, 364.
24. *Ibid.*, 364.
25. Leigh, *op. cit.*, 35.
26. Lovelace, *op. cit.*, 184–5. Letter dated May 7, 1843, from Lady N. Byron to Selina Doyle.
27. *Ibid.*, 185. Letter dated May 13, 1843, from Lady N. Byron to Lady Wilmot-Horton.
28. *Ibid.*, 186. Letter dated May 18, 1843, from Lady N. Byron to Lady Wilmot-Horton.
29. *Ibid.*
30. *Ibid.*
31. Leigh, *op. cit.*, 35.
32. *Ibid.*, 36.
33. *Ibid.*
34. *Ibid.*
35. *Ibid.*
36. *Ibid.*

CHAPTER 16

1. Leigh, *op. cit.*, 36.
2. *Ibid.*
3. Lovelace, *op. cit.*, 188. Letter dated May 27, 1843, from Sir George Stephen to Earl of Lovelace.
4. *Ibid.*
5. *Ibid.*
6. *Ibid.*, 189. Letter dated May 28, 1843, from Earl of Lovelace to Lady N. Byron.
7. *Ibid.*
8. *Ibid.*
9. *Ibid.*, 192. Letter dated June 4, 1843, from Lady N. Byron to Earl of Lovelace.
10. *Ibid.*, 190. Letter dated May 28, 1843, from Lady N. Byron to Lady Wilmot-Horton.
11. *Ibid.*, 191. Letter dated June 2, 1843, from Dr. William King to Lady N. Byron.
12. Leigh, *op. cit.*, Part II, 25.

CHAPTER 17

1. Lovelace, *op. cit.*, 193. Letter dated July 14, 1843, from Rt. Hon. Stephen Lushington to Lady N. Byron.
2. Lovell, *op. cit.*, 412–424. Extracts from *Conversations with Lord Byron* by Thomas Smith. Also manuscript included in *Medora Leigh: History*

and Autobiography, along with manuscript of M. Leigh's *Autobiography* and various letters (Morgan Library).

3. Leigh, *op. cit.,* ed. Mackay, Part II, 25.
4. Lovelace, *op. cit.,* 193. Letter dated July 14, 1843, from Rt. Hon. Stephen Lushington to Lady N. Byron.
5. *Ibid.,* 193–4.
6. *Ibid.,* 194.
7. Leigh, *op. cit.,* ed. Mackay, Part II, 26–7.
8. *Ibid.,* Part II, 27.
9. Lovelace, *op. cit.,* 195. Letter dated July 26, 1843, from Sir George Stephen to Lady N. Byron.
10. *Ibid.,* 195. Letter dated July 4, 1843, from Earl of Lovelace to Lady N. Byron.
11. *Ibid.,* 199, footnote.
12. *Ibid.,* 199. Letter dated August 18, 1843, from Rt. Hon. Stephen Lushington to Lady N. Byron.
13. Leigh, *op. cit.,* ed. Mackay, Part II, 28.
14. *Ibid.,* Part II, 38.
15. *Ibid.,* Part II. Letter dated August 14, 1843, from E. M. Leigh to the Hon. William Osborne and Hon. D'Arcy Osborne.
16. Moore, *op. cit.,* 506. Manuscript John Murray August 12, 1843.
17. Lovelace, *op. cit.,* 197. Letter dated August 14, 1843, from Earl of Lovelace to Lady N. Byron.
18. *Ibid.*
19. Leigh, *op. cit.,* ed. Mackay, Part II, 37.
20. Lovelace, *op. cit.,* 196. Letter dated August 6, 1843, from The Hon. Mrs. George Lamb to Lady N. Byron.
21. Leigh, *op. cit.,* ed. Mackay, Part II, 27.
22. *Ibid.,* Part II, 37.
23. *Ibid.,* Part II, 37.
24. *Ibid.,* Part II, 36.
25. Lovelace, *op. cit.,* 200. Letter dated August 20, 1843, from Lady N. Byron to Rt. Hon. Stephen Lushington.
26. Mayne, *op. cit.,* 366.
27. Gunn, *op. cit.,* 251.
28. *Ibid.,* 204. Letter dated September 26, 1843, from Lady N. Byron to Lady Wilmot-Horton.
29. Leigh, *op. cit.,* ed. Mackay, 38. Letter dated October 12, 1843, from E. M. Leigh to Captain Barrallier.
30. O'Mahoney, *op. cit.*
31. Lovelace, *op. cit.,* 205. Letter dated December, 1843, from Sir George Stephen to Lady Byron.
32. de Regie, *op. cit.,* 92.
33. *Ibid.,* 94–5.
34. *Ibid.,* 95–6.
35. Lovelace, *op. cit.,* 205. Note by Lord Lovelace.

CHAPTER 18

All facts in this chapter unless otherwise noted are from *Le Secret de Byron* by Roger de Vivie de Regie, 117–124.

  1. Lovelace, *op. cit.*, 205. Note by Lord Lovelace.

CHAPTER 19

All facts in Chapter 19 are from *Le Secret de Byron* by Roger de Vivie de Regie with the exception of Note 1.

  1. Broughton, *op. cit.*, Vol. II, 283. E. M. Leigh's Will 48–9. Letter regarding the headstone on her grave 46.

CHAPTER 20

  1. Lovelace, *op. cit.*, 210. Letter dated September 12, 1849, from Lady Wilmot-Horton to Lady N. Byron.
  2. Encyclopedia Brittanica, 11th Edition: Wills.
  3. Lovelace, *op. cit.*, 211.
  4. de Regie, *op. cit.*, 133.
  5. *Ibid.*
  6. *Ibid.*
  7. Lovelace, *op. cit.*, 210. Letter in French dated February, 1857, from G. de Waroquier to Lady N. Byron.
  8. de Regie, *op. cit.*, 180.
  9. *Ibid.*, 200, 202.
 10. *Ibid.*, 169.
 11. de Regie, *op. cit.*, 170–6. All facts in paragraph from this book. References to Elie, 184–5.
 12. Trevanion family tree (Courtesy Christine Hawkridge).
 13. *Ibid.*
 14. Personal letter to me from Rosamund Clerk, granddaughter of Ada Trevanion.
 15. *Ibid.*
 16. de Regie, *op. cit.*, 96–8.
 17. Moore, *op. cit.*, 506.
 18. *Ibid.*, 507. Also Broughton, Vol. VI, 150.
 19. Moseley, *op. cit.*, 194.
 20. Henry J. H. Bashall, *The Oak Hamlet* (London, 1900).
 21. Mayne, *op. cit.*, 399.
 22. Moseley, *op. cit.*, 221.
 23. *Ibid.*, 215.
 24. *Ibid.*, 211. Also Mayne, 434.
 25. Moseley, *op. cit.*, 197. Letter dated August 22, 1845, from Lady Love-

lace to Babbage. "Mr. Hawkins says there is nothing the least alarm-ing—."

26. Moore, *op. cit.*, 450. Teresa Guiccioli's comments regarding Col. Wild-man at Newstead.
27. Mayne, *op. cit.*, 388.
28. Mayne, *op. cit.*, 397.
29. *Ibid.*, 405–6.
30. *Ibid.*, 408.
31. *Ibid.*, 414.
32. *Ibid.*, 435.
33. *Ibid.*, 438.
34. James T. Fields, *Yesterdays with Authors* (Boston, 1872). Letter from Miss Mitford.
35. Moseley, *op. cit.*, 211.
36. Mitford letter. See Note 34.
37. Mayne, *op. cit.*, 435.
38. Moseley, *op. cit.*, 212.
39. *Ibid.*, 212.
40. *Ibid.*, 213. Letter dated August 12, 1852, 6 Cumberland Place, from Augusta Ada Lovelace to Babbage.
41. *Ibid.*, 220.
42. Mayne, *op. cit.*, 436.
43. Fields, *op. cit.*, Mitford letter. See Note 34.
44. Jameson, *op. cit.*, 279.
45. *Ibid.*, 282. Letter dated February 13, 1854, from Lady Byron to Mrs. Jameson.
46. *Ibid.*, 280.
47. Kemble, *op. cit.* Letter to "Hal" from 2 Park Place, Manchester.
48. Mayne, *op. cit.*, 437.
49. *Ibid.*, 437.
50. Stowe, *op. cit.*, 212.
51. *Ibid.*, 245–6.
52. *Ibid.*, 235.
53. Mayne, *op. cit.*, 429.
54. Maurois, *op. cit.*, 558.
55. Moore, *op. cit.*, 451.
56. Stowe, *op. cit.*, 243.

Bibliography

The factual material not enumerated in the footnotes can be found in almost all biographies of Byron which are in most public libraries. Many of these biographies are included in the list of sources.

The sources which are numbered are from material found in special libraries: The Pierpont Morgan Library, Huntington Memorial Library, Harvard Library, British Museum, etc., or occasionally in the reference rooms of larger public libraries. Other footnotes have been culled from books dealing with subjects other than Byron or Elizabeth Medora Leigh, but which have information germane to this biography.

The following are sources consulted.

Broughton, Rt. Hon. Lord (John Cam Hobhouse). *Recollections of a Long Life*. 6 vols. London: John Murray, 1909–1911.

Browne, Mary. *Diary of a Girl in France*. New York: Dutton, 1918.

Carr, Philip. *The French at Home*. New York: Lincoln MacVeagh, 1930.

de Regie, Roger de Vivie, *Le Secret de Byron*. Paris: Emil-Paul Frères, 1927.

Dodd, Anna Bowman. *In and Out of Three Normandy Inns*. London: Lovell, 1892.

Elwin, Malcolm. *Lord Byron's Wife*. New York: Harcourt, Brace & World, 1962.

Erskine, Stewart (Mrs.), ed., *Anna Brownell Murphy Jameson, Letters and Friendships*. London, 1915.

Gunn, Peter. *My Dearest Augusta*. New York: Atheneum, 1968.

Kemble, Frances Ann. *Records of Later Life*. New York: Holt, 1884.

Leaves From the Greville Diary. New York: Dutton, 1929.

Leigh Family Papers. London. British Museum. Additional Mss 31037.

Leigh, Medora, *Autobiography*. See Mackay.

Lovelace, 2nd Earl of (Lord Wentworth), *Lady Noel Byron and the Leighs.* Privately printed, 1877.

Lovell, Ernest J. *His Very Self and Voice, Collected Conversations of Lord Byron.* New York: Macmillan, 1954.

Mackay, C. *Medora Leigh, A History and Autobiography.* New York: Harper & Brothers, 1870.

Marchand, Leslie. *Byron.* 3 vols. New York: Knopf, 1957.

Maurois, André, *Byron.* New York: Grosset and Dunlap, 1930.

Maxwell, Sir Robert, ed. *The Creevy Papers.* New York: Dutton, 1904.

Mayne, Ethel Colbert. *The Life and Letters of Anne, Isabella, Lady Noel Byron.* New York, Charles Scribner's Sons, 1929.

Milbanke, Ralph (Earl of Lovelace) *Astarte.* Privately printed, 1905. Another edition edited by Mary Countess of Lovelace, London: Christophers, 1921.

Moore, Doris Langley. *The Late Lord Byron.* London: John Murray, 1961.

Moore, Thomas, ed., *Letters and Journals of Lord Byron with Notices of His Life.* London: John Murray, 1830.

Moseley, Mabeth. *The Irascible Genius, Life of Charles Babbage.* London: Hutchinson, 1964.

Murray, John, ed., *Lord Byron's Correspondence.* London: John Murray, 1922.

Sedgewick, Anne Douglas. *A Childhood in Brittany 80 Years Ago.* New York: Century, 1919.

Stowe, Harriet Beecher. *Lady Byron Vindicated.* Boston: Fields, Osgood and Co., 1870.

White, R.J., *Life in Regency England.* New York: Putnam, 1963.

Wright, Laurence, *Clean and Decent.* New York: Viking Press, 1960.

Quennell, Peter. *Byron: The Years of Fame.* New York: Viking Press, 1935.

Quennell, Peter, ed., *Byron, A Self Portrait, Some Letters and Diaries Hitherto Unpublished.* Vols. I, II. New York: Charles Scribner's Sons, 1950.

Extracts from *The History of Esher* by Ian G. Anderson, *Literary Associations of Esher and Thames Ditton* by C. K. O'Mahoney, *The Oak Hamlet,* an account of the history and associations of the village of Ockham, Surrey, by Henry J. H. Bashall, *The History of Surrey* by E. W. Brayley. All collected and sent to the author by Derek Brown, District Librarian of Esher, Surrey.

Various letters from private individuals relative to E. M. Leigh, Trevanion, etc. Material relative to the Trevanion family collected by Christine Hawkridge North, Senior Assistant Archivist, County Record Office, Truro, Cornwall.

Index

315